The
Changing
Global Order

B

The
Changing
Global Order

World Leaders Reflect

Edited by
Nathan Gardels

First published 1997

2 4 6 8 10 9 7 5 3 1

Blackwell Publishers Inc.
350 Main Street
Malden, Massachusetts 02148
USA

Blackwell Publishers Ltd
108 Cowley Road
Oxford OX4 1JF
UK

Library of Congress Cataloging-in-Publication Data

The changing global order / edited by Nathan Gardels.
    p. cm.
    Includes index.
    ISBN 1–57718–072–0 (alk. paper)
    1. World politics —1989–   2. Social history —1970–   3. Economic
history—1990–   I. Gardels, Nathan.
D860.C438   1997
909.82—dc21   97–10144
                                                CIP

British Library Cataloguing in Publication Data

A CIP catalogue record for this book is available from the British Library.

Printed in Great Britain by T. J. International, Padstow, Cornwall
This book is printed on acid-free paper

Contents

Foreword

In this age when the media has all but given up on serious discourse about ideas that matter, *New Perspectives Quarterly* and its weekly Global Viewpoint column for the Los Angeles Times Syndicate – from which the contributions to this volume are compiled – are a remarkable exception.

Over the past decade, this small "high-brow" journal has managed to spin a global intellectual web through a commentary and feature interview service that appears regularly before 30 million readers in 15 languages through the pages of many of the globe's top newspapers on all continents, from Germany's *Die Zeit* to *La Stampa* in Italy, to *O Estado de São Paulo* in South America, to *Yomiuri Shimbun*, Japan's largest daily.

Unlike any other effort I know, this creative combination of serious thinking from the world's best minds and most authoritative voices, presented in a style and format accessible to a mass media audience, has been able to link the topical issues of the day to the deeper issues of civilization at the end of the twentieth century.

For all the talk these days of globalization, very few publications can claim to have the perspective that *NPQ* and Global Viewpoint actually possess. The datelines of columns and interviews are as often from Beijing Khartoum and Moscow as from Paris, London or Washington.

The book is divided into five parts, the first two of which look back at the main geopolitical events of the twentieth century and the other three of which look ahead to geocultural and other conflicts sure to arise in the next century.

"The Parted Paths of Postcolonialism" looks at the disillusion with decolonization and revolution, the retreat to political Islam, and the rise of Asia. "Defrosting the Old Order" recounts the end of the Cold War and the early post-communist years with many of the key historical players, including Mikhail Gorbachev and Margaret Thatcher.

"Population, Migrants, and Megacities" looks at the critical environmental and population issues that have not traditionally been part of foreign policy concerns during a century bitterly divided over ideology.

"Globalization and Empires of the Mind" examines how the boundaries of the nation state are eroding from beneath and from above, whether by the restoration of local trade routes, consumer loyalties to companies over countries, the omnipresence of Hollywood films, or e-mail on the Net. Above all, part IV illustrates how America's global presence has moved far beyond the institutions of its foreign policy.

"Terror, Democracy, and Peace after the Cold War" looks at the new nature of the geopolitical order when terrorists possess mass destruction weapons, when loose nukes and unemployed (or just unpaid) atomic talent leak from the former Soviet Union, and when the concern over human rights and democracy has shifted to Asia and the Arab world.

Naturally, I do not always agree with the views presented in this collection. However, I wholly embrace the stunning presentation of this diversity of views in one context. Together they illuminate the world we are leaving behind and the one coming into view.

Zbigniew Brzezinski
Washington D.C.

Preface

The defrosting of the Cold War order has left behind a skewed world in which the American presence is uniquely global. As the century ends, the United States remains not only the sole superpower that can fly its B-52 bombers 19,000 miles from Guam to attack Iraq on a moment's notice; through the likes of Hollywood, Microsoft, and CNN it also dominates the metaworld of images, icons, and information. Where once there was containment, now there is entertainment. MTV has gone where the CIA could never penetrate.

Though the embers of the empire's wounded nations continue to smolder, the Soviet Union itself is no longer even on the map. Europe has stalled in self-absorption as it labors to thread its diversity through the needle eye of a single state. Triumphant for now, in the twenty-first century the ideal of Anglo-Saxon free markets will surely face the same challenge of social justice that gave rise to Marxism in the first place. The inequality is too vast to last: In 1995, 538 billionaires possessed as much wealth as 45 percent of the planet's population combined, some 2.3 billion people.

The legacy of the other great episode of the second half of the twentieth century, decolonization, has also unfolded in vastly different ways for different regions of the planet. East Asia is realizing its aspirations to the point of arrogance. Most of Africa, on the other hand, suffers a fate worse than imperialism. While Internet usage is already overloading phone lines in California, scientific reason has yet to meet Allah in the Arab world, which everyday seems to be sinking further into the defensive ideology of political Islam. Latin America has so far not escaped the backdraft of corruption and the tremendous weight of poverty.

To be sure, patches of order are appearing here and there like *zen* gardens in the crush of Tokyo but, mainly, swaths of pandemonium will cover the world in the times to come. Loose nukes and refugees, migrants and megacities, Aum Shinrikyos and Hezbollahs are rapidly occupying center stage. Over it all, the bondmarket arbitrates.

This book, compiled from essays and interviews first published in *New Perspectives Quarterly* (*NPQ*) and distributed to newspapers worldwide through the Global Viewpoint service of the *Los Angeles Times* Syndicate, traces these transformations of the last part of the twentieth century. From Singapore to the Sudan, from Moscow to Havana, key political players and thinkers of the period put their voices on record for *NPQ* – one of the only truly global publications in an age where there is plenty of data spinning around the planet, but precious little meaningful communication.

This book is not a compendium, but a collage. It is a sum of fragments of what Hegel would have called the unfolding "world mind" that, together, speaks more than the parts. No one perspective can possibly be authoritative or broad enough to capture the essence of the autumnal decades of our century.

If you haven't known *NPQ* or Global Viewpoint, this collection is the best introduction. If you do know them, it is valuable in itself to have the enduring thoughts presented in these essays and interviews under one cover, all wrapped up and ready for that rare moment when you can sit down beneath the reading lamp to contemplate the numbing rush of events taking us to the brink of the new millennium.

Nathan Gardels
Editor
Los Angeles, California

PART I

THE PARTED PATHS OF POSTCOLONIALISM

The nationalist dreams that brought about decolonization in the wake of world war are by now covered in dust and blood. Every new state got its own national airline, but more often than not the local despot could never deliver development. With famine, civil war and genocide, many states in Africa today suffer a fate worse than imperialism. In the Middle East, the failed project of Pan-Arab socialism has resurrected the politics of Gód and tradition. In struggling to leave its history of poverty and repression behind, most of Latin America can't seem to take one step forward without taking another one back. Corruption and weak institutions hold it back.

East Asia is the exception. Through sheer economic energy and numbers of people, it is ascending once again, promising to leave behind human rights and pluralism with the stained legacy of Western colonialism.

The general stagnation and regression of what Ryszard Kapuscinski calls "historical societies" does not take place in a vacuum. As they lick their past wounds, the "republic of the future," as Octavio Paz calls the United States, is relentlessly speeding ahead. Two worlds on the same planet, one fast and one slow, are spinning apart in opposite directions. One world is toiling still to stave off hunger, the other – encompassing America, as well as parts of Europe and Asia – is chomping at the byte to cross over into cyberspace.

In part I, some of the most astute observers of the latter half of this century take a look at what, in the days when we still believed the gap would close instead of widen, used to be called "the third world."

1

1 / One World, Two Civilizations

Ryszard Kapuscinski, foreign correspondent *extraordinaire* and literary journalist, is one of the great observers of the second half of the twentieth century.

Among his many works are two seminal books, *The Emperor*, about the fall of Haile Selassie of Ethiopia, and *Shah of Shahs*, about the Iranian revolution. Kapuscinski, who has returned to Poland after decades of wandering across Africa, Latin America and Central Asia, is presently at work on his reflections about Idi Amin of Uganda, completing his trilogy on dictators.

In times of crisis the importance of the individual is mini- **WARSAW** mized because of the tension caused by big forces. Big forces involve the interests of the whole. Big forces mean a big mass and a big mass means the removal of the individual. It means the neglect, the non-importance, of the individual. Through manipulation and mass organization the individual becomes only an element of great social forces, without a name and without hope. Most of humanity has experienced the twentieth century under this dark shadow of big forces.

In a country with internal calm, in a stable society, there is a feeling that the space ahead is open. There is hope. One can pronounce his hopes and express himself because he's an individual. That's not true in a situation of crisis and instability. Only big anonymous forces move things.

In a large demonstration, or in a large crowd, a person sees that he doesn't count. He is lost completely. He sees that his spirit has no meaning. He is a machine made to march, to move, to fight.

There is a fantastic description of a crowd scene by one of the Russian journalists of the nineteenth century. He describes how the Czar had a military parade outside of Moscow in a large open field. As a big crowd gathered there the army started to hand out some free bread. There was such pressure when the huge, hungry mass moved that many individuals were crushed. The crowd was so big that the dead people were moved along together with the living. In this crowd, it was of no importance if you were dead or alive.

Crisis is always represented by crowds. In a crisis there are such important things involved that no one pays attention to the individual. History is always bigger and more important than individuals. History is the master, but not as Marx said, "created according to man's will." Rather, people are always faced with a situation where they don't know what they're creating. This is the paradox of history. And the tragedy of modern times.

Crisis means everyone is dissatisfied – that's why there is tension. Everybody is unhappy. And if we are unhappy as a social force, then our private unhappiness is dissolved in this big social unhappiness. Our personal unhappiness exists, but becomes unimportant. Nobody pays attention.

The more space history takes for itself, the less there is for the individual. The individual is anonymous. In the Cambodias or Rwandas or Bosnias the mass graves have no markers. Millions of people died of hunger, disease and genocide, but we are unable to mention a single name.

I once wrote a poem called *About Man*.

In Warsaw, during the Nazi occupation, many executions took place on the streets. Today, these places are marked by plaques. The commemorative plaques say, for example, "on the fourth of September, in this place, the Nazis executed *about* 4,000 people." The poem says that no. 3,024 or no. 3,068 is something that can be identified at least by number, but what *about* people? In this *about* situation, a person doesn't count; he's of no importance. This is the destructive force of history.

History has caused the paralysis of what used to be called **THE** "third world" societies. These sad societies produce **HANDICAP** nothing but violence, hatred and death. It is a heavy burden **OF HISTORY** that handicaps development.

In historical societies, everything has been decided in the past. All their energies, their feelings, their passions are directed toward the past, dedicated to the discussion of history, to the meaning of history. They live in the realm of legends and founding lineages. They are unable to speak about the future because the future doesn't arouse the same passion in them as their history. They are all historical people, born and living in the history of great fights, divisions, and conflicts. They are like an old war veteran. All he wants to talk about is that big experience of crisis which carried such a deep emotion that he was never able to forget about it.

All historical societies live with this weight clouding their minds, their imagination. They must live deeply in history; this is how they identify themselves. If they lose their history, they lose their identity. Then they will not only be anonymous. They will cease to exist. To forget about history would mean to forget about themselves – a biological and psychological impossibility. It is a question of survival.

Yet, to create a new value, a society has to have a clean mind that will enable it to concentrate on doing something directed at the future. This is the tragedy in which historical societies are trapped.

America, by contrast, is a lucky nation. It has no problem with history. The American mentality is open to the future. As a young society it can be creative with no burden of history keeping it down, holding its leg, tying its hands.

The danger for America, and the danger for the whole world, is that American development is so dynamic and creative that, by the beginning of the next century, it will be a completely different world on this same planet. Everyday, America is producing more and more elements of a completely new civilization which is further and further from the civilization of the rest of the world. The gap is not only a matter of wealth and technology, but of mentality.

CYBERSPACE VS. DECAY   The position and rule of dynamic America and the paralysis of historical societies – this is the big problem for the future of mankind. Unlike the vision we all held twenty years ago, the world is not converging, but spreading apart like the galaxies. This is the world we will have at the end of the twentieth century – one world, but two civilizations.

Despite 50 years of decolonization and attempts at development we remain unable to find a way to shrink this division, to make the North and South more equal. The gap will be greater at the beginning of the next century than at the beginning of this century. Ecological devastation widens the gap further as pesticides poison, toxics spill, sewage seeps, and lakes dry up in the historical societies. The Ebola virus and AIDS take up where civil war leaves off.

When I first went to Africa thirty years ago, I could find some modern agriculture, infrastructure and medicine. There was more or less a parallel with the Europe that had been destroyed by war.

Today, even what was left from colonialism in Africa has deteriorated. Nothing new has been built. Meanwhile, America is entering cyberspace.

POST-COLONIAL DEAD END   After the Second World War there was a great awakening of consciousness in the Third World countries. For Africa and Asia particularly, the war proved that the master countries, like Britain or France, could be beaten. Also, the centers of power in the world shifted from Germany, Japan, and the French and British empires to the United States and the Soviet Union – countries that were not traditional colonial powers. These developments convinced the young nationalists in the Third World that they could achieve independence.

The fight for independence had three stages. First came the national liberation movements, especially in the largest Asian countries. India obtained independence in 1947 and China in 1949. This period ended with the Bandung Conference in 1955, where the first political philosophy of the Third World – "non-alignment" – was born. This philosophy was promoted by the great and colorful figures of the 1950s – Nehru of India, Nasser of Egypt, Sukarno of Indonesia.

The second stage, in the 1960s, was characterized by great optimism. It was the period when decolonization spread rapidly with the non-alignment philosophy as its guide. In 1964, fourteen African countries achieved independence.

In the third stage, beginning in the 1970s, the great optimism which had accompanied the birth of nations began to be dashed. The belief that national independence automatically meant economic independence and cultural independence proved to be a utopian and completely unrealistic conception.

A fourth stage was opened up by the Iranian revolution, which emerged as a reaction to the optimistic efforts for development. The technocratic character of modern values and the industrial plans of the optimistic period ignored the crucial dimension of historical societies – the ethical and religious values of tradition. The traditional-historical societies refused this new way of life because they felt it threatened the most elemental part of their identity.

The rapid importation of technology into Iran, for example, was also perceived by Iranians as a humiliation for a people with such a long, traditional culture. Because they were not able to learn the technology, they felt ashamed. This humiliation caused a very strong reaction. The Iranians nearly destroyed the sugar factories built by European specialists because they felt such fury. Because it was something foreign, they felt the technology was built-in to dominate them. Change was so rapid that they were unable to accept it.

The great Iranian masses that followed the Ayatollah Khomeini found the grand economic plans of the Shah and his Westernized advisers inefficient in terms of leading them to Heaven, to Paradise. As a result, even more emphasis was placed on older values. People defended themselves by hiding in these old values. The old traditions and the old religion were the only shelter available to them.

The emotional and religious movements we see in reaction today across the Islamic world are only the beginning. The Iranian Revolution opened a new period in Third World countries – the period of cultural decolonization. But this counter-revolution cannot succeed. It is not creative, but defensive. It remains defined by what it resists. It leads to paralysis. Meanwhile, America moves on at relative light speed.

Nothing will change unless the historical societies learn to create, to make a revolution of the mind, of attitude, of organization. If they don't destroy history, it will destroy them.

2 / State, Father, and God in the South

Mahmoud Hussein is the pen name of the two Egyptian intellectuals, Baghat Elnadi and Adel Rifaat, who edit the *UNESCO Courier*. They also produced and directed the film, *Versant du Sud*.

The societies of the South have emerged from a long and **PARIS** memorable past. But as the twentieth century draws to a close, they are the product of a history that is not exclusively their own. Certainly, they bear the marks of cultures with religious and traditional foundations that take for granted the pre-eminence of the group over the individual. At the same time, however, they have been irreversibly transformed by the colonial experience which gradually led to the disintegration of their community institutions and paved the way for the emergence of the modern individual.

As the individual was progressively weaned from his ancestral solidarities, he became psychically an orphan, culturally a hybrid, and politically deprived of most of the rights and prerogatives of citizenship.

Today societies such as Egypt are in a feverish fluctuation between outside influences and inside culture, between tradition and progress. The individual is endlessly torn and tormented with conflicts. It is through this existential wound that we can understand the true essence of the societies of the South.

Indeed, there is a fundamental difference between the individual who emerged in the Europe of the Renaissance and the Enlightenment and the individual who emerged in all those societies dominated by European colonialism. In Europe, individuality meant liberty, progress, initiative, creativity; for the colonized, individuality meant alienation, loss of any frame of reference, and bewildering solitude.

In the South the birth of individual self-awareness was a process filled with pain and conflict inflicted by the colonizer in a series of shocks – people were forced to live their individuality before they could come to terms with it intellectually, and with conceptual instruments that were alien to their culture.

Before colonialism, people had two interlocking systems of reference that claimed their allegiance. The first was the domain of the clan, tribe, village, and neighborhood. For each person, these constituted the primary dimension of his being. Second, the religious domain linked together the meaning of life, the secret of eternity, the fear of the political, and peace of the spiritual.

When the colonial penetration was completed at the turn of the twentieth century, the South's system of reference was shaken and traditional economic institutions were disturbed. The challenge was total.

It was mainly in the cities that the individualization process gained strength. As the dislocation of the pockets of community life coincided with the introduction of modern social organization – bureaucratic administration and professions – a growing number of people found new intellectual references and new economic supports which centered on the individual's responsibility for his own actions.

Transformation was effected above all through the modern school. Introduced by colonial powers that did not hesitate to violate tradition, the new schools replaced traditional religious schools that soon lost their prestige, their teaching discredited. The modern school was the capillary system through which a new mentality was introduced. That modern mentality slowly but surely separated the circuits of rational intelligence from those of faith, giving the first impetus to an experimental and critical approach. In doing so, it etched the concept of individual awareness.

But this awareness stood alone when it was called upon to confront the omnipotence of the colonizer. Indeed, the confrontation only intensified the individual's feeling that he was torn between two worlds – the colonizer simultaneously aroused his secret admiration and humiliated him. The colonizer spread new horizons before him even as his innermost impulses were shattered. He offered him access to modern rationalism, but in doing so forced him to betray remaining vital truths. The colonizer introduced the tools of change, but kept the colonized in a status of endless subjugation.

Communications networks began to take root in towns, linking together these awakening individuals who, without breaking off their attachment to their communities, began to live lives beyond the reach of those ties. Different parts of town opened up to each other; cafés, clubs, and associations bloomed; books and journals circulated, contacts and discussions crossed frontiers of tribe, family, craft, organizations; ideas constantly circulated; general priorities emerged. Public opinion was born.

The collective entity that emerged was not simply the combined echo of all other awakening subjects. The collective was the object of transference, a superego sublimating the feelings of individual impotence; it was a point of refuge for those defenseless individuals who saw all the hallmarks of their identity tottering under the scornful eye of the colonizer. Individuals sought to create around themselves a new point of reference in which they could recognize each other and also gain recognition from the colonizer.

Thus there emerged a third circle – national identity – to supplant the earlier circles of allegiance in clan or ethnic and religious identity. At the urging of the emancipated middle-class intellectuals, nationalism slowly grew out of the embrace of the first two, using secularization of political life as leverage. **FROM CLAN TO NATION**

What would be the specific reference points around which national character could be defined? The answer was a living language able to adapt to new forms demanded by modernity – a literary, artistic, philosophical, scientific, and technical heritage rooted in the familiar landmarks of a people but that could survive outside of the religious world; a transposable code of values; a shared memory of past events, mythic or historic, on the basis of which political discourse could create a temporal vision of the past.

These elements were combined into a coherent discourse by leaders of national liberation movements. After the Second World War, the modern state carved out by colonialism became the repository of national spirit for a society that was still too incomplete and fragile to assume its own destiny.

This state had to impose its authority over society, attempting to subdue the chaotic forces that surged through it. The state had to remain above society in order to arbitrate its conflicts yet penetrate it if it hoped to install a lasting legitimacy. It had to recognize the forces of inertia and conservatism which persisted within the religious and traditional communities while still working to encourage the development of a middle class capable of reinforcing the state's hold on society and eventually opening the country to the modern world.

In the face of such an unstable transition, a country usually needed a strong figure who could embody the nation's common interests; a voice that would resound deep within the popular consciousness; a figure of unity who could overcome the lost fellowships and personal impotencies – who could make it possible for each individual to find himself in communion with all the others.

FROM STATE TO FATHER The Father figure – Nahhas Pasha, Nasser, Bourguiba, Nehru, Sukarno – stood as the guardian over the anxious individual, shielding him from the uncertain future, the growing anonymity of society and the frightening diversity of the world.

This figure thus fulfilled two essential functions. On the

one hand, he reproduced at the level of the entire nation the structure of the grassroots community, whose members could recognize one another and win recognition in other people's eyes through the link with the Father. On the other hand, the Father figure accelerated the disintegration of that community's own form of expression, providing in exchange the comforting assurance of belonging to a national identity, gradually freeing politics from the influence of religion, steering people's minds away from the eternal and locating the collective destiny in historical time.

The individual was thus governed by the Father figure over which he had little control. The private dimension of his life also began to demand more self-management which presented the individual with increased solitude and anxiety with every passing day.

This was a period of anguished growth for the individual. His collective self-awareness before others continued to deepen, his sense of personal dignity began to sharpen. He began to observe society and the world with a more objective eye. And yet the field of his fundamental rights was a wasteland, the extent of his political liberties tightly controlled.

He was expected to assume responsibility for his daily life without the opportunity to assume responsibility as a citizen. He was accountable to the state but could not demand the same accountability in return.

For all intents and purposes he was a citizen, yet he was shorn of that margin of real initiative – political rights – that determines the conditions of his existence.

So long as the Father continued to be identified with the need for national unity, and so long as this unity was felt to be vital for protection against an external threat, the individual could find only a tentative significance in his prerogatives as a citizen. Only with discomfort and a sense of infringing on sacred rules did he ask questions about his fundamental liberties.

By the end of the 1970s, the affirmation of individual autonomy began to pick up speed as the models and standards of the world market penetrated the national market. The influence of the Father or his heirs faltered as the state lost its ability to mobilize on ideological grounds.

Society thus began to split up, dividing among those who integrated successfully into the new international economic environment, accepting the cultural and psychological context, and those who were the victims of this integration and began to oppose it.

The majority of the middle class – civil servants and professional people who did not have access to the public trough of self-enrichment, or frustrated students always ready to answer a strike call – found themselves driven out of the privileged brackets of the social body. Their standard of living deteriorated and they reluctantly found themselves in a new political and social situation, cheek by jowl with the working class, the disinherited and those groups still bound to the traditional economy.

For the intellectuals and the urban lower middle class, the new situation was a rude awakening of disillusionment and broken promises. The hybrid formulas underlying the nation state were fast losing legitimacy and credibility. They would soon fall under the crush of economic failures, social and ethnic injustices, and the many interrelated dissatisfactions that the state had engendered.

The opposition movements that then developed demanded an end to the hybrid nature of the state and the re-establishment of moral and political unity that the state had ceased to embody. They put forward programs to re-establish value systems that would regain the sense of identity and integrity that society was losing. These opposition movements ultimately faced real alternatives: Either the re-establishment of an order based on pro-national values of religion and communal traditions, or the pursuit of a more radical modernity in the form of a secular democracy.

FROM FATHER TO GOD The first option, of which Islamic fundamentalism is the most striking example, aims to utilize the system of religious values (or ethnic or tribal values) as the source of political legitimacy, but then denies this legitimacy to each and all the country's citizens. The citizens are reduced to being believers – political discourse is once more a mere profession of faith.

Fundamentalism is popular at the present time because it speaks to all those who are frustrated with the modernist stage of national development and because it restores a sense of fraternity lost in the struggle against the harsh, implacable laws of the market. Fundamentalism also offers the authentic as an answer to all things foreign; and it preaches morality amidst an environment of corruption. And above all, it satisfies because it relieves the individual of the unbearably heavy burden of doubt and risk, of individual responsibility and solitude. In exchange it offers them collective certainties sanctioned by holy writ.

The fundamentalist option will see its chances grow day after day because in an accelerating world that is less and less egalitarian, the countries of the South have lost the bargaining power that they once held in the balancing act between East and West. Their structural unemployment marginalizes half of their populations, and the future is more and more closed off, even for university graduates. Overcome by events, those in authority are often tempted to give up and just enrich themselves.

The option of human rights and democracy, defended by a courageous intellectual elite in conditions that often border on the clandestine, is at odds with the current trend. It assumes an intellectual, cultural, and political maturity that depends on each individual citizen taking upon himself the risks of his personal destiny.

At this moment in history, the essential difficulty with the democratic choice rests on the fact that the conditions that will foster it have not yet been established at either the national or the international level. The requisite socio-economic equilibria will not be found, for example, within any of the Arab or Islamic countries (with the exception of the oil-rich states) unless conditions in the world at large are changed. This assumes, in the long run, that the industrialized countries would be willing to make sacrifices in their present standard of living by adjusting the price of commodities on the world market, through debt relief and development aid.

Stranded out on a limb, the most important need in the coming years for the individual in the South is for the solidarity of other democratic and universalist currents in both the North and the South. Without this link, the circle of progress will break and the whole historical idea of the modern individual will again become untenable.

3 / God Is Not a Head of State

Jean Daniel, the editor-in-chief of *Le Nouvel Observateur*, has been at the centre of French intellectual life for the last three decades. He is also an administrator of the Louvre Museum. He prepared these reflections for the second gathering of *Intellectuels du Monde*, held at the Rajiv Gandhi Institute in New Delhi.

The issues are basic: Should we render unto Caesar that **PARIS** which is Caesar's, separating the temporal from the spiritual? Or, if we believe that such a separation is impossible, are we led to the conclusion that religious belief in a divine order should dominate civic organization? Must we then consider a theocratic state as legitimate? If we grant this, the issue boils down to whether such a theocratic state can respect the minorities within its jurisdiction if they hold a different religion from that of the state, or if they have no religion at all.

However, if we consider that a separation between the spiritual and the temporal is desirable and possible, we are forced to ask ourselves about the role of a secular state. Can one have political ethics with no spiritual basis, or laws without any transcendental affirmation? Or, is the state merely meant to organize the coexistence of the various religious communities? The issue is then to discern the categorical imperatives of a federal government, such as natural and civil rights. In other words, can the ethics of a godless secular state be lastingly legitimate and effective?

GOD AND STATE There are at least two examples of pure theocracies in the world today: Iran, which practices Shi'ite Islam, and Saudi Arabia, which practices Sunnite Islam. There are other less "pure" examples elsewhere in Islam and in Israel where theocracy has been amended or somewhat modified by the influence of democracy.

Iran is seen to persecute its minorities on occasion while Saudi Arabia merely forbids the worship of any faith other than the state religion. This state religion is intolerant because it takes itself to be divine and universal, and it leans toward ethnic and religious grouping and even ethnic and religious cleansing. (One could claim that totalitarian communist states also practiced a state religion, since only the priests of their single party were considered capable of deciphering the sense of history.)

On the other hand, we have witnessed in the West an anti-theocratic movement beginning with the English Revolution in 1679, followed by the American Revolution in 1787, and the French Revolution in 1789. From the idea of *habeas corpus* to the Declaration of the Rights of Man, the machinery emerged for the death sentence passed on God. A denial of God as head of state was proclaimed.

I am talking here, of course, about the God of monotheism. From the point of view of another of the world's most important civilizational traditions, India, our Western revolutions were not needed to separate the spiritual from the temporal. There is nothing in the sacred writings of Hinduism, Buddhism, Jainism, or Sikhism which regulates the lives of its citizens – nothing that compares with the Jewish Torah, the Catholic doctrines and the Muslim *shari'a*. This does not mean, of course, that people are not deeply imbued with religion. In fact the opposite is true.

Interestingly, the modern West and India enjoy a form of secularity close to the definition of religion found in Greek and Roman antiquity. To Aristotle and Cicero religion was seen as separate from civil administration or the state. The gods were omnipresent but they were not necessarily obeyed.

What, then, has happened to our secular states where politics and religion no longer seem to know their respective places? Does Indian fundamentalism stem from the reaction to a Hindu identity threatened by imported monotheism, albeit now secular?

According to the great French scholar Sylvain Levi, there is also nothing in the sacred writings of polytheistic India to incite intolerance, even less, violence. Nevertheless it seems the Indian state has been reduced to arbitrating in so-called wars of religion – even though this democratic sanctioning has no legitimate popular consensus.

It appears that the United States has often found itself in circumstances similar to India: Religion is totally separate from the state although its citizens are broadly organized into religious groups and multicultural communities. The Great American Dream in recent times has become somewhat sterile, a colorless and neutral legal administrator of intercommunity conflicts. In the aftermath of the implosion of the Soviet system, and after the Gulf War experience which left the US sanctioned by the world community as the singular superpower, America is wondering if its citizens have less in common than they have differences. They all come together not under the banner of assimilation or oneness, but of coexistence.

THE INDIVIDUAL BORN

Religion is, of course, separate from the state in France too. But the beheading of Louis XVI meant more than just a symbolic death for the Godhead of State. I shall even dare to suggest that in a way the individual, transformed into a citizen, was born in France between 1789 and 1791, even if almost two centuries went by before he reached maturity. The invention of the modern individual was a hugely presumptuous creation – the free-thinkers, radicals and Voltairians had been content to rally against the power of the Catholic Church, while remaining mistrustful of the people.

The Revolutionaries and members of the Assembly created this Promethean idea of the sovereign individual taken out of his religious context, his origins, his environment and his social class. The Republican state in this view is not merely the arbitrator for the various communities which have no legal or official entity – it is the expression of popular sovereignty by free and equal individuals.

At the end of the twentieth century, group interests – "communities" – are starting to spring up again France, sometimes joining together to lobby for some reform or other. This tendency toward "communitarianism" is undoubtedly as alarming for Europe as it is for the United States. We can see in Lebanon and the former Yugoslavia where this kind of convulsion leads.

POST-COMMUNIST COMMUNITARIANISM

At the end of the twentieth century, we have entered what can be called the era of "communitarianism." Why is this? Three reasons come to mind:

- What we have forgotten is that man is a religious being. He is more than Aristotle's political animal or Hobbes' wolf. He is, and always has been, a social and religious being. The "individual" was an invention, a construction. He appeared late in human history, preceded by the community, without which he cannot exist. He keeps wanting to get away from it, but at the same time keeps wanting to get back into it.

  The French Hellenist Jean-Pierre Vernant admitted that he had spent his life thinking, like Marx, that nations and religions were doomed by history. Later he realized that he could understand little about his subject, ancient Greece, unless he resigned himself to accepting the solid permanence of both concepts within man.

  It is evident by now that everything in modern life which too brutally rips an individual from integration into his religious community ends up causing a reaction, sometimes even a regression.

- For some time now we have been going through a crisis of Enlightenment Reason that emerged with the birth of the individual. The cult of Reason, the progress of Science and also the organized cult of History and its

Chosen People (or Class), replaced transcendence that was worshipped and experienced in a religious manner. As we know, the cult of Reason even led to totalitarian ideologies. There is no longer any point in dwelling on how Stalin's successors brought back Russian-style chauvinism and an eschatology where "the Future" supplanted "the Beyond."

This crisis of Reason does not just come from its derived ideologies or even the scientific limits that scholars have recently noted. According to Emmanuel Levinas, it stems from the tremendous outcome of the two ideologies of Progress – liberalism, which ended up in Nazism, and Stalinism. It is clear that the crisis of Reason leads either to a temporary nihilism or a permanent need for transcendence.

- Our century has not just snatched from the gods all civic powers, the ability to destroy mankind, to re-create man and to reproduce himself *ad infinitum* through bio-technology; this century also enjoys a ubiquity of images, the obliteration of space and time with air waves and satellite transmissions. What kind of "new man" will emerge from this mediasphere? We have no idea, but we do know that there is only one Earth, one world, one planet, one media space.

From a philosophical point of view it is disconcerting to think that nothing human can remain unknown to us. But awareness of the unique nature of our world does not mean achieving unity. Quite the opposite. And the upheavals we must suffer before we achieve this unity will be terrifying.

Population movements, soaring birthrates, the unprecedented mingling of peoples, the mixing of cultures and the babble of the world's language – all give rise to nervous reactions and bewilderment. Remember that Babel, far from being a tribute to multilingual cosmopolitanism, was a curse. The tower of Babel is a tower of punishment and misery.

Rather than happily accepting our fate as one planet Earth, we wonder who we are, preferring to be what we were – or what we thought we were. We run after what is called "authenticity," which often means re-inventing our own roots and claiming to have rediscovered our fathers' religion, a religion whose message we sometimes selectively use to reject others.

THE NEED TO BELIEVE The need for something religious is felt by some as a lack and by others as nostalgia. It might be regret for a world of continuity and the kind of immanence where an animal feels an integral part of its community, like "water in water." To Georges Bataille it is a need for intimacy with things and with others. It may also be regret for a transcendental and original state, like the fulsome soul in Plato's universe, or Paradise before the Fall.

Mircea Eliade emphasized the rituals in ancient Greece, India, and Christianity – reconstructed for the circumstances – which symbolically fulfilled the desire to return to the supposed era of founding myths.

If we contemplate the compelling logic of the reasons I have just given we can grasp the fragility of those secular regimes which claim to counter or ignore it. We can also understand how if even the most totalitarian system manages to satisfy man's basic religious needs and yearning for origins it can be assured of a future. We can see clearly the essence of despotism and the precarious nature of democracy.

My interpretation here is rather pessimistic and the reader is in no way obliged to share it. However, it is useful to remember that the religious act existed before religious faith, and that the construction of a system of belief often corrected what was imperfect in natural religion. For example, the sacrifice of Abraham would lead, through the customs practiced by the Chaldeans, to human sacrifice. In other words, there are plenty of reasons for taking into account man's naturally religious side, but there are even more for resisting the drift back to a natural state where temporal and spiritual were fused.

The religious act colors, nourishes, and impregnates the political act, but religion cannot on its own inspire the political organization of the secular city. It is vital to take into account the indomitable nature of the religious act, but it is quite another thing to submit the people's institutions – the great achievement of man's dignity – to any manifestation of religious belief.

4 / Islam's Second Awakening

Hassan al-Turabi, leader of the Islamic National Front, is the eminence behind power in Sudan and a central influence on the Islamic movement throughout the Middle East. In this rare interview that we conducted in the Summer of 1994, Al-Turabi says the Islamic awakening in North Africa is due to the failure of Arab nationalism and African socialism. He also argues that, according to the tenets of Islam, Salman Rushdie is not guilty of the apostasy for which he was condemned. He also predicts that an Islamic revolution will succeed in Algeria.

Though Al-Turabi denies exporting terrorism, the United States government considers Sudan a key host of terrorist activity around the world – Carlos the Jackal was tracked down in Khartoum and abducted by French intelligence agents in 1995 to stand trial in Paris.

Abdullahi An-Na'im, an Islamic Sudanese dissident and head of the Cairo-based Africa Watch human rights group, disputes the moderation Al-Turabi professes in this interview. "Despite its appeal to a religious rationale," says An-Na'im, "the National Islamic Front ideology is the other side of the coin of Stalinism: the same combination of totalitarian utopian vision, opportunistic exclusivist politics and ruthless methods of coerced social engineering."

NATHAN GARDELS As the fervour of the Iranian revolution fades, you are said by many in the West to be the "new Khomeini," the new bearer of the flame of Islamic fundamentalism. What do you think of that perception?

HASSAN AL-TURABI Well, people in the West are fond of personalizing the Islamic revival. No doubt, they will ultimately reduce it to a conspiracy to export Islamic revolution, of which I am the leading villain. But there is nothing of the sort.

I merely represent a new, mature wave of the Islamic awakening taking place today from Algeria and Jordan to Khartoum and Kuala Lumpur. As first evidenced in the Iranian revolution, this awakening is comprehensive – it is not just about individual piety; it is not just intellectual and cultural, nor is it just political. It is all of these, a comprehensive reconstruction of society from top to bottom.

This widespread Islamic revival has been given impetus by the vacuum left by a bankrupt nationalism, especially Arab nationalism, and African socialism. The post-colonial nationalist regimes had no agenda but to throw out the imperialists. Once they achieved their goal, they had nothing to offer the people. Then they turned to socialism as an alternative to the imperial West. Now, like everyone else, the Islamic world is disillusioned with socialism.

The Islamic awakening began to build in South Asia and the Arab world, as well as in Iran, in the 1950s – participating in some administrations in the 1970s. Perhaps due to the limitations of language and access to the sources of Islamic law, the expansion of Islamic consciousness came somewhat late to North Africa and then south of the Sahara. The Gulf war, which brought foreigners into the vicinity of our sacred religious centers in Saudi Arabia, gave an enormous boost to the movement in North Africa, not only among the general population but also among the elites.

The new and critical factor about the Islamic awakening of recent years is that the elites in the army and government – the so-called "modern" sector – are themselves becoming Islamicized.

This has already happened in the Sudan, and is in the process of happening in Algeria. In 1985 the Sudanese army, led by Defense Minister General Abdel Rahman Siwar el-Dahab, intervened to stop Islamization. But their efforts led to an uprising by junior officers who supported Islamization. I have no doubt the same thing will happen in Algeria. The Islamization of the modern sector is the prevalent trend throughout the region.

GARDELS You include Malaysia in your web of Islamic awakening. But one has a very different impression of the Islamic current there than in, for example, Iran. Islam in Malaysia is much more open, liberal and tolerant, whereas in Iran there is the totalitarian effort to impose *Shari'a*, the Islamic code governing all aspects of life.

AL-TURABI Although these two countries have experienced the Islamic awakening, each has taken a different form. Much has depended on the nature of the challenge from the West. In Iran, the challenge was very sharp, so the Islamic movement became obsessed with the West. The US identified so closely with the Shah's effort to introduce the post-Christian–West lifestyle – materialistic, sexually licentious, highly emancipated in terms of drinking alcohol – that Ayatollah Khomeini and his followers became fixated on confronting "the Great Satan."

Also, the movement in Iran was very unusual in that it was led by traditional Shi'ite scholars, the *mullahs*. Since they are a minority sect in Islam, they organized a separate, alternative leadership structure.

The hostility of the Shah's regime, like the hostility of the Roman Empire to the early Christians, gave rise to an analogous church structure. Unlike the rest of Islam, the Shi'ite individual could only relate to God through the *mullahs*.

In Malaysia, decolonization came about rather gently. So the people there focused less on the common enemy than on common ideals. The awakening there has thus been more constructive than Iran's revolutionary reaction.

GARDELS What does Islamic rule offer Sudan that neither nationalism nor socialism did?

AL-TURABI Like all religions, of course, it provides people with a sense of identity and a direction in life, something shattered in Africa since colonialism. In the African context in particular, it offers a sense of common allegiance.

Islam provides a focus for unity and a minimum consensus in the face of regionalism and tribalism which have been so devastatingly rampant in Africa. The idea of the "nation" has offered nothing in this regard. Everyone knows that African nations are only the legacy of colonialist cartographers.

Moreover, the Islamic code of *Shari'a* provides the people with higher laws and values, which they obey out of belief and not because they are enforced by government.

In the wake of the collapse of materialist totalitarianism in the Soviet Union and Eastern Europe, the West has talked endlessly about the rebirth of "civil society," that sphere of activity beyond the reach of government. But only when Muslims lost the *Shari'a* as their binding law under colonialism did they suffer the bitter experience of absolutist government.

Under *Shari'a*, no ruler could suppress his own people. So the individual was protected and society was autonomous. People felt that the norms that governed the society were their norms because they were God's laws.

The colonialists did away with that, introducing a sense of alienation between people and government with their secular laws divorced from indigenous values and internal norms. That alienation remained as the legacy of colonial rule. Even if there were formal elections, people just elected their tribal relatives, or voted for those who would give them money. There was no representation.

In the absence of *Shari'a* in poor, largely illiterate societies like Sudan, corruption ruled because there was also no accountability or moral checks on government. The public sector squandered its resources and brought the people nothing. Only when all subscribe to the moral code of Islam in public affairs can corruption be eliminated.

Finally, and fundamentally, neither nationalism nor socialism could mobilize our societies to develop. Religion can be the most powerful impetus for development in social situations where profit and salary incentives are insufficient.

In societies that lack opportunity, people have no motivation to go to school or to seek knowledge. Islam provides that motivation because it mobilizes people to pursue divine ends. The appeal of God reaches their heart. The pursuit of knowledge becomes an act of worship.

When people are taught that agriculture is their *jihad*, their holy struggle, they will go for it in earnest. *Be good to God and develop agriculture.* That is the slogan that is transforming Sudan from near-famine to self-sufficiency in food.

To the rich West that may sound strange. But what role did Puritanism play in carving America out of the wilderness? What role did the Protestant Ethic play in the development of the European economies? Religion is a motor of development.

GARDELS   To get a tangible sense of the brand of Islamic rule you promote, let me ask about four areas where Islamic fundamentalism has clashed with the West: the rights of women, the rights of non-Muslims, the penal code under *Shari'a* and the case of Salman Rushdie.

AL-TURABI   First, women. It is true that a very powerful tradition developed in some Islamic countries which segregated women from men and deprived them of their rights of sharing equally and fairly in society.

With the new revival of Islam, women are gaining their rights because no one can challenge the Koran in the name of local custom or convention. In Sudan in particular, the Islamic movement campaigned for giving women their political rights. Now, women not only have equal educational chances, but are playing substantial roles in public life – some have gone to parliament. Women returned to the mosque, as well.

As a way to protect women, since they might constitute a temptation to men, there was a time when convention had it that they should stay home. But that is not what religion taught. Of course, accordingly, women must dress modestly, covering their heads and bodies in public. Men also have to dress decently. Both must act properly toward each other.

Forcible female circumcision, another customary practice in parts of the Sudan which often led to the death of women, has faded away due to the Islamic awakening. To the extent it is practiced at all today, it is practiced symbolically. Many in the West have identified this cruel custom with Islam. But it has nothing to do with Islam. It was, in fact, called "Pharonic circumcision."

On the rights of minorities, under *Shari'a* there is a guarantee for non-Muslims of freedom of religion and cult. Private life, including education and family, are immune from interference by Islamic state law. Under *Shari'a*, if they happen to live together in one area, a minority is entitled to a large measure of administrative autonomy. Their relationship to the Muslim majority can be organized according to a covenant that spells out and regulates reciprocal duties and obligations, defining what is common and what is private.

Under such covenants in Islamic history, for example, alcohol was free to be consumed in the Jewish or Christian quarters while prohibited in Muslim quarters.

The *Shari'a* itself is not one standard code observed worldwide in a monolithic way. It is applied in a decentralized way according to varying local conditions. Different Muslim communities have different schools of law. These Islamic principles of governance are being invoked to settle the war with the non-Muslims of southern Sudan.

Shari'a will be applied in the north, where the Muslims dominate, but in the south, where Christians and pagans make up the majority, the criminal provisions of *Shari'a* will not apply.

On the penal code, when Major General Gaafar Mohammed Nimiery applied the *Shari'a* penal code in a makeshift manner back in the 1980s as a political gesture to demonstrate his Islamic commitment, it brought worldwide condemnation of cruelty and abuse of human rights. As a result, many in the West think that, under the rule of *Shari'a*, every act of theft will result in such punishments as the severing of hands or even execution.

In reality, few such sentences have been imposed because, under properly administered Islamic law, the degree of proof required is very high. And there are other considerations – the value of the stolen property, the absence of any extenuating circumstances like dire need, or repentance and restoration of property.

The whole idea is to associate severe punishment with major theft as a deterrent in order to morally educate the people. Petty theft is punished no more severely than in most of the world. In spite of the severity of punishment under Islam, the crime scene in the United States, with all its violence, is a worse alternative.

Homicide law is even more flexible under *Shari'a* than the English law, which was formerly enforced in Sudan. For example, even when the charge is intentional homicide, if there is conciliation between the parties or compensation paid, the perpetrator may actually be pardoned and go free. *Shari'a* also de-emphasizes prison sentences because such punishment is subversive of character and extends beyond the culprit to the innocent family members.

On Salman Rushdie, in Sudan, he could not be convicted of apostasy. Although Islam is very universal in its implications, it does accept territory as the basis of jurisdiction. Thus, the jurisdiction of an Islamic state does not extend beyond that state. Those living abroad are not subject to Islamic law, but to international treaty obligations between states.

Within Muslim states, it has been a traditional view that public apostasy is punishable by death, subject to trying to persuade the perpetrator to change his mind and recant. But, from the early days of Islam, apostasy completely coincided with treason, because warring societies were based on religion and someone who publicly abused his religion would objectively join the other party as a combatant.

Today, in the Sudan, such intellectual apostasy as Rushdie's is not punishable by death. It must involve active subversion of the constitutional order.

GARDELS   These responses all sound seemingly moderate, but isn't it a fact that opposition parties have been banned in the Sudan?

AL-TURABI   The case of Sudan today is not, of course, the ultimate model of where the Islamic awakening should end up. The

Sudan is an Islamic state-in-process and today is going through many emergencies as a result of the war in the south. Security is at risk. Masses of people are streaming toward the urban centers searching for food and relief. Under such circumstances, one can't maintain the ordinary due process of law.

We have been through so many cycles of uprisings and coups in the past several years that the equation between freedom and order must, at the moment, have a balance tilted toward stability and order that it wouldn't have in times of peace. Such abnormality in the time of war is, so to speak, normal. After all, the Americans imprisoned nationals of Japanese descent during the Second World War.

The social change taking its course may be rough, but all changes are like that. They are transitional features that arise from the tension of an old order dying and a new one being born.

And where there is suppression, as in Algeria, it will mean revolution instead of peaceful evolution. Peaceful change through persuasion and sincerity is the path dictated by Islam. But what if there is no alternative to revolution?

GARDELS You have been accused of exporting Islamic revolution in consort with Iran. Sudan has also been accused of becoming the new haven for terrorists.

AL-TURABI The Iranian relationship with Sudan, which is minor, has been present for the last three years. But, so what? Iran of late is opening up to everyone. They've reconciled with Saudi Arabia, Morocco and even the Europeans. Since we are a professed Islamic state like itself, what is so surprising about Sudan's relationship with Iran?

Moreover, Sudan has been shunned by some in the West, so it has turned East. Not only to Iran, but to Malaysia, Indonesia, Pakistan, and China.

Sudan itself cannot export revolution. No doubt, because of the African and Arab aspect of Sudan as well as our well-articulated programs and theories, the Sudanese example does radiate. But we have no money to finance revolution abroad or spread it by military conquest. The Sudan is not engaged in subverting other nations.

As for harboring terrorists, let me say this: We have no interest in terrorism. The Koran is very explicit against individual acts of terrorism. It says that the Islamic cause must build patiently, even in the face of persecution, until acquiring statehood. Then the Islamic state is entitled to defend itself.

Most of the terrorist movements in the Middle East were far closer to European leftism and nationalism than to the tradition of Islam. They were inspired by groups in France, Germany and Ireland. As far as I am concerned, Islam can have nothing to do with terrorism.

The Islamic awakening has reached a new stage. It is no longer interested in confronting the West, in fighting with the West. The West is not our preoccupation. We are concerned with the constructive regeneration of our societies by mobilizing our souls and our minds, not fighting "Great Satans." Except when a policy is directed against Islam, the West is not the enemy for us.

5 / When Allah Meets Galileo

Farida Faouzia Charfi is one of North Africa's most outspoken women scientists. Dr Charfi is Professor at the Faculty of Sciences and the Institut Preparatoir aux Etudes Scientifiques in Tunis. She writes regularly in scientific journals on the optical and electronic properties of semiconductors and electromagnetism.

Most Arab-Islamic countries are today passing through a **TUNIS** serious political and cultural crisis. After the failure of Arab nationalism and the lost illusion of rapid economic and social development, a certain fringe of the population is seeking refuge through a return to the sacred.

For a traditional society to accept modernity is to accept the wrenching dislocations caused by any deep-seated and radical change. This wrenching experience may be bearable when it is the price to be paid for development. But, if development proves beyond reach, the whole deal goes sour.

Since economic improvement has not arrived on time and as promised in the Arab-Islamic world, conservative traditionalists took advantage of this perceived betrayal to spread their fundamentalist ideology by force. The Iranian Revolution or the coup of the Islamists in Sudan came about according to this dynamic. Elsewhere the Islamists are also attempting to impose their religious order by violence.

The assassinations of intellectuals and foreigners in

Egypt or Algeria, like the numerous death sentences against writers, stem from practices once believed to have faded into the past. These acts reveal that the fundamentalists are confined in a world that is foreign to modern man. In those countries where fundamentalism has taken hold among the youth in the universities, it is striking to observe that the fundamentalist students are in a majority in the scientific institutions. This situation astonishes Western observers because they tend to believe that a scientific mind is of necessity modern. At first glance, one would expect to find the majority of fundamentalists among jurists and men of letters since the humanities and social sciences, unlike the physical sciences, can provide a thread of continuity with the past.

This, however, is only an apparent paradox. The humanities, literature, and philosophy allow a global view of problems in time, through the history of ideas, and in space, through the comparative study of different civilizations. As such, these disciplines encourage a certain open-mindedness. The exact sciences can, of course, ensure the same open-mindedness – but only if they are correctly taught and if they are not cut off from their theoretical content to the extent of being reduced to mere technique. It has been observed, furthermore, that fundamentalists are even more numerous in the engineering than the science faculties. They are, in other words, more users of the results of science than creators.

Contrary, then, to what one would expect, a scientific education does not equal modernization of the mind. Islamists are not at all well adapted to modernity. Indeed, traditionalists and Islamists resist assimilation because their aim is the opposite: to gain control of state power in order to "re-Islamicize" a society corrupted by Western values.

The Islamists do not recommend a "return" to what existed before, as do the fundamentalists in the strict sense of the term; rather they seek a political reappropriation of society and modern technology. In short, Islamic fundamentalists want to govern society with ideas of the past and the technical means of modernity.

During a pre-election meeting in 1991, the Algerian

fundamentalist leaders did not hesitate to use laser technology to inscribe on a cloud in the sky, the sacred formula "Allah is Great" so as to let the crowd believe that they were conversing directly with God.

* * *

At root, the Islamic fundamentalists do not accept the theoretical foundations of modern science. They reject the modern scientific culture from its very origins – when the Earth was first ejected from its central position in the cosmos.

GALILEO MEETS ALLAH

Ptolemy's model, which had been accepted for fourteen centuries in the entire Mediterranean basin, was cleansed of its fixed celestial spheres as the symbol of perfection and divinity. Copernicus reduced the Earth to a planet, a roving body with the same status as the other planets of the solar system. Around 1915, Shapley decentered the solar system by placing it toward the periphery of our galaxy. The sun for him was only one among the billions of stars that inhabit our galaxy, not the immutable face of God. Modern science in these ways demolished the system of privileged reference posited by religion.

Islamic society has not contributed to these conquests of knowledge. It has remained outside the research work that has been the basis of scientific modernity.

One form of reaction by Islamists to their absence from the momentous discoveries and redefinitions of modern science has been to overemphasize the contribution of Arabs while expressing some reservations on the very real contribution of Westerners to scientific advancement. Thus, it will be insistently affirmed that the laws of optics stated by Descartes were entirely the fruit of the work done by Ibn al-Haytam.

It is certainly true that the mathematical sciences have progressed thanks to the Arabic contribution, but their contribution in the field of astronomy has been overestimated. They developed astronomical instruments and enriched the repertoire of astronomical observations. For a modern scientist, though this contribution is not insignificant, it is not decisive. The fact is that Arabs have not put forward any new representations of the world; they have not begun to challenge Ptolemy's ancient model.

SELECTIVE MEMORY OF THE ISLAMISTS What is extremely significant in this connection is that the fundamentalists do not lay claim to the whole of the Islamic heritage, in particular, the rationalist philosophy propounded by Ibn Rochd (twelfth century), who was called Averroes by the Latins. Ibn Rochd is known for his commentaries on the writings of Aristotle and for his philosophical work which contributed to the separation of faith and knowledge, religion and philosophy.

"Nothing proves better divine wisdom than the order of the cosmos." Ibn Rochd wrote. "The order of the cosmos can be proved by reason. To deny causality is to deny divine wisdom, for causality is a necessary relation. The only function of reason is to discover causality and that which denies causality denies reason and does not grasp science and knowledge." These words were set down in Ibn Rochd's famous work, *Self-destruction of Self-destruction*, a reply to Ghazali's work (eleventh century) *Self-destruction of Philosophy*.

By affirming that divine law requires the rational study of things and that there is, therefore, no contradiction between divine law and philosophy, Ibn Rochd offered an answer to the anti-rationalist views of Ghazali.

For Ghazali the world is not eternal. God has existed without the world and then along with the world. His will is free and unbounded. God is the exclusive cause of everything in this world. In "Self-destruction of Philosophy," Ghazali rejects all submission of nature to laws that would bind the will of God: "The cosmos is voluntary. It is the permanent creation of God and does not obey any norm. . . . The first master is God and knowledge is transmitted by revelation in the first instance and then through the prophets . . ."

For Ghazali, the only knowledge there can be is that which stems from revelation: "the principle of the natural sciences is to recognize that nature is in the service of the Omnipotent: It does not act of its own volition but is used in the service of its creator. It is in this way that the sun, moon, stars and the elements are subject to the divine order: nothing in them allows them to act spontaneously. . . . Although unconnected to religion, mathematics are the basis of the other sciences. Therefore, he who studies them runs the risk of being infected by their vices. Few can deal with these calculations without succumbing to the danger of losing faith."

Ghazali's views are present in today's fundamentalist discourse. They refuse to admit that man has formulated a representation of the universe based in the discovery of fundamental physical laws. To confer such power on men is unacceptable to them.

For the fundamentalist, all the mysteries of nature are explained in the Qu'uran. God governs nature, which cannot therefore be beyond His control by the autonomous functioning of physical laws. This view of Ghazali and of fundamentalists today was opposed by Ibn Rochd's conception: "The reason for their negation of natural causality arises from the fear of knowing the world to be born of a natural cause and yet, if they only knew that nature is created and that nothing better proves the existence of the Maker than the presence of this perfectly organized object . . ."

Ibn Rochd, persecuted for his views, was condemned to silence. Many of his books were burned. Fortunately, his works were later rediscovered and translated into Hebrew and Latin in the West.

For centuries in the Muslim world, Ghazali's thought prevailed. Fundamentalists therefore prefer technology, which leaves little room for doubt, to science that incites one to reflection. Paradoxically, then, the writings of someone like Ibn Rochd that are more than ten centuries old are more in conformity with the rational spirit of our times than the views that are held currently by our "scientific" Islamists.

At the end of the twentieth century it is difficult not to **BACK TO** recognize the advances, for example, in physics or of **THE MIDDLE** biology. Islamists admit that which does not risk **AGES** challenging the explanations given in religious texts. Out of the progress in biology, they are content to retain the consequences of the development of medicine; but the theory of the evolution of the species does not need to be taught. Out of the progress in physics, the remarkable development of the means of communication are willingly retained, but they are ill at ease with the finite value of the speed of light.

To partially accept fundamental laws of physics is to render the whole theory incoherent. The rational step is to propose another theory that is logically coherent; this requires an analysis of the principles that underlie theories and their relations and not a simple rejection of some of them. In order to undertake such work, an open mind that is free of all constraints is necessary.

To explore, understand, criticize, innovate, and create without forbidding any question, without banning any field and giving the imagination free play – all this implies that one has freed oneself from all dogma. This is unfortunately not the case in the Islamic world, where reference to the sacred is inevitable and where the most socially correct thing is to be in conformity with Islam rather than to believe in God.

SACRED ACTS OF INTOLERANCE It is in the name of this unavoidable reference to the sacred that scientific knowledge is mutilated. But it is also in the name of this unavoidable reference to the sacred that freedom of expression and imagination is restricted to the extent of condemning authors to death.

It is in the name of the sacred that in June 1992, Egyptian militants assassinated Faraj Fouda, a writer whom they considered an apostate. It was in the name of God that the fundamentalists launched the campaign against a university professor, Nasr Hamed Abou Zeid, also accused of apostasy, to force a separation from his wife. Such acts reveal for all to see how fundamentalism lowers intelligence to the level of emotional and visceral reflexes.

This irrational step constitutes an important curb on the cultural and scientific development of Islamic countries where scientific thought is in many ways less free than it was during certain periods of the Middle Ages. It was in

Christian Europe from the thirteenth century onward that modern thought was developed. It allowed the passage from the holy text to the text that is interpreted, evolved, thus leaving room for reason.

It has been pointed out in comparative studies of Islam and Christianity that the point of arrival of the former was the point of departure for the latter. The history of opening up in Christianity was the history of closing down in Islam.

It is time again for the rehabilitation of Ibn Rochd in order to open up Islam just as the rehabilitation of Galileo contributed in a significant way to the development of modern scientific thought. If Islam cannot manage in this era to separate knowledge from belief, it will find itself further and further separated from the rest of the world racing by into the next century.

6 / God and the Political Planet

Régis Debray, the French writer and philosopher, first came to world attention when he was imprisoned in Bolivia for his links to Che Guevara and for his book on Cuba, *Revolution Within the Revolution*. In later years, Debray was a top foreign affairs adviser to French President François Mitterrand and is now engaged in constructing a new intellectual discipline, which he calls "mediology." His latest book in English is entitled *Manifestos On the Media* (Verso, 1996).

PARIS   In Cairo, Tunis and elsewhere along the rim of the Mediterranean, the first headway made by Islamists in the student world occurred initially in technical institutes, then in engineering faculties, and finally in scientific universities – in other words in the most modernist sectors and those most exposed to the outside world.

But did our sociologists not tell us that all things religious emanated from the soil, from history and from tradition? Had our historians and philosophers not proclaimed a century ago, that technological and scientific progress, industrialization and communications would without doubt erase nationalistic and religious superstitions? Don't we daily speak about the "opposites" inherited from the nineteenth century: the sacred vs. the profane, the irrational vs. the rational, archaism vs. modernity, nationalism vs. globalism?

Apparently, we got everything wrong. Our modernist vision of modernity has itself turned out to be only an archaism of the industrial age. The anachronistic and the archaic all have their place in modern politics because "modern" does not designate a location in time but a position in the terracing of influences, or determinations: not the outmoded but the substratum; not the antiquated but the profound; not the outdated but the repressed. It is not by mere chance that such a large number of contemporary cultural mysteries can only be penetrated through the x-rays that reveal out primitive traces.

In fact, terms that are antithetical in the mind of modern sociology appear instead to be in correlation with each other. Every imbalance caused by technological progress seems to lead to an ethical readjustment. Hence, the confusion between the homogenization of the world and assertion of differences, between intellectual knowledge and emotional roots, between economic imperatives and spiritual aspirations.

When the birthplace becomes blurred, the threat of death looms large. We no longer know "where we are" for we no longer know from whence we came. People discover they are lost and the list of "believers" lengthens. There is an intrinsic relationship between the disappearance of points of reference and the rise in myths of origins.

It is true that industrialization is antireligious because it relocates people through the rural exodus, the shift in employment, the immigration and emigration of foreign labor, the increased social mobility, and the loosening of moral codes dependent upon close community.

But it is because of this very dislocation that, in industrialized countries, the pursuit of relocalization of the imagination is relentless through movements seeking regionalization or ethnic affinity. Even the ecological ethos of the age is "think global, act local."

In agrarian countries subjected to industrial rape, a no less convulsive return to presumed sources of identity destroyed by technological standardization takes place. The Shah's Iran liberated by Khomeini comes immediately to mind. In short, the modernization of economic structures leads to a rise, rather than a decline, in archaic attitudes of mind.

ONE PLANET   Planetary reunification has, in a sense, indeed taken place: The world is one, and the interconnection between its parts is ever more apparent. But at the very moment that economic life has become planetary, cracks are appearing in the political planet. There are surprising cross-currents: An obsessional neurosis concerning territory confronts the increasingly free flow of commerce; the freer flow of information begets cultural self-assertion.

Our village is, at the same time, ever more planetary and chauvinistic. One exists because of the other; that is why we are experiencing the age of nationalism, separatism, irredentism, and tribalism whose hidden face is that of segregation, war and xenophobia. The urge toward division which principally threatens large multinational states of a federal or confederal nature has not spared even the earliest "civilized" and centralized states of Europe.

The combination of the economic integration and political disintegration of the world calls for a deeper examination of the interdependence of the two. The rise in religious fervor can be interpreted as a backlash against leveling in the economic sphere, leaving the field open to the imposition of cultural boundaries, both as an outlet for the expression of differences and as a brake on technical uniformization. Identity lost in one field is regained in the other. Imposed globalism incites pre-meditated particularism as an antidote to homogeneity. The macro-spaces of dispossession lead to a loss of the sense of belonging, made up for by the micro-space of sovereignty.

Splintering politics counter-attack integrating economics. The transfer of skills to external, uncontrollable decision-making centers gives rise to a compensatory tilt toward withdrawal and internal autonomy. Globalization must be appreciated under its twin aspects of withdrawal and redeployment, of contraction and expansion, of de-culturalization and re-culturalization. In Europe this was all manifestly clear in the debate over the Maastricht Treaty on integration.

The appearance of localisms does not negate globalization. On the contrary, it is a product of globalization. Each new device for uprooting liberates a mechanism of defensive territorial implantation, necessarily of a sacred nature. The soil and the sacred go together.

It is as if there were a thermostat regulating collective identification, a mysterious anthropological mechanism that, through extremism, heals the wounds inflicted by dislocation on the cultural integrity of human groups.

THE SPIRITUAL PENDULUM IN HISTORY

The twentieth century saw an unprecedented infusion of religions into politics, mostly through the great secular mythologies of class struggle and nationalism. Since the failure of our utopias and substitute millenarianisms with a universalist claim, we have witnessed the offensive of the old, local millenarianisms. The latter are trusted as far more consistent and less prone to "falsification."

The disinvestment in the political field by those who have been disillusioned is now opening the way to invest-ment in the "City" – in the ancient sense of a tribal grouping – by the revealed religions according to their natural, terri-torial inclination. This can be seen as a backward swing of the spiritual pendulum in history.

The liberal, mercantilistic and minimalist state is, there-fore, playing into the hands of the clergy who will not relent until the universal secularism of modern times gives up completely. "We destroy only that which we replace," Auguste Comte prophesied.

Religion turns out after all not to be the opium of the people, but the vitamin of the weak. How is it possible to divert the poorest of the poor from taking recourse to this vitamin if democratic states have no mystique to propose other than material improvement?

We must see that it is precisely due to the lack of a freely granted civic religion, the lack of an agnostic spirituality, the lack of credible political and social ethics that, once again, clerical fanaticisms are prospering.

Today, the greatest ally of obscurantism is the spiritually empty economism of our prosperous liberal societies. If our cynics up there at the apex of power were less concerned with the Dow Jones Index there would undoubtedly be fewer devotees, down here, in the mosques and basilicas.

7 / Islam:
Postman of Civilization

Haris Silajdzic was prime minister of Bosnia from 1992 through 1995. Silajdzic, whose father headed the largest Mosque in Bosnia and whose maternal grandfather was a religious judge, had a Koranic education and studied in Libya. His remarks here are adapted from a conversation with Flora Lewis, Paris-based contributing editor of *NPQ*'s weekly column for the *Los Angeles Times* Syndicate, Global Viewpoint.

SARAJEVO Islam today is not the Islam of fifty years ago. Each in its own way, Muslim societies as different as Bosnia, Iran, Egypt, Malaysia, and Pakistan – all worlds in themselves – are trying to step into modernity.

But there is tension. While the revolutions of literacy, telecommunications and travel have exposed ordinary Muslims to the glamorous material symbols of modernity, such a reality remains beyond the reach of all but one or two percent of the population.

So there is frustration, and anger. To fill this gap between dreams and reality, people cling to what they trust most: their cultural identity and their religion. As a religion Islam is especially comforting because it is comprehensive. It provides answers for all situations in life, including an answer to the spiritual vacuum of the West.

When this all–encompassing faith is presented by some in an aggressive manner, animated by anger and frustration, it is viewed by the West as dangerous "fundamentalism." Like the Muslims of the East, the heads of Westerners these days are so overloaded with information that they can only organize their world with labels and by resorting to prejudice.

Images of distant places are taken for reality. Whether looking West to East or vice versa, grasping complexity seems a luxury our fast-paced times will no longer afford. The rush of the media is bringing people together as never before, but people are not ready. Man's nature is incremental. He needs time to absorb change and adapt, to acculturate.

Information can be helpful, but it can also be dangerous if the speed of the deluge only creates false ideas, anxiety and suspicion. If we want to survive, we will all have to slow down and live with less.

THE TRAIT OF TOLERANCE

Certainly intolerance can be found in the Islamic world, particularly among those mired without hope in impoverished living conditions, just as it can be found within the actual history of all the great religions. In properly assessing any faith in today's complex world, though, one must look to the fundamental message. Throughout its history, the message of Islam has been one of inclusiveness, not exclusiveness.

Indeed, the trait of tolerance has led to Islam being called "the postman of civilization" because it has linked so many disparate cultures together with its message. Though Islam emerged from the harsh desert, it became the faith of the great mercantile cities with their diverse populations – Baghdad, Damascus, Tashkent, Baku, Cairo. Unlike the exclusive farming civilization of the European heartland, Islam grew and strengthened as an open civilization of the Mediterranean.

The Muslim trait of tolerance has characterized Bosnia throughout its long history, which is why I don't fear that, even in the face of the "biological fundamentalism" of ethnic cleansing campaigns by the Serbs and Croats, Bosnia will succumb to aggressive fundamentalism. Today, the majority of the people in Bosnia want a completely autonomous religious society separated from the government, which is my view as well.

Even before Islam came to Bosnia, we were known not only for our tolerance, but as dissidents and heretics. The Bosnian Church was considered so heretical that Martin Luther called it "proto-Reformationist." We were not forced to convert to Islam by the Ottoman Turks, as many think, but we converted *en masse*, and voluntarily, because of the widespread disenchantment of the population with Christendom.

8 / Recolonize Africa?

Ali Mazrui, one of Africa's leading intellectuals, wrote and hosted the acclaimed BBC television series *The Africans: A Triple Heritage*. Author of over twenty books, Dr Mazrui is editor of Volume 8 of the UNESCO *General History of Africa: Africa Since 1935* and has been a member of the Eminent Persons Advisory Council of the Organization of African States since 1992.

Much of contemporary Africa is in the throes of decay and **PRETORIA** decomposition. Even the degree of dependent moderni-zation achieved under colonial rule is being reversed. The successive collapse of the state in one African country after another during the 1990s suggests a once unthinkable solu-tion: recolonization. To an increasing number of Africans, this was the bitter message that emerged from the horri-fying events in Rwanda.

While Africans have been quite successful in uniting to achieve national freedom, we have utterly failed to unite for economic development and political stability. War, famine, and ruin are the post-colonial legacy for too many Africans.

As a result, external recolonization, albeit under the banner of humanitarianism, is entirely conceivable. Countries like Somalia or Liberia, where central control has entirely disintegrated, invite inevitable intervention to stem the spreading "cancer of chaos," in the phrase of United States Agency for International Development director Brian Atwood.

The colonization impulse that is resurfacing, however, is

likely to look different this time around. A trusteeship system – like that of the United Nations over the Congo in 1960 when order fell apart with the Belgian pullout – could be established that is more genuinely international and less Western than under the old guise. Administering powers for the trusteeship territories could come from Africa or Asia as well as from the rest of the UN membership. The "white man's burden" would, in a sense, become humanity's shared burden.

In the twenty-first century, for example, might Ethiopia (that will by then presumably be more stable than it is today) be called upon to run Somalia on behalf of the UN? After all, Ethiopia was once a black imperial power, annexing its neighboring communities. Why should it not take up that historical role again in a more benign manner that has legitimate international sanction?

Might Egypt re-establish its big brother relationship with the Sudan? Might the UN implore post-apartheid South Africa to oversee war-torn Angola?

Surely it is time for Africans to exert more pressure on each other, including through benevolent intervention, to achieve a kind of Pax Africana based on regional integration or unification of smaller states. Some African countries will simply need to be temporarily controlled by others. Inevitably some dysfunctional countries would need to submit to trusteeship and even tutelage for a while, as Zanzibar did when it was annexed by Tanganyika in 1964 to form Tanzania. If Burundi and Rwanda had been similarly united into a larger state where the balance between Tutsi and Hutu would have been part of a more diverse population, the savagery we've witnessed over the past months would very likely not have happened on the scale it has occurred.

If recolonization or self-colonization is the path that lies ahead for Africa, there must be a continental authority to ensure that such an order does not merely mask base aims of exploitation.

What I propose as a longer-term solution to problems exposed by today's crises is the establishment of an African Security Council composed of five pivotal regional states, or potential pivot states, that would oversee the continent. This Council would have a Pan African Emergency Force, an army for intervention and peacekeeping, at its disposal. And there would also be an African High Commissioner for Refugees linked to the UN High Commission. While Africa accounts for one-tenth of the world's population, it accounts for one-half of the world's refugees.

The African Security Council that I envision being formed in the coming decades would be anchored in the north by Egypt and in the south by South Africa. Although it is presently experiencing very troubling times, Nigeria would be the pivotal state in West Africa. Its size and resources could give it the weight of India if it can find political stability.

In East Africa, the pivotal country is still in doubt. Ethiopia, among the most fragile of the largest African states today, is the most likely anchor because of its size. Though Kenya is more stable, it is far smaller.

In Central Africa, the presumed regional power of the future – Zaire – is today itself in need of trusteeship. If Zaire can avoid the collapse into chaos in the near future, it will be one of the major actors in Africa in the twenty-first century, taking Burundi and Rwanda under its wing. Zaire has the population and resources to play a major role. In the next century it will even surpass France as the largest French-speaking nation in the world.

As permanent members of an African Security Council, these five states would coordinate among each other and with the UN.

In tandem with the efforts of the UN to establish a peaceful world order, Africans need an African peace enforced by Africans, from Angola to Rwanda and Burundi.

Regional integration is the order of the day in Europe, in North America, in East Asia and even, tentatively of course, in the Middle East. If Africa too does not follow this path, the lack of stability and growth will push the entire continent further into the desperate margins of global society.

These are no doubt frightening ideas for proud peoples who spilled so much blood and spent so much political will freeing themselves from the control of European powers in this century. To be sure, self-colonization, if we can manage it, is better than colonization by outsiders. Better still would be self-conquest. But that implies an African capacity for self-control and self-discipline rarely seen since before colonialism.

9 / Does Africa Matter?

Yoweri Museveni, the president of Uganda, has emerged, along with Nelson Mandela, as one of the visionary leaders of the new Africa. These remarks, delivered at a meeting of the World Economic Froum in Davos, Switzerland were later expanded by Museveni into an article for the Fall 1995 issue of *NPQ*.

Africa is really a victim of her great endowments. Much of **KAMPALA** tropical Africa is endowed with tremendous natural resources. Above all, this part of Africa is endowed with plenty of fresh water, good soils and sunshine all year round. In some parts of Africa, like Uganda, where the elevation of the land adds to the equation, we have day temperatures of between 22 and 28 degrees Celsius all year round. We do not have the radically different seasons of other parts of the globe – boiling hot in one part of the year and freezing cold in another. Before the onset of technology, this was a tremendous advantage.

This very pleasant climate, however, has its own disadvantages, one of which is that many of those who are indigenous to this climate take its advantages for granted. Generally they have a complacent attitude and are sometimes extravagant with our natural resources because they do not know that they are scarce and treasured in other parts of the globe.

The second disadvantage is that the climate of tropical Africa, which is good for man, is also good for many of man's enemies – malaria, ticks, fungi, and other kinds of parasites. Therefore, in the days before modern medicine was available, the population tended to remain small. In spite of the recent high rate of population growth, Africa, with a land area of 30 million square kilometers, has a population that is smaller than India's which has a land mass more than ten times smaller than Africa.

The small population of past times was a disadvantage for two reasons. First of all, a small population in the midst of abundant natural resources will not be forced to become innovative: they will become complacent. Second, the evolution of more complex political formations will not be an imperative because there will be no good reason why one clan or tribe should go to conquer another one if they have enough resources where they live.

This was not a problem as long as the local constellation of tribal states lived by itself, without the appearance on the scene of groups from other continents where scarcity of natural resources and other difficulties have forced them to be more disciplined and organized. If the latter appear on the scene, then the former will, initially at least, find it difficult to maintain their sovereignty. This is exactly what happened in Africa, especially tropical Africa. The small tribal states were confronted by more organized groups from Europe and the tribal states lost their sovereignty.

EUROPEAN DISTORTIONS The European intrusion in our affairs cost us 500 years of development and created the many distortions that we are still grappling with even today.

Two of the distortions stand out in my mind. The first one is the destruction of the artisan class of Africa that resulted from colonialism grabbing the African market. The agricultural iron implements and other household items that used to be the prop of the African artisan socioeconomic class were replaced with European manufactured goods. The artisan class, which was on the verge of metamorphosing into a middle class, was wiped out. Therefore, colonialism, in spite of the few, peripheral advantages it brought, such as literacy for some parts of tropical Africa, caused a very serious social regression.

Without a middle class, entrepreneurship, if there has been any at all, has been foreign – European and Lebanese in West Africa, or Indian in East Africa. The absence of a middle class has also negatively impacted on African security and integration. A middle class has cosmopolitan interests and is more integrative in the search for markets and raw materials. It is the absence of a middle class that explains phenomena like the catastrophes in Somalia, Rwanda, and Burundi, where people who speak the same language, have the same culture and religion, have been killing one another. The cause if not tribalism: It is social underdevelopment.

The second distortion is the structures of political power that were inherited from colonialism. In order to ensure compliance and servility, the masters created a dual system of control throughout the colonial administration. On top, you always had European officers with African auxiliaries below them. In the colonial administrations you had European officers on top and African clerks and interpreters below them; in the hospitals you had European doctors (very few at that time) and below them you had African dressers and medical assistants; in the army (and this is most important) you had European officers on top and African sergeants below them.

Owing to the emergence of the communist camp in Eastern Europe and China, the mutual weakening by the imperialist powers because of the first and second world wars, and to the massive Afro-Asian anticolonial struggles, colonialism suffered either outright defeat, as in Vietnam, or was forced to withdraw with a degree of residual grace by the "granting" of independence.

Unfortunately, in most cases in Africa, the people who were "granted independence" were not the population at large. The Asian countries were luckier in that the independence movements were led by intellectuals representing sizable local middle classes. People like Jawarhalal Nehru and Mahatma Gandhi come to mind. However, in most of Africa power was "granted" to the very colonial auxiliaries who had been menial subordinates in the colonial system.

Therefore, the clerk became the prime minister; the hospital assistant became the minister of health; and the sergeant became the field marshal. This is how we got our Idi Amins, Said Barres, Bokassas, and others. There were some intellectuals like Julius Nyerere and Kwame Nkrumah, but they had no sufficient local backup and cross-fertilization to evolve sustainable policies. They were lone messengers in a wilderness of social and political underdevelopment.

Because of the effects of colonialism, therefore, three types of regimes emerged in Africa. One type was led by the colonial sergeants like Amin and Bokassa, characterized by ignorance and buffoonery. The second type was led by intellectuals like Kwame Nkrumah of Ghana, Julius Nyerere of Tanzania, Gamal Abdel Nasser of Egypt, and Leopold Senghor of Senegal.

Although these were men of ideas, their countries lacked an energizing, entrepreneurial middle class. They, therefore, tended to either be clients of this or that ex-colonial or superpower and continued to concentrate solely on producing raw materials for the former colonial industries. Some relapsed into populism, thereby amplifying the views of the only social force available – the peasants – who did not dream of entrepreneurship but of sharing the available poverty. This distortion in the ideological evolution of the post-colonial state was compounded by the rivalries between capitalism and communism. Everybody had to declare whether he was pro-East or pro-West. You were not supposed to be pro-Uganda or pro-Africa. You had to declare yourself to be pro-West or pro-East in order to qualify for material support from the relevant superpower camp. Local issues, including human rights, could not be properly addressed in such an atmosphere.

The third type of regime was a small minority, like the one in Zimbabwe. Robert Mugabe, partly forewarned by the populist disasters in other African countries (because he and his country's independence came later on the scene) and partly responding to local pressures by the white middle class, desisted from excessive interference in the economy by the state. Some dosage of protectionism, put in place by the fascist Ian Smith, continued as a constraint to rapid, rational economic growth. All the same, countries like Zimbabwe have maintained reasonable economic growth and are now classified as middle-income countries.

*   *   *

These were some of the precursors to the present so-called **AFRICA** "African crisis" – only African in part but, otherwise, also **TODAY** caused by exogenous factors.

Does this mean that Africa does not matter? Certainly not. If anything it means that Africa is the giant of the future – I would even say the near future. I say so because if Africa could survive all these onslaughts that have been hurled at her for the last 500 years, then nothing can destroy her. Furthermore, it means that if Africans could survive the slave trade, colonialism, incompetence, and the criminality of their local leaders; it means that Africa requires little to re-assert herself thanks to our geography, our natural endowments and our tough but poorly-led peoples. The black people of Africa who 6,000 years ago gave the human race one of the earliest civilizations, the Egyptian civilization, are in the process of emerging from their long nightmare.

Uganda is an example. In the last eight years our economy has grown at an average rate of six percent per annum, and inflation rate has been reduced from 240 percent in 1986 to only seven percent by 1995. Over the last three years, we have licensed 970 new enterprises potentially worth $1.5 billion. Last year Uganda registered a record inflow of more than one billion US dollars. This may not appear much if you compare it with Taiwan's $165 billion of annual export earnings. However, if you consider that Uganda was only earning $285 million in 1970 before the onset of Amin's regime, you will be able to see what appropriate policy stimuli can do for a country.

Apart from Zimbabwe and Uganda, there are some other African countries, like Ghana and Mauritius, which have scored impressive rates of growth. It is, therefore, indisputable that the African giant can wake up and assert itself.

To sustain this assertion, five factors are necessary:

- Liberalization of markets so that sovereignty is restored to the four direct producers of wealth – the farmers, the artisans, the manufacturers, and the people working in the services sector.
- Making the African common market operational so that African producers can access a sufficiently large market to absorb what they produce and help them lower unit costs.
- A democratic order to ensure that people are free of dictatorship, as well as ensuring that economic rationalization is not distorted by the corruption that goes with dictatorship.
- An adequate infrastructure that does not have to be developed only by the state.
- An educated population that will have the capacity to utilize technology in order to transform our natural resources into wealth.

All of this, of course, is on the assumption that the remnants of the colonial state, with its sergeants-turned-field-marshals and clerks-turned-presidents, have been dismantled in a sufficiently large part of Africa. When these conditions are obtained across the whole of Africa, as they now are in a few cases, it will not be necessary to pose the question of whether Africa matters or not. The smell of profits will drive not a few businessmen once again to that great continent as they did in the past. However, on this occasion, the relationship will be a mutually beneficial one, not a parasitic one.

10 / Leaving History Behind in Latin America

Alejandro Foxley was Chile's Finance Minister in the first civilian government of Patricio Aylwin after General Agosto Pinochet left the Palacio de la Moneda. Foxley is largely credited with Chile's "growth with equity" development model that has been called Latin America's "middle way," much as Sweden was labeled Europe's "middle way" in the early days of the Cold War because it chose neither communism nor capitalism.

Under Foxley's guidance, the Chilean government remained on the path of orthodox monetarism, fiscal conservatism, and privatization set by General Pinochet but, at the same time, initiated an aggressive social spending program and an incomes policy to close the gap between rich and poor.

Too great a gap between rich and poor leads to political **SANTIAGO** instability. That is the history of Latin America. In the 1990s, we want to leave that history behind.

It is for this reason Chile has followed a development model of "growth with equity" after democracy was restored in 1989. Economic growth has raced ahead at an average of 6.5 percent a year. The Chilean state has a budget surplus and inflation has stabilized, yet we have diminished, not increased, the number of poor people.

Private investment drives economic growth. In 1993, foreign and domestic investment reached 27 percent of GDP, a rate higher than in Hong Kong or Taiwan. Unemployment by that year was only 4.5 percent.

There are no tricks here. If growth with equity is what a nation wants, taxes have to be increased on those who are better off. The government must then commit to devote all revenues from the tax increases to bringing up the bottom end of society.

For those who followed the first Clinton campaign in the United States, the slogan "investing in people" may sound familiar. But we were saying that years ago as the Christian Democrats campaigned to take the reins of power from General Augusto Pinochet. We pledged then to raise taxes and devote them entirely to spending on housing, health care, and education for the poor.

When in power, we did what we promised. In 1993, we spent more than $6 billion of Chile's budget in the "social sector," a figure that amounts to more than 15 percent of GDP.

We also raised the minimum wage by 36 percent – now the equivalent of $120 per month – and the family allowance.

As a result of these policies, we have been able to reduce the number of people living in poverty from 45 percent of the population (at the time the military yielded the government) to 33 percent of the population by 1993. Over one million people were able to escape destitution.

According to the "purchasing power" methodology now used by the World Bank to measure standards of living, today Chile has an average income of $6,000–$7,000 per capita.

TAX AND SPEND = GROWTH AND EQUITY The orthodox monetarism of the "Chicago School" and Milton Friedman were forced upon Latin America by the debt crisis of the 1980s. The countries of Latin America were so swamped by debt that restructuring was necessary, whatever the consequences.

By the early 1990s, however, it was absolutely clear that this remedy for what ailed Latin America was not sustainable unless it incorporated a very active concern with social development.

The orthodox economists and their neoliberal allies whose ideas shaped Chile's approach under the junta –

those in the United States and Britain known as "supply-siders" of the Reagan and Thatcher revolutions – argued that taxes must be reduced to "grow" the economy.

I want to make just the opposite argument. Political stability and infrastructure, the two pillars of sustained growth, have to be bought with higher taxes. In Latin America, taxes have to be increased in order to grow. In Chile we have demonstrated it can be done: We raised taxes and continued to grow at more than 6 percent a year.

Why? First, for countries that have now shifted from import substitution to export strategies, a vital component of long-term growth is an efficient and modern infrastructure. Chile is exporting 37 percent of its national product. In order to achieve efficiency and high returns, we must have very good roads, ports, airports, telecommunications, and transport systems. And our workers must have training to compete in the international economy.

Only the government can fulfill these functions. And in order to finance these expenditures without running a fiscal deficit, taxes must be raised.

Second, for the private sector to increase investment over the long run, and not just in a surge during the course of privatization, businesses must know that there will be long-term political stability and government credibility.

Naturally, it is the instinct of any businessman not to want higher taxes. At the same time, he also knows that the government must have revenues for infrastructure and to reduce the destabilizing gap between rich and poor, so he is willing to buy stability with taxes.

In Chile, not only has the business class accepted higher taxes, but they have increased their investment (by 33 percent from 1990 to 1993), driving unemployment below 5 percent.

So, where is Art Laffer and the Laffer Curve? Where are all the others who said that investors would flee if higher taxes were imposed, or that unemployment would rise because a higher minimum wage would force businesses to collapse under the burden of their wage bill?

In Chile, we have found a "middle way." We are playing

by the old rules of the global free-market economy with our orthodox monetary and fiscal policies. But taxation is progressive to finance our social policies, which are in turn bolstered by an incomes policy that puts a floor under the working poor.

AN ECONOMIC COUP Could a democratic system have pulled off the economic coup in Chile that the military junta did? Could democracy have successfully made the switch from an import substitution to an export strategy, from a pervasive state to privatization, from loose money to tight money?

History does not write its own alternatives. We cannot know what might have happened if Chile had not fallen under dictatorship. Experience has shown, though, that to make radical economic reforms in Latin America you need either an authoritarian government or a high degree of political consensus. If a democracy is to manage an "economic coup," the quality of politics must be very high.

In Chile, the Christian Democratic government became more popular after implementing policies – an anomaly in most politics – even though we have not been populist in any sense and we have not inflated the economy to keep the electorate happy. We have been able to maintain public support for our economic opening because the public knows we are making every effort to direct resources toward alleviating poverty and consolidating a middle-class society.

A modern public values this kind of sensitivity very highly. They don't expect all problems to be solved at once. They do want to see the will and the commitment on the part of the political class to make society work for all its members.

11 / Torture Without Inflation

Mario Vargas Llosa is one of Latin America's most popular writers. Mario Vargas Llosa ran for President of Peru against Alberto Fujimori in 1989 and has since become one of the most severe critics of that regime.

Included among his works are *Aunt Julia and the Script Writer* and *In Praise of the Stepmother* (1990).

I spoke with Vargas Llosa in the summer of 1993.

NATHAN GARDELS You were one of the first and most energetic proponents of privatization in Latin America. How do you assess the changes that have taken place in recent years on this vast Spanish-speaking continent?

MARIO VARGAS LLOSA An intellectual revolution has taken place in Latin America. For the first time in our history there is a broad consensus in favor of a predominant role for civil society and private enterprise; a consensus in favor of privatization not only in the economic sphere, but in the institutional life of society as well.

This is new. Our tradition – and it is a very old one – has been that all aspects of life must fall under the responsibility of the state. The state was seen as the solution for everything; it was thought to be the only guarantor of efficiency and justice despite the opposite experience of the state being the source of inefficiency and corruption.

Of course, this transformation of mentality has not yet decisively won out. Populism still lurks about and there is a lot of confusion about the nature of the privatization that is necessary. But if we compare where we are today with where Latin America was a mere ten years ago, the change is more than remarkable.

On the other hand, I think we Latin Americans are missing an extraordinary opportunity to use privatization not only as a technical measure to transfer the responsibility of creating wealth from the state to private hands, but as a means to disseminate private property as broadly as possible among the population.

When I have spoken of privatization, my idea has always been that the workers, the poor and the dispossessed of Latin America who were outside the system of property ownership should be brought in. Without widespread dissemination of property ownership, it has long been clear, modernization cannot take hold in any society.

What has mostly happened with privatization efforts in Peru, Mexico, and Argentina is little more than the transfer of monopolies from the state to the largest private owners. This contradicts the moral reason for privatization, which is the opening of markets and the creation of competition that will drive the process of wealth creation.

Too often privatization has just been used to replenish bankrupt states with fresh resources through the corrupt sell-off of assets to cronies of the political leaders.

Privatization ought instead to be the key tool of modernization for social as well as economic reform. It ought to be the means of giving people both a stake in the system and autonomy within the society. If formal political participation is not accompanied by direct participation in the market economy through ownership, democratization will not lead too far.

During the recent privatization in England, for example, people at least were enabled to buy shares in former state companies such as British Telecom, or buy their state-owned council houses and flats (apartments) at a good price.

In Latin America where the economic differences are so enormous, social stability will be little improved unless the poor obtain some property of their own. Only in Chile has this begun to happen.

With the kind of privatization now being generally pursued, the chief benefits of growth accrue exclusively to a very tiny elite. This is a big mistake because ten years from now there will be a reaction against the market and privatization. Populism will then again find propitious ground in Latin America.

In Brazil, populism is already making significant headway **GARDELS** against the market orientation of the rest of the region . . .

Brazil is way behind. It still has too much old populist poli- **VARGAS** tics and mercantilistic economics. **LLOSA**

But even in Mexico, where the advances of reform have been far reaching, social inequality remains so enormous that it threatens to frustrate the process of modernization.

The only way to avert this outcome is to make sure that the market becomes rooted in the practical life of most people. Only grass-roots modernization will do the trick. Otherwise everything is reversible because economically disenfranchised people just will not believe in the market as the instrument of progress.

Chile, as you suggest, is one place where things are **GARDELS** different. The gap between rich and poor is closing, not widening. Unemployment has fallen below 5 percent and the government has made special efforts to stimulate the formation of "microbusiness," where only a few people join together to make a small business that can provide a decent living.

There is no question that chile is in the avant-garde of Latin **VARGAS** America. It has improved not only statistically, but socially. **LLOSA** And politically it has advanced much further than Mexico or Argentina. I mean, Chile is a modern democracy. Leaders in the region should take notice.

Would Chile's "economic coup" – the switch from an **GARDELS** import-substitution to an export economy, privatization, balanced budgets, tight money – have been possible under democracy? Could it have been so efficiently executed if

General Pinochet didn't have the society under his armed thumb?

Maybe Fujimori can do the same thing for Peru?

VARGAS LLOSA I certainly don't accept that. This is wrong. Freedom is not divisible. That is why I have been criticizing Fujimori since his *autogolpe* on April 5, 1992.

In Chile it is true that the economic reforms took place during a dictatorship. But this is not a model. The building up of a market economy in England or the United States did not require a dictatorship. Why, then, do we need dictators for this purpose in Latin America?

It is true that the market reforms are taking place much more rapidly in Latin America than even in England under Thatcher. But that is because our state sector was much bigger and more had to be done. In order to get the benefits, we know we need to move fast. Gradualism has been tried too often in Latin America, and it doesn't work. So, you need radical reforms.

But radical reforms are not incompatible with democratic practice if politicians are honest and ask for a mandate. Costa Rica, to take one example, modernized without destroying its democratic practices.

We can also not accept the idea that we need a dictatorship to have a market economy because dictatorships in Latin America have traditionally been deeply corrupt. You can't have modernization of a country if government is nothing but a system of corruption.

Democracy is the best way to fight corruption because corruption can only be eliminated if the institutions of governance are opened to scrutiny and public criticism.

What happened in Chile was an exception not only because they gave civilians a free hand to shape the economy, but unlike other Latin American dictatorships, the Chilean military was not populist. Traditionally, Latin American dictators have favored a strong, authoritarian intervention by the state in every aspect of social and economic life; and they never hesitated to inflate away their unpopularity.

Of course, Argentina is attempting a more radical economic **GARDELS**
opening than Chile or Mexico in a relatively open, competitive, democratic environment.

But I am very nervous about Argentina because the level of **VARGAS**
corruption is too high. There have been so many scandals **LLOSA**
with the way privatization has been handled. Argentina
is the case par excellence of the transfer of monopolies from
the state to the private sector, as in the case of the de-
nationalized telephone company.

Fujimori, of course, is highly popular in Peru today because **GARDELS**
of his strongman approach. The public has delegated their
trust to him to save Peru because they think that democracy
was just too messy and because it did not eliminate corruption or end Shining Path terrorism.

Fujimori is not cleaning up corruption; he is giving it a new **VARGAS**
lease on life. And Peru has returned to the worst of times in **LLOSA**
Latin America in terms of human rights abuses. The army
has a free hand to kill and torture whomever they
summarily and arbitrarily choose.

What is happening now in Peru is a classic case where
practically everything – the judiciary, the media, the
Congress – is controlled by the state.

So the official image of the country is the one modeled
by the regime. This image is positive, but it hasn't much to
do with the reality.

Although I don't totally believe the polls, I do admit that
the regime is popular, but mainly out of rejection of the
memory of the hyperinflation, demagoguery, and chaos of
the Alan Garcia period. At least there is some order now
with Fujimori and inflation is down.

But this kind of nostalgic order is destined to collapse
and will, I fear, bring down with it the modern idea of the
free-market economy.

This is why we must be very strong critics of the
Fujimori approach. If it catches on – some are calling for
"the Fujimorization of Brazil" – all the progress of the
past decade can be reversed. All across Latin America

there are generals watching Peru with great enthusiasm.

Peru, for them, is the new model of dictatorship for the twenty-first century: the military using a civilian leader who instead of sloganeering about socialism talks about private enterprise. This is not democracy. This is not modernization. This is torture without inflation.

In the end this new model of authoritarianism will have the same result as the old one: It will only bring about more corruption, more social inequality and destabilizing public disaffection. If the Fujimori model spreads, it will stoke the flames of extremism and ruin the new hope born in Latin America during the past decade.

12 / From Mosque to Multimedia: *Hollywood, Islam and the Digital Age in Asia*

Mahathir Mohamad, the prime minister of Malaysia, has been called "the master planner" of Asia by *Time* magazine. We spoke in January 1997 in Beverly Hills, California, where the renowned Islamic nationalist leader was visiting to woo Hollywood's burgeoning digital industries to Malaysia's new Multimedia Super Corridor.

Many people remember Malaysia as an old rubber colony, **NATHAN** then a country that has grown more prosperous, as has **GARDELS** much of East Asia, by the route of low-wage manufactured exports to the West.

Now, suddenly, great new symbols of Asia's ascendence are rising out of the Malaysian jungle. Like New York's Empire State building at the outset of this century, the gleaming Petronas Towers in Kuala Lumpur – now the world's tallest skyscrapers – announce what many believe to be the coming Asian century.

Then, there is the Multimedia Super Corridor, which aims to make Malaysia a central player in the Information Age. You are also talking about a paperless "electronic government," telemedicine and "cyberlaws."

In the bigger picture, what does all this mean for the role of Asia's developing countries in the world?

MAHATHIR Like others in the region, for the past decades Malaysia has
MOHAMMAD been industrializing. We have been successful to an extent
where we are short of workers. As many as 1.7 million
people, in a country with a population of 20 million, are
foreign workers. Our "gleaming" skyscrapers are paid for
by us, not by anybody else. They are built because we can
afford them. That is a long way from being a producer of
rubber and tin.

Now we have to take the next step into the Information
Age. And this requires a special approach that is not just
about upgrading the old manufacturing industry, but about
a new, collaborative way of doing business through
networking and webs of relationships. We want to create
the most conducive environment in the world through our
Multimedia Super Corridor, or MSC, for digital commerce
– replete with a rapid-track permit process, tax-free incentives, an unprecedented 2.5 to 10 gigabits per
second-capacity fiber optic backbone and cyberlaws that
absolutely protect intellectual property.

This approach recognizes a fundamental new reality:
Where countries once competed with one nation's trade
surplus resulting in another's trade deficit, in the future
both countries can benefit because networks of companies
collaborate across borders to deliver value to customers.
Thanks to the mobility of capital, goods and information,
for the first time in history companies and countries can
escape the competitive zero-sum logic and mutually enrich
each other.

For a limited time, there will be a relatively level playing
field where developed and developing countries can work
together to their mutual benefit.

This is because many of the developed countries are
locked into obsolete industrial infrastructure, legal frame-
works and vested interests that stubbornly stand in the way
of the change. A country like Malaysia can more easily
leapfrog ahead to the Information Age because these
interests have not had time to entrench themselves.

In addition, Malaysia's multicultural edge – Islam,
Confucianism and Hinduism – provides us with cultural
access to others.

I fully expect that the "multicultural web" emanating from the MSC will extend beyond Malaysia's borders and out across our multicultural links to our neighbors.

Component manufacturing can then be done in China, on machines programmed from Japan, with software written in India and finance coming from Malaysia. The product may be assembled in Penang and shipped to global customers direct through our new airport, which will be the largest in Asia.

GARDELS One remarkable fact about Malaysia's industrialization over the past two decades is that, while the economy has grown more than 7 percent per year, social inequality has narrowed. The UN reports that the incidence of poverty in Malaysia from 1970–1993 fell from 49 percent of the population to 14 percent.

That is very different from the record of, say, Latin America. What is the secret?

MAHATHIR In Malaysia, we are very concerned with social stability. Therefore a more equitable distribution of income has been a high priority. Everybody in society should move along at the same time – that is our conviction.

In this context, the first objective of our economic policy was to eradicate poverty among all races. Our approach in doing this was to create industries that would employ a lot of people. Labor intensive industries – not cheap labor – enable people to earn incomes on which they can live. This policy in Malaysia accounts for our attraction to foreign workers, who come from elsewhere in Asia where they cannot earn a decent wage.

The second objective was to remove the identification of race with economic function . . .

GARDELS . . . what they call "affirmative action" in the United States.

MAHATHIR Yes. In a multicultural society like ours, this is absolutely critical.

We have succeeded in both of these objectives. Malaysia is, as a result, a balanced society. In fact Nelson Mandela visited to study our efforts to see how they might apply to South Africa.

This approach will remain central to Malaysia as we move into the Information Age.

GARDELS Singapore also talks about being a hub of the Information Age. Yet, like the Chinese, they have tried to censor access to the Internet.

After visiting Singapore, Microsoft's Bill Gates said "they want to have their cake and eat it too," – they want both cyberspace and control of information – "but no place is an island anymore."

Like [former Singapore prime minister] Lee Kuan Yew, you are also known as a critic of the excesses of the Western media. How will you cope with free-for-all media flows necessary for the MSC to succeed while also maintaining the cultural integrity of Malaysia society?

MAHATHIR I would be lying if I said I was not worried about pornography, hatred and violence being disseminated by the Internet, causing all kinds of upheavals. People all over the world are concerned about the more obnoxious things that appear on the Internet.

At the same time, it is almost impossible to censor unless there is a code subscribed to by the world community as a whole. That is something we will encourage. In the meantime, in Malaysia we will not censor the Internet.

On the other hand, the normal laws of the country still apply. If, for example, you download some pornography from the Internet and start distributing it all over the country, you will be breaking the law. If someone advocates the violent overthrow of the government on the Net and then this is distributed through a pamphlet around the country, we cannot accept that.

If you are to get something through the Internet and it is not distributed, that is your business. We will not interfere.

GARDELS As a devout Muslim, aren't you worried that by linking up so aggressively with the media revolution emanating from

America – digital and otherwise – you will be inviting what many in the Islamic world consider cultural domination by the secular West?

Today's entertainment is almost entirely American in its **MAHATHIR** cultural content. The characters are American, their problems are American, their dialogue is American. Most of the rest of the world experiences this at a superficial level. Because of the glitz and special effects, that may be enough for now. That is why action movies are the most popular outside America.

But technology will make these advantages disappear. Digital entertainment based on action and special effects can be developed anywhere. Digital action heroes will become more and more realistic.

This reality converges with another. As developing countries get richer, they will want more local content for their entertainment. Themes may be universal, but Asians will increasingly prefer entertainment that is localized in its languages, myths, music and characters. We are already seeing this in television in Asia; sooner or later the same trend will be true in movies and computer games. People everywhere want to link their entertainment with their own material aspirations. As they become secure through their success, they will look for deeper fulfillment. They want to improve themselves, to be touched by something more than materialism or escapism.

This is a realm of religion, culture and moral values which requires a context that goes well beyond America's pop culture. In Asia, the major cultures are Confucianism, Islam and Hinduism, each with a rich history that can be a deep source of creative content. Technology can allow new characters to be electronically created that embody these ideas and touch people at a deeper level.

In digital entertainment, there are many more ways of bringing things to life than simply putting words in the mouths of actors or having amazing special effects.

While Asian Islam is highly dynamic and open, Arab **GARDELS** Islam is stagnant socially, economically, and in scientific development, threatened by the grip of fundamentalism. Why such a difference?

MAHATHIR   The Arabs are still hung up about having been dominated by other countries. In Malaysia, we go back to the roots. Islam brought about the flowering of culture and the sciences for a very long period of time. The great early mathematicians were Muslims. If Islam could do that even back before the Middle Ages, why not now?

We are taking that course in Asia. Progress, science, technology, and, for that matter, democracy, are not the monopoly of anybody, and they are not inconsistent with being Muslim.

GARDELS   Hassan al-Turabi, the fundamentalist Muslim leader of the Sudan who is regarded as the militant heir to Khomeini, has declared "a new Islamic awakening" in his part of the world, including Algeria.

It seems, though, that the real Islamic awakening is in Asia.

MAHATHIR   I would say so. Even Arabs now talk about the great changes taking place in the Islamic countries of the East, whereas, before, Islam was synonymous with the Arab world. And after all, Asia is where most of the world's Muslims are, in Malaysia and Indonesia.

GARDELS   You are both Muslim and Asian – the two civilizations which Harvard professor Samuel Huntington, probably America's most influential post-Cold War intellectual, identifies as prime candidates in the "clash of civilizations" with the Christian West.

Yet you are talking about a "borderless world" and "multicultural information webs" that supplant all that.

How does your vision of the world compare with Huntington's?

MAHATHIR   I disagree with his assumption that in all times and all places in history there must be conflicts between huge blocs of people. I don't believe that. Of course, there will be plenty of conflicts between small groups of people, brush fire wars and the like.

But to think in terms of one segment of the world confronting another, that is old fashioned.

Also, there is not one "Asian civilization," but many Asian cultures. Of course we are proud of our accomplishments, but just because we are Asian does not mean we are loyal to all things Asian. I would not be proud of something wrong done by Asians just because they are Asians.

I even reject the idea of a coming "Asian century." The next century will be a "world century" because borders are breaking down. In a global village you cannot afford to have confrontations which divide one half of the villagers against the other half. People are no longer loyal to any one group.

So, this idea of a "clash of civilizations" is based on very narrow thinking.

That doesn't sound like the old "anti-Western" Mahathir **GARDELS** who has called for an East Asian trading bloc that excludes America and scolded the "lazy" Europeans for trying to ruin East Asia's competitive strength by harping on human rights and ecological concerns.

I am only "anti-West" to the extent that some people in the **MAHATHIR** West are anti-Eastern. We are criticized all the time in the name of free speech. But when we reply we are regarded as saying something which is wrong, of being anti-this or that.

It is our right to call it as we see it, East or West. I've often criticized Japan. And when we saw the brutality in Bosnia getting less attention by the West than some minor violence in some remote area, I had to comment.

If you subscribe to free speech, you have to accept the unpleasantries that come along with it. The difference is that most Eastern countries avoid criticizing other countries. If they don't say nasty things to me, I don't say nasty things to them. So, no, I am not anti-West, just outspoken.

My proposal for the East Asian Economic Caucus is nothing more than for a gathering of East Asian countries to discuss common problems. Many of these problems are caused by people outside of East Asia making decisions which affect us. Are we not allowed to talk with each other about these issues, when you have the North American Free Trade Area and the European Union? And yet, I'm told East Asians cannot talk to each other. Every time the EAEC is mentioned, it is called a trade bloc against America. It is not.

For example, the G-7 decided to push up the value of the Japanese yen as a way of coping with the trade problems of the West. The value went up two-and-a-half times what it was before. Since Malaysia has borrowed a lot in yen, we had to pay two-and-a-half times more, plus the interest. Since no one in the West is going to consider us in their decisions, we must do that ourselves. We have to have a forum where we can explain to Japan that if they make us poorer by pushing up the yen, then they are going to lose their markets in East Asia. Japan will then have to balance its policies accordingly.

13 / China Can Say No to America

Zhang Xiaobo and Song Qiang are the editors as well as contributors with four other young Chinese writers to the most-discussed new bestseller in China entitled *China Can Say No – Political and Emotional Choices in the Post Cold War Era* (May, 1996). The book, which has not yet been translated from Chinese, is consciously modeled after the famous 1991 tract by the Japanese nationalist, Shintaro Ishihara, *A Japan That Can Say No.*

A generation of Chinese has totally and uncritically **BEIJING** absorbed Western, particularly American, values. Lately, however, the tide has begun to turn. More and more people in China are looking East, instead of West to find a future. Because of the growth of the Chinese economy and the legacy of China's rich cultural traditions, many of us maintain that China should aspire to take its place as a world power instead of lamely emulating Western society as, for example, Japan has.

The bold expression of this point of view in our book *China Can Say No* has drawn sneers from Western observers as well as China's own established "intellectuals," such as Su Ziaokang, whose consistent put down of China comes from looking East through Western eyes. But those who sneer have not been able to propose any way of their own for China to become democratic and more prosperous, yet which does not compromise our national dignity. Those who criticize the fact that "America bashing" has become fashionable in China ignore the fact that "China bashing" has always been fashionable in America.

In fact, Chinese intellectuals are now in the process of seriously examining and rejecting the pro-Western views of the older generation, particularly those in exile such as the physicist Fang Li Zhi or the journalist Liu Binyan. They have long lost touch with realities in China and can never again be an inspiration to Chinese youth. Nor will they have a part to play in future changes in China.

In writing down such views in our book – which includes chapters entitled "We Don't Want MFN" and "I Won't Get On a Boeing 777" – we and the other contributors are not "confessing our sins" about once being attracted to the ways of the West. We are only pointing out a dangerous fact: The sense of loss and resentment at this overwhelming Western influence in the Third World is a breeding ground for a growing, anti-Western post-colonialism. As a consequence, saying "no" to America will become more and more common in the world, particularly in Asia.

Our book openly condemns Japan for, in essence, defecting from Asia. We argue that Japan should not be a permanent member of the United Nations Security council and suggest, sarcastically, that the UN may as well give two seats to the United States instead. Further, our book makes the case that China has the right to claim damages from Japan for its invasion and occupation of China and exposes, for the first time, the resentment of Chinese students over former Communist Party General Secretary Hu Yaobang's over-optimistic invitation to 3,000 Japanese youth to visit China.

Critics of *China Can Say No* have noted that we make no secret of our appreciation of Vladimir Zhirinovsky, the Russian nationalist. But our view is that if we can permit an open airing of views by national black sheep such as Su Zaozhi, who has said "if only I could change my blood," then we should also allow those who think like Zhirinovsky in our country. After all, the emergence of differing views in the debate is just a reflection of our future democratic political situation.

Examining the state of United States–China relations, we are pessimistic about the future. The younger generation China can't stand America's disingenuous preachiness on human rights (haven't we all seen the video of Rodney King or of the immigrant workers being mercilessly beaten by police in Riverside, California?) or its irresponsible threats on trade sanctions and Taiwan. In turn, we take a critical look at the weak and vague stance of China in international relations, calling on the Chinese authorities never to give an inch to the "Anti-China Club" which exists in America. China should be more like Cuba, which has admirably stood up against America.

No doubt our views on Taiwan will worry the Americans and some people in Taiwan because we encourage Chinese youth to prepare to solve the Taiwan issue by force. The theory that the people of Taiwan have the right to determine their own political future is "absurd." This is not meant to be a provocation, only a reaction to the arrogance of the American Congress who think it is their vocation to "protect" Taiwan.

There should be no illusion that relations will be qualitatively improved by visits from high-level American officials. Barring revolutionary change in American foreign policy, the confrontation between China and America will be a protracted one.

Though the neo-isolationist strain apparent in American thinking may eventually be self-defeating for the United States, we believe it could nonetheless also be constructive in dampening America's indulgent self-exaltation. Certainly, the commercial greed and impotence before terror revealed during the Olympics in Atlanta should shake America from its illusion of being the sole world leader from here to eternity. This is especially noteworthy because the "Anti-China Club" in the United States vetoed Beijing's chance to host the Summer Olympic Games for the year 2000 in that city because "we couldn't handle it."

At the end of the twentieth century, Chinas has once again become a world power in its own right. It need not play second fiddle to anyone. The next generation coming to power in China is prepared to say no, and won't hesitate to do so when it is in our interests.

14 / America Is No Longer Asia's Model

Lee Kuan Yew, the senior minister of Singapore, is still the eminence behind power in that city-state where he was prime minister from 1959 to 1991. I spent one long, sweltering afternoon with Lee in September, 1995 at Istana, the former British governor's residence in Singapore. Despite the frankness of the exchange on some sensitive topics, our entire exchange was published in the *Straits Times* of Singapore. My own reflections, "Singapore: Post-Liberal City of the Future," which later appeared in the *Washington Post*, are also included in this volume.

NATHAN GARDELS For the first time in 500 years, the West is no longer the formative influence on world affairs. According to the World Bank, China will be the world's largest economy by the year 2020. Is this the last "Western" century?

LEE KUAN YEW Not so fast. I wouldn't put it so apocalyptically. First of all, when we are talking of Asia, we are really talking of China. Asia's influence on the world without China would not be all that much.

Now, China may well become the world's largest economy, but will it become the most admired and the most influential society? Will it have the technology, the standard of living, the quality of life, the lifestyle that others want? Have they got songs, lyrics and ideas that engage people? That is going to take time.

What will not take a long time is for China, and hence Asia, to say to the West "stop pushing us around." When Britain was eased out of its position as the world's number one power, America took over effortlessly. It was uncomfortable for the British, but they gave way with grace. Britain needed America's help in two world wars. She paid dearly for that help and had to dismantle her empire. So the American takeover was accompanied with much grace on both sides.

As Harold Macmillan put it, the British decided to play the role of the Greeks to the Romans; in other words, to help America with Britain's experience, just as the Greeks helped the Romans run their empire. Washington was the new Rome for Britain. Both shared a common language and a common culture, at least originally.

But now, for America to be displaced, not in the world, but only in the Western Pacific, by an Asian people long despised and dismissed with contempt as decadent, feeble, corrupt, and inept is emotionally very difficult to accept.

The sense of cultural supremacy of the Americans will make this adjustment most difficult. Americans believe their ideas are universal – the supremacy of the individual and free, unfettered expression. But they are not – never were.

In fact, American society was so successful for so long not because of these ideas and principles, but because of a certain geopolitical good fortune, an abundance of resources and immigrant energy, a generous flow of capital and technology from Europe, and two wide oceans that kept conflicts of the world away from American shores.

It is this sense of cultural supremacy which leads the American media to pick on Singapore and beat us up as authoritarian, dictatorial; an over-ruled, over-restricted, stifling and sterile society. Why? Because we have not complied with their ideas of how we should govern ourselves. American principles and theories have not yet proven successful in East Asia – not in Taiwan, Thailand or South Korea. If these countries become better societies than Singapore, in another five or ten years, we will run after them to adopt their practices and catch up.

And now in America itself, after thirty years of experimenting with the Great Society programs, there is widespread crime and violence, children kill each other with guns, neighborhoods are insecure, old people feel forgotten, families are falling apart. And the media attacks the integrity and character of your leaders with impunity, drags down all those in authority and blames everyone but itself.

GARDELS   Zbigniew Brzezinski has said, "What worries me most about America is that our own cultural self-corruption – our permissive cornucopia – may undercut America's capacity not just to sustain its position in the world as a political leader, but eventually even as a systemic model for others."

LEE   I wouldn't put it in that colorful way, but he is right. It has already happened. The ideas of individual supremacy and the right to free expression, when carried to excess, have not worked. They have made it difficult to keep American society cohesive. Asia can see it is not working.

GARDELS   In other words, "Extremism in the name of liberty is a vice."

LEE   Those who want a wholesome society safe for individual citizens to exercise their freedom, for young girls and old ladies to walk in the streets at night, where the young are not preyed upon by drug peddlars, will not follow the American model. So we look around, at the Japanese or the Germans, for a better way of doing things.

Though America is no longer a model for social order, many other parts are obviously worth emulating. The way American companies have responded to competition from the Japanese and bounced back, for example, in manufacturing automobiles through increased productivity – that is worth emulating. How Americans raise venture capital, take risks and start up new firms. I don't see that in France, Germany, or Japan.

That is not just creativity of ideas, but the ability to

bring the new ideas to fruition and test them in the marketplace. That is all greatly admired around the world. But this free-for-all, this notion that all ideas should contend and there will be blinding light out of which you'll see the truth – ha!

Isn't that innovative spirit, the capacity for initiative, part **GARDELS** and parcel of a society where all individuals are free to create?

No it is not. The top 3–5 percent of a society can handle this **LEE** free-for-all, this clash of ideas. For them, you can turn an egg on its head and ask, "Will this work?" But if you do this with the mass of people in Asia, where over 50 percent of the people are not literate and the other 50 percent are just barely literate, you'll have a mess.

The avant garde may lead a society forward; but if the whole society becomes like the avant garde, it will fall apart. Let the avant garde lead the way, and then when they have debugged the system, others can follow.

In this vein, I say, let them have the Internet. How many Singaporeans will be exposed to all these ideas, including some crazy ones, which we hope they won't absorb? Five percent? OK. That is intellectual stimulation that can provide an edge for society as a whole. But to have, day by day, images of violence and raw sex on the picture tube, the whole society is exposed to it, it will ruin a whole community.

Isn't that an outmoded view in the Information Age? I cite **GARDELS** Shimon Peres: "The power of governments was largely due to the monopoly they had over the flow of knowledge. But ever since knowledge has become available to all, a new dynamic has been set in motion and cannot be stopped. Each and every citizen can become his own diplomat, his own administrator, his own governor. The knowledge to do so is available to him. He is no longer inclined to accept directives from on high as self-evident. He judges for himself."

LEE   That is true only to a point. Every lawyer knows the law, yet every lawyer at the bar knows who are the better lawyers and who are the best.

The more knowledge there is, the more people know who is best qualified to do the job. In a cabinet meeting, every minister gets the same information. But the ministers who tip the balance in reaching a decision are not the ones who have clever arguments, but those whose judgments are respected because repeatedly, from experience, they have been proven right.

It is not the information that makes the difference, but better use of information through better judgment. We are not all equally gifted or talented. This will still be true in the information society.

GARDELS   I spoke here to the editor of the *Business Times of Singapore* who, as you know, was taken to court and jailed by the government because his paper published leaked information on Singapore's business statistics a day before their scheduled release.

The editor told me he was not bitter and understood why the government took him to court. Lee, he said, wanted to establish a point of principle that the media in Singapore would not be allowed to erode the institutions of authority, as has happened in the United States since the Pentagon Papers were leaked and published.

LEE   That is right. One of America's great problems is that the authority of its key institutions has been undermined by the media. Now maybe Nixon's Vietnam War policy was wrong, but the publication of the Pentagon Papers undermined the war policy. America was fighting a war! Soldiers were being killed! Why help the enemy? Why undermine the morale and confidence of the fighting men and women?

Ever since then, disgruntled insiders have felt free to leak information on matters high and low and the press has felt free to publish all sensitive information with impunity. Is it a wonder that there is a problem with governance in America? People in government are fearful of having their as-yet-unformed thoughts leaked out. When they are leaked in the midst of policy-making, they look half-baked and the government loses the confidence of its people and of its allies abroad.

What would have happened if all of General Colin Powell's hesitations and thoughts and disagreements with General Norman Schwarzkopf were published in the middle of the build-up for the war against Saddam? Under the American rules today, anything goes. We had to put a stop to that in Singapore before it began to happen. We said no. We are not going on that path.

GARDELS The case you brought against the *International Herald Tribune* for suggesting there was a "pliable judiciary" was also to make a point of principle about media responsibility?

LEE The judiciary is a pillar of society that can't be maligned without proof. If there is corruption, let it be proved. The *International Herald Tribune* was responsible in publishing the article when their own correspondent in Singapore admitted in a sworn affidivit that the Singapore judiciary is independent. So they lost the case and had to pay a fine.

In Singapore, as in Britain, if demafatory statements are not true, they are legally actionable. In America, if is not true, so what? That is freedom of the press! That is to the disadvantage of America's leaders.

So you have this miasma of sleaziness, crookedness or immorality about them all, justified or not. The British haven't gone that far. When, as happened recently, a paper insinuated that John Major was carrying on with a lady, he sued them for libel and they had to apologize. He was right to clear his reputation. He cleared that doubt – though his popularity didn't rise because his interest rates are still too high.

GARDELS America's most prominent futurist, Alvin Toffler, has said, "I used to think of Lee Kuan Yew as a man of the future. Now I think of him as a man of the past. You can't try to control information flows in this day and age." Bill Gates of Microsoft said something similar: "Singapore wants to have its cake and eat it, too." They want to be wired into cyberspace, but keep control over the information that affects their local culture.

"But no place is an island anymore," Gates says. Not even Singapore. If you get the Internet, you will get Madonna's lewd lyrics and *New York Times* columnist Bill Safire calling you a dictator. Are you a man of the past, or a man of the future? Can you have your cake and eat it, too?

LEE   I know two fundamental truths: First, in an age when technology is changing so fast, if we don't change we'll be left behind and become irrelevant. So you have to change, fast. Second, how you nurture the children of the next generation has not been changed, whatever the state of technology.

From small tribes to clans to nations, the father–mother–son–daughter relationship has not changed. If children lose respect for their elders and disregard the sanctity of the family, the whole society will be imperiled and disintegrate. There is no substitute for parental love, no substitute for good neighborliness, no substitute for authority in those who have to govern.

If the media is always putting down and pulling down the leaders, if they act on the basis that no leader deserves to be taken at face value, but must be demolished by impugning his motives and character, and that no one knows better than media pundits, then you will have confusion and eventually disintegration. Their attacks may make good copy and increase sales, but will make it difficult for society to work.

Good governance, even today, requires a balance between competing claims by upholding fundamental truths; that there is right and wrong, good and evil. We cannot abandon society to whatever the media or the Internet sends our way, good or bad. If everyone gets pornography on a satellite dish the size of a saucer, then the governments of the world have to do something about it or we will destroy our young and with them human civilization. Without maintaining a balance, no society has a future.

Censorship, then, is the affirmation of community values?   **GARDELS**

I would put it in slightly stronger terms. It is community   **LEE**
approval or disapproval. When I was a student in England,
I used to read little notices in the newspapers that so and so
could not be invited to Buckingham Palace because he had
been divorced. Now, they bring women they are having
extramarital affairs with to Buckingham Palace.

A certain barrier has been brushed aside. But such social
conventions and sanctions have an important function, to
uphold standards in a community. If I want to copulate in
my front yard, I cannot be allowed to say it is my own
business. If everyone does it, the children would be brought
up confused. So the government and society must say "stop
it." That is the value of social sanctions – they are a necessary way of making everyone understand that some kind of
behavior is off limits.

PART II

DEFROSTING THE OLD ORDER

The signal episode of the second half of this century was the rise and demise of the Cold War order. The fall of the Berlin Wall, German unity and the end of the Soviet Union are events to which a date can be affixed; the defrosting of the old order is a long process that continues to unfold in any manner of ways, from ethnic bloodletting to the return to power of old communists through democratic elections to the trials and tribulations of the United Nations.

In a remarkable collective memoir of the dramatic events leading to the collapse of the Soviet empire (recorded shortly before the death of the former French president in 1995), George Bush, Margaret Thatcher, François Mitterrand, and Mikhail Gorbachev recount to each other their doubts and decisions in those days that shook the world.

The other articles and interviews in this section follow the contortions of the post-Cold War period, from Russia's humiliation by NATO expansion to Fidel Castro's stubborn brand of socialism on one island to the failure of the UN in Bosnia.

15 / What Did We End the Cold War For?

Margaret Thatcher, Mikhail Gorbachev, François Mitterrand, and George Bush sat down together recently at a resort in the Colorado mountains in February 1995 for a private reminiscence about their respective roles in ending the Cold War. The meeting was at the invitation of former President George Bush and The Forum for International Policy.

This fascinating collective memoir was first published in newspapers around the world through *NPQ*'s "Summing Up the Century" series for the *Los Angeles Times* Syndicate.

SDI and the Collapse of the Soviet Union

There was one vital factor in the ending of the Cold War: **MARGARET** Ronald Reagan's decision to go ahead with the Strategic **THATCHER** Defense Initiative (SDI).

The point of SDI was to stop nuclear weapons from reaching their objective. The first nation that got it would have a tremendous advantage because the whole military balance would change. So, it was of supreme importance.

This was a completely different level of defense. It required enormous computer capability, which he knew at the time the Soviet Union could not match. And that was the end of the arms race as we had been pursuing it. I told

Mr Gorbachev when he first visited me that I was all for President Reagan going ahead with SDI and that some of our scientists would help if needed.

From that particular moment, everything was not so easy in my relationship with Mr Gorbachev. At the same time it was clear that (with Gorbachev) we could negotiate in a different way with a different kind of person who was beginning to allow people in the Soviet Union to have freedom of worship and freedom of speech. So the end of the Cold War had a great deal to do with Ronald Reagan and a great deal to do with Mr Gorbachev.

MIKHAIL GORBACHEV I cannot agree that the SDI initiative had this much importance. SDI-type research was also done in our country. We knew that in the defense sector we could find a response. So, SDI was not decisive in our movement toward a new relationship with the West. If you accept that reforms in the Soviet Union started under the pressure from the West, particularly as a result of the implementation of SDI, that would distort the real picture and offer the wrong lesson for the future.

Of decisive importance were the changes within the Soviet Union. They necessarily preceded any change in our external relations.

We had to go a long way from a critical reassessment of the Communist model that was forcibly imposed on our country and that was sustained by repressive measures. With technological progress and the improvement of the educational and cultural level, the old system began to be rejected by people who saw that their initiative was suppressed, who saw they were not able to realize their potential.

Therefore, the first impulses for reform were in the Soviet Union itself, in our society which could no longer tolerate the lack of freedom, where no one could speak out or choose their own party or select their own creed. In the eyes of the people, especially the educated, the totalitarian system had run its course morally and politically. People were waiting for reform. Russia was pregnant.

So, the moment was mature to give possibility to the

people. And we could only do it from above because initia- **FRANÇOIS**
tive from below would have meant an explosion of **MITTERRAND**
discontent. This was the decisive factor, not SDI.

From the first moment Ronald Reagan mentioned SDI to
me I made known my firm opposition. I believed this was
an excessive project, and it has since been abandoned.

The best way to take up the new stage with the Soviet
Union was through disarmament, not armament. The
point of nuclear strategy is not to have a bomb land, but to
ensure that it is not launched. The issue is assuring deterrence so that no one would dare trigger a nuclear war; the
issue is not trying to win a nuclear war.

When, in 1986, the parliamentary majority changed in
France and the opposition came to power, they placed SDI
in the forefront of their program. When Mr Chirac, whom
I had appointed as prime minister, said, "Well, we are going
to implement SDI," I responded, "Mr Prime Minister, if
you want to remain prime minister more than 24 hours
don't mention SDI again." And he never did.

In the Soviet Union, the need for change went back long
before Gorbachev arrived on the scene. Nikita Khrushchev
and even Leonid Brezhnev were sufficiently intelligent to
transform trends into habits. They made reforms; but the
purpose of reform was to guarantee their power. For this
reason, Soviet public opinion never trusted or believed in
reform. That changed with Mr Gorbachev. Under him
reforms were carried out for the sake of reforms. That is the
difference.

I supported SDI, but you have got to remember that **GEORGE**
Ronald Reagan was very idealistic on nuclear weapons. **BUSH**
Ronald Reagan felt SDI was a way to reduce nuclear terror.
As you remember, he offered to share the technology with
all countries.

At Reykjavik, he and Mikhail almost hammered out a
deal to get rid of nuclear weapons altogether. And Margaret
had a fit about it, as did a lot of people in the United States.
I suspect François wasn't too pleased either because of the
French deterrent.

I disagree with Margaret, though, about the degree to which it forced reform or accelerated change inside the Soviet Union. We had huge defense budgets at that time and they continued on through my administration. SDI was part of that, but it was nothing compared to the overall deployment of nukes all around the world.

THATCHER I am very sorry that the SDI program has been severely reduced. In the post-Cold War world some nuclear materials are finding their way into the hands of states that sponsor terrorism. This is just when SDI would be most useful – when it would not have to face a whole barrage of nuclear weapons (which would have been almost impossible to do effectively) but only a few, which it could stop. Today we have a totally new danger for which SDI was, in fact, a very considerable reply.

*　　*　　*

The Fall of East Europe and German Reunification

GORBACHEV During the Chernenko funeral, when I spoke with George Bush (then Vice President) and Margaret Thatcher, I was also talking with the leaders of the Eastern European countries. I said to all of them: "I want to assure you that the principles that used to just be proclaimed – equality of states and non-interference in internal affairs – will now be our real policy. Therefore you bear responsibility for affairs in your own country. We need *perestroika* and will do it in our own country. You make your own decision." I said this was the end of the Brezhnev Doctrine.

I must say they all took a rather skeptical attitude. They thought, "Well, Gorbachev said something about troop reductions at the UN. He is talking about reform at home. He must be in bad shape. He will improve things a little, and then the Soviet Union will go back to its old ways. This is playing the game that is usual with Soviet leaders."

During my years in power we stuck to the policy I announced. We never interfered, not militarily and not even politically. When Gustav Husak from Czechoslovakia and others came to us, we told them we would help them to the extent possible, but "your country is your responsibility."

We were skeptical (about Gorbachev's proclamations on **BUSH** non-interference). We were cautious. We were prudent. We didn't want to provoke something inside these Eastern European countries that would compel the Soviet leadership to take action.

I remember going to Poland as Vice President to visit General Wojciech Jaruzelski who, incidentally, felt that, of all the Eastern European leaders, he was personally closest to you. We had difficulty figuring out how much freedom would be permitted. And I think Jaruzelski also had difficulty figuring that out.

The events in Poland were highly symbolic, but no more. **MITTERRAND** The trade unions were awakened with Solidarity, but the Soviet Union never stopped controlling the evolution of events there as it did in Czechoslovakia. What brought everything down was the inability to control the fantastic migration out of East Germany into Hungary and Czechoslovakia, and later to West Germany. That was the end for the Soviet empire.

If Gorbachev had chosen to use force in those countries under Soviet sway, none could have resisted. But he made it known that he considered that option an historical blunder. The very moment that Gorbachev said to the president of the GDR (East Germany) that he did not intend to use force to solve the crisis, that this was a new day and a new deal, that was the end. This was when the big shift occurred. The fault line was not in Warsaw or Prague. It was in East Berlin.

So, the Communist leaders in Germany continued to be Communist leaders, but they no longer led anything. This was a truly popular, peaceful revolution against which they could do nothing.

After that, it all broke down, leading to the transformation of Europe and to German unity.

BUSH When the Berlin Wall came down, we didn't know whether there were elements inside the Soviet Union that would say "enough is enough, we are not going to lose this crown jewel, and we already have troops stationed there."

In an interview at the time in the Oval Office, I was asked why I didn't share the emotion of the American people over the fall of the Berlin Wall. Leaders of the opposition in Congress were saying that I ought to go and get up on top of the Berlin Wall with all those students to show the world how we Americans felt.

I felt very emotional, but it was my view that this was not the time to stick our fingers in the eyes of Mikhail Gorbachev or the Soviet military. We were in favor of German unity early on and felt events were moving properly.

So, we didn't want to do something stupid, showing our emotion in a way that would compel elements in the Soviet Union to rise up against Gorbachev.

GORBACHEV We were not naïve about what might happen. We understood that what was underway was a process of change in the civilization. We knew that when we pursued the principle of freedom of choice and non-interference in Eastern Europe that we also deprived the West from interfering, from injecting themselves into the processes taking place there.

As for what was happening within the Soviet leadership at the time, I wouldn't have been able to launch the far-reaching process of reforms alone. There was a group of reformers around me in the very first months of being in office and we set out to change personnel, including in the Politburo and in the provinces, and replace them with fresh forces. It was also at this time – in 1986 and 1987 – when I thought that we should expand the democratic process. If we didn't involve the citizens the bureaucrats would eventually suppress all reforms. Without these changes I would have met the fate of Khrushchev. Of course, it was not a smooth process.

Unlike George Bush, I was opposed to German unification **THATCHER**
from early on for the obvious reasons. To unify Germany
would make her the dominant nation in the European
community. They are powerful and they are efficient. It
would become a German Europe.

But unification was accomplished, really, very much
without consulting the rest of Europe. We were always
amazed that it happened. My generation, of course,
remembers that we had two world wars against Germany,
and that it was a very racist society in the second. Those
things that took place in Germany could never happen in
Britain.

I also thought it wrong that East Germany, whom, after
all, we fought against, should be the first to come into the
European Community, while Poland and Czechoslovakia,
whom we went to war for, had to wait. They should have
been free in 1945 but were kept under the Communist yoke
until the collapse of the Soviet Union and, even now, are
not sufficiently integrated into Europe and suffer from
protectionism.

To be very frank, we had our differences with Lady **BUSH**
Thatcher and François Mitterrand. Perhaps it was because
I didn't share their concerns based on the histories of the
two world wars. Maybe it is because America is removed
and separated.

But I felt that German unification would be in the fundamental interest of the West. I felt the time had come to trust
the Germans more, given what they had done since the end
of the Second World War.

I was convinced, also, that Helmut Kohl would not take
a united Germany out of NATO. I was convinced he
would opt for the West and not neutrality between NATO
and the Warsaw Pact as Mr Gorbachev wanted. The whole
process moved faster than any of us thought, including
Chancellor Kohl. President Mitterrand was in the middle
of all this . . .

The issue was whether unification was a certainty, or could **MITTERRAND**
it be prevented?

Permit me to paint a short historical frame for my thinking at the time.

Through the centuries French leaders, and the rest of Europe's leaders, thought it was appropriate to maintain a division of the German people among kings, princes, bishoprics, divergent interests, Prussia, the Rhineland, Bavaria. But history went through and the Reich built itself a nation. This people without borders who were looking for boundaries for such a long time found them.

The first Reich became strong between 1870 and 1919. Then there was a second Reich which was victorious and then defeated. Millions died. The destruction of Germany itself was extraordinary. But the search for boundaries wasn't over.

The initial objective of Hitler in *Mein Kampf* was to gather all the Germans, scattered as they were from the Sudetenland to Austria and as ethnic concentrations all across Europe. He originally thought it would be a mistake to make war with England because there was no land for a Reich there. But there was land available east of the Ukraine. So, Hitler thought then, there should be no move westward. Yet in power he did the opposite. And that is when they began to lose. Germany was destroyed and divided again.

So, the Germans themselves had a century of memories of horrible destruction from whenever they tried to get together. It was thus possible after the Second World War to realistically dream that you could divide Germany even further. Charles de Gaulle wanted to split Germany into five components. He knew that if you go back through the last centuries of history, the Germans were divided into many more parts – Hannover, Wurtemberg, Bavaria and a few others dominated by Prussia for only a short time after the Battle of Sadowa in 1866. The links were not really very strong, historically speaking.

Despite all this, and despite the artificial division into East and West, when the Berlin Wall came down in 1989 the German nation existed. In legal terms, the borders were recognized by the outside world. The German Democratic Republic as well as the Federal Republic were recognized as sovereign countries.

So the issue by 1989 to 1990 was not whether German unification was good or not for France – certainly it was safer to have a Germany of 60 million rather than a nation of 80 million. It was more convenient to have Germany divided.

But there was nothing anyone could do. Not the super-powers. Not the East German military. There was no coup. There was no rioting. The wall just fell. There was a popular revolution in which the people in the streets imposed their views on the whole world.

Thus while Margaret and I shared the same historical fears about a unified Germany, we differed here. I believed it was a done deal that no one could undo. As early as July 1989 I was saying that if Germany wanted to reunify democratically, after a universal vote and peacefully, then it was inevitable. And that is what happened.

In the end there was a rush to reunification that over-ruled all treaties. In that process each of us had a viewpoint we held as more important than the other's.

The United States was thinking primarily of NATO. I was thinking primarily in terms of borders. I did not want Germany to become unified without recognizing both its eastern and western borders.

Germany certainly did not know what it should do. When Chancellor Kohl went before the Bundestag in November 1989 and proposed his ten points on how to cope with what had happened, reunification was not one of the ten. He was thinking then of a confederation between East and West Germany.

GORBACHEV The German question was the nerve center of our European policy. You will recall that the Soviet position after the Second World War was that Germany should be united – but as a democratic, neutral, and demilitarized country. But that did not happen.

When West German President Richard von Weiszacker came to see me when I had first become general secretary and asked about my views on Germany, I told him that as result of the war and the system created after the war, two

Germanys were an historic reality. History had passed its judgment. Perhaps Germany would reunify in five or ten – or a hundred – years. That was my position then.

At the same time, the Helsinki Process, begun in 1975, was underway. That consolidated the postwar realities, among them of a divided Germany, and made it possible for us to normalize relations with Europe. We then became engaged in widespread cooperation with West Germany. Together, East and West Germany were our biggest economic and trade partners. The Federal Republic, to my mind, had also settled all those frontier issues President Mitterrand raised by signing treaties with Poland and Czechoslovakia. All this created the groundwork for the movement to a new situation.

Of decisive importance, though, was the launching of *perestroika* in the Soviet Union. It affected public opinion in all the central and eastern European countries, but especially in East Germany.

When I went to the GDR to participate in the 40th anniversary celebrations in October 1989 there was a torch-light parade organized by the leaders. The marchers were carefully selected from 28 districts around the GDR. They were people who were supposed to be "reliable." But they began to shout slogans demanding democracy and *perestroika* for the GDR.

The Polish premier came to me and said: "This is the end." This had become the reality. And politicians have to accept realities.

For us the German reunification issue was the most difficult one. For President Bush and the US Administration the key issue was the future of NATO. And, today, as we see how NATO is being pushed forward instead of a European process of building common institutions, we understand why it was their concern. That is a problem.

The president of France was concerned about borders and territory. Mrs Thatcher had geopolitical concerns about who would dominate Europe. Everyone had questions.

But I can tell you those questions cannot even be compared with the problems the Soviet leadership was facing given our enormous sacrifices during the war. So, for us, taking the decision on German unification was not easy. We had to go a very long way. We thought the process would take a long time and would be coordinated with the building of new European institutions under the umbrella not of the Americans, but of a European process.

Like Chancellor Kohl, we thought that initially there would be some kind of association of German states, a confederation perhaps.

Then history began to speak when the masses created a new reality more rapidly than any of us were prepared for. Suddenly all these questions were put in a new frame.

We had ended the Cold War and said, as George Bush and I did in Malta, that we would no longer regard each other as enemies. We had come a long way in opening freedom in our country. We dismantled the totalitarian system, launched *perestroika* in the Soviet Union and reforms in Eastern Europe. The entire world had moved into a new stage of development.

Was all this to be sacrificed by trying to stop what the Germans themselves wanted by moving in troops? No. Only the political process was available to us. And the political process is constrained by the realities of what the people want. We had to recognize the free expression of the Germans.

President Bush was right about Germany. The Germans had accepted democratic values. They had behaved responsibly. They had recognized their guilt. They had apologized for that past, and that was very important.

So, as difficult as it was, it was inevitable that the Soviet leadership took decisions consistent with this reality.

Our concern was not simply NATO. We were very **BUSH** concerned about the question of eastern borders. I personally worked with Chancellor Kohl and the Polish leaders on this. The Poles wanted a treaty which Chancellor Kohl wasn't prepared to agree to until the unified Congress of the Bundestag could vote on it.

Kohl came out with his ten-point plan on November 28, and you and I met on December 2 in Malta. If I am not mistaken, you told me then that whatever the Germans themselves wanted to do – self-determination – was okay with the Soviet Union. That relieved our concerns about the use of force.

The only differences we had on German unification, I readily confess, were with Margaret.

GORBACHEV Yes, indeed I said that to you at Malta. I said the same thing to Chancellor Kohl a little while later, in January and February. But, still, my position was that German unification should be a protracted process. At Camp David in 1990 we also pressed the Soviet view that a united Germany should remain neutral between the pacts. And I saw, at the Vienna discussions, that (Soviet foreign minister Eduard) Shevardnadze was alone on the neutrality position.

So, we agreed there at Camp David that we would each proclaim what we thought, but that it was for the German people to decide. The united Germany decided that it wanted to be a member of NATO, and I had to accept that given reality.

THATCHER There had obviously been some discussions between us and I think a number of people shared my fear that there is something in the character of the German people which led to things which should never have happened. To this day, I cannot understand why so many Germans, why these remarkable people who are so highly intellectual – their science is marvelous, their music is wonderful, they have a high degree of efficiency in industry – let Hitler do what he did.

As President Mitterrand said, Germany only became one country in 1870, and then it started wars. There is something in that which I still fear. When you get some of the Germans demonstrating against immigrants in rather terrible ways, then that fear all comes back.

Now, I feel you facilitated the reunification. You could say it was inevitable. It wasn't. Political leaders are not there to accept reality. I think we are there to change inevitability – certainly into love of freedom. And you did move in the right direction morally.

In any event, now Germany is once again very powerful. Her national character is to dominate. Added to Germany, you now have Austria in Europe, making the German factor bigger.

President Mitterrand and I know. We have sat there at the table very often indeed. Germany will use her power. She will use the fact that she is the largest contributor to Europe to say, "Look, I put in more money than anyone else, and I must have my way on things which I want." I have heard it several times. And I have heard the smaller countries agree with Germany because they hoped to get certain subsidies. The German parliament would not ratify the Maastricht Treaty unless the central bank for a single currency was based there. What did the European Union say? Yes, you shall have it.

Now, that is flatly contrary to all my ideals. Some people say you have to anchor Germany into Europe to stop these features from coming out again. Well, you have not anchored Germany to Europe, but Europe to a newly dominant Germany. That is why I call it a German Europe.

This flies in the face of the history of what has happened to empires in Europe in this century: They all collapsed. The German empire collapsed in war. The Austro-Hungary empire collapsed in war. The Turkish [empire] collapsed in war. That collapse of empire was followed by political collapse.

President Mitterrand and I speak up for political reasons. We brought our colonial territories up to independence with a rule of law. And so the French empire went, the British empire went, the Dutch empire went. So did the Belgian, the Spanish, and the Portuguese. In their stead you now have 187 nation states.

Later, the Soviet Union collapsed.

So the essence of this century has been the collapse of empire. You only have two now left: China, which will never give Hong Kong self-determination and still lays claim to Taiwan, and the European Union, which is succeeding in diminishing parliamentary sovereignty and the rule of law, for which we fought, in favor of the biggest bureaucracy the world has ever known. And all this with Germany as the dominant one – I don't like it.

In the end, my friends, it will not work. The modern thing is the nation-state – loyalty to the nation-state in cooperation with others in a common market. I didn't vote for a common market to have our parliamentary sovereignty taken away, to have laws thrust upon us which our parliament cannot overturn. The age of empire is over. This will not last.

GORBACHEV Yes, I, too, like Mrs Thatcher, was thinking about the dangers associated with German unification. But I was acting at that time in full accord with my moral position and with my political analysis. And we did sign treaties that placed obligations on a unified Germany regarding the ground rules of international behavior and borders.

Like Mrs Thatcher, I was also struck by the more recent events in certain parts of Germany where reactionary elements were provoking clashes between Germans and migrants.

And I must say that public opinion in our country, and public opinion as well as the government in Germany, responded in a very responsible way.

I went to Germany at the time of these events [the fire-bombing of the home of Turkish immigrants in 1992 – ed.] and spoke to a group of 35,000 workers at a Volkswagen factory. I told them that when the Soviet leadership had taken a positive decision on German unification we assumed that Germany had changed, that the German people were committed to democracy, that Germany would be cooperating with other nations and sharing the responsibility for the future of Europe, that the German people would not be provoked into clashes with migrants.

I must say that the workers responded with applause that could have made the roof fall in. I have this hope for Germany.

You mentioned China. We should not take an absolutely pessimistic view toward China. China is changing not only in its economy. I also believe a democratic process is beginning in China. That will gain momentum and the problems

Mrs Thatcher mentioned will be addressed within that framework.

Now, on Mrs Thatcher's case against the European institutions, let me make this point. If the world remains without ground rules and without institutions we will, again, have to face new conflicts, we will have new divisions, will have new suspicions.

That is why we need a pan-European process. We need the structures that monitor conflicts so as to prevent them. Otherwise there will be behind-the-scenes dealings like those that took place in Yugoslavia and Bosnia by Germany, Austria, the United States and Russia. All of them were engaged behind the scenes rather than working together according to the rules, as all of us here did with President Bush at the time of the Iraqi aggression.

When you forget about the European process, then, as we've already seen, you see the temptation of some nations to fish in troubled waters.

THATCHER   I agree with you about China. I, too, believe that once you are given economic freedom that political freedom will follow. It will come in the future almost as night and day. It has been the course of history.

Now, certainly the great event of our time has been the collapse of communism. But that is not synonymous with the coming of democracy. Democracy is more than about majority voting. You must have the rule of law and a sense of justice adjudicated by an independent judiciary or a parliament elected to make the laws.

And you have to have a market economy so people can make their own decisions about what to produce and what to buy. And you have to have private property.

Mr Gorbachev and I used to talk about this. When he was still in power he tried to get a law through the Supreme Soviet to give title to land to citizens and companies. You could not get it through. And to this day such a law has not been passed by the Russian parliament. So, if you buy land or make contracts in Russia today there is still no rule of law to protect your property. This is my warning.

The transition from tyranny to democracy takes longer

than we had ever thought. We should have been better prepared.

* * *

Self-Determination and the Virtues of Empire

GORBACHEV The Soviet Union, so to say Greater Russia, evolved as one country. I had concluded that the Soviet Union was a unique country and not a classic empire with a metropolis and colonies. Its destiny, I therefore believed, was not to meet the fate of all other empires.

This was an association of many nations and ethnic groups with the Slavic nations at its nucleus. For many centuries Russia evolved outward in a concentric way, interfacing with other cultures and civilizations. It showed itself to be capable of integrating with others, of creating a country in which various peoples, though they sacrificed part of their sovereignty, also benefited from union. Russia made it possible for these peoples to protect, preserve and revive their cultures, to create their own intelligensia, their own economy.

Everyone assumed that the country would continue as one. This was my conviction as well.

It was my view that it would be extremely difficult if we tried to divide up the country. Seventy-five million people – a third of the Soviet Union's population – lived outside of their ethnic republics. If we broke up they would all be foreigners overnight. And we had a common energy system, common railroads, education, science, and defense.

In the place of a bureaucratic, centralized state, I thought we should try to make the union a real federation, as proclaimed in the Soviet constitution, by redistributing competencies and authority among the members of the federation. To create a real federation supported by the people: that was my logic.

Even though we acted too late in reforming our country, the leaders of all the republics were eventually prepared to sign the new Union Treaty on August 20, 1991, before the whole process was broken by the attempted coup.

The Baltics were a special case. For many centuries the Baltic countries had been associated with Russia. After the October Revolution the Soviet government initially recognized their independence but then, in the secret Ribbentrop–Molotov annexation treaty, that was canceled, though some in the Baltics welcomed incorporation into the Soviet Union. Although the United States and others recognized the former status of the Baltic states, I believe they generally understood that this problem of Baltic independence was an internal matter.

We knew that while some republics would sign the Union Treaty, there would also be those with whom we would have to begin negotiations – which we thought would take a period of three to four years – to address problems of territory, population, the economy, and defense that would arise from going their separate ways. During the years of *perestroika*, we adopted legislation that provided a mechanism for secession. So we were thinking about a differentiated approach for different republics.

The amazing thing was that, in the spring of 1991, even the Baltic leaders, even Vytautas Landsbergis, began to send messages to us that they would be ready to put aside for some time their declarations of independence to think about some association with the Soviet Union within the framework of the Union Treaty.

When I was in the Crimea as the signing date of August 20 approached, Yeltsin called me to complain that he was being criticized for agreeing to sign a document that would preserve the Soviet empire. I told him I was being criticized for dismantling the Soviet Union!

The fact that I was right at the time about reforming the federation and not breaking it apart is shown by the current situation. They all thought that, having abandoned the other republics, they would become rich in two or three years because of their resources. Now, they are all in bad shape.

All the republics are independent states and members of the United Nations. We have to accept this reality. But I believe there will be a process of reintegration. The present governments are not doing much to pursue this, and people are unhappy about it. They want to integrate their economies and share some mutual defense.

I would welcome this as I believe others in the international community also would. France has always understood that for the vast space of the former Soviet Union to be integrated means stability. And it would necessarily mean democracy and reform in that vast area because conflict would be too dangerous.

BUSH   The question of the Baltics was extraordinarily difficult for us. It was the one issue we worried might really drive a serious wedge between Mikhail Gorbachev and ourselves. We had never recognized the Baltic annexation, and we had a very emotional, domestic constituency of Lithuanians, Latvians, and Estonians – wonderful, patriotic people – who craved independence for their countries. I found Mr Landsbergis a very difficult man. But no one insulted me more than one Estonian-American who called me Neville Chamberlain because I refused to go to the barricades and call for immediate independence of the Baltic states. I was accused of coddling Mr Gorbachev, of not being willing to stand up for freedom.

I told Mikhail how difficult it would make it for US–Soviet relations if he used force in the Baltics. We were for independence in the Baltic states, and he knew it. But I still feel that if we had exhorted the Lithuanians, the Estonians, and the Latvians we could have set back all the progress in Soviet–American relations. It would have adversely affected Europe as well.

MITTERRAND   We, too, had never recognized the annexation. France and Great Britain were also the depositories of the gold assets of the Baltic states, which we returned to them with interest a few years later after they became independent.

However, I understood the Soviet viewpoint for several reasons.

First, the claims of the Baltics were the first to go toward the dismantlement of the Soviet Union that so many other states were seeking. And you never know if you can apply the brakes to the disarray (with a federation arrangement or the like) once the process starts. But the Baltic states were rushing the process. This made everything difficult.

Let us also recognize that throughout the great periods of Russian empire – of Peter the Great, of the Soviet empire – they had acquired free access to the Baltic and to the Black Sea, and through the Black Sea to the Mediterranean. With the passage of time as the Soviet Union unraveled, they could see those openings shrinking.

Today they have only a small parcel on the Baltic. And east of the Crimea, just a little bit.

One could easily see that for the chief of the Soviet state it was a problem of patriotism and preservation of the Soviet legacy. So, I thought at the time, let us not put Mr Gorbachev in a morally and politically untenable situation. So President Bush and I decided we would tackle the matter in a subtle, diplomatic way in order not to place Mr Gorbachev in difficult straits. We understood that he wanted to transform the entire Soviet Union, but too much haste before he could set up the legal and political confederation framework could doom his efforts.

Yet, in the end, the splintering commenced. And we have just seen in Chechnya how this process still unfolds with internal threats to the unity of Russia.

GORBACHEV Of course, the Union Treaty was not signed, though it was ready to be signed, and all of this was eventually scuttled and frustrated. The hard-liners and coup-plotters knew that democracy in the federation would mean the end of their careers. They wanted to keep the power and privileges they had for decades.

On the other side, Yeltsin's view of himself was very high. He thought, perhaps, that he could play this card (of taking Russia out of the union) in order to defeat me. So he acted behind my back, behind the back of the president of the Soviet Union. They even informed President Bush first about their decision to dismantle the Soviet Union, and not me.

This was setting the record straight. But it is of historical importance to understand why in the broader picture the Soviet Union splintered.

The problem of national identity, I believe, is the most acute problem in the world today. Of course there are some ambitious politicians who try to exploit this problem to their own ends, but it is more than that. This problem has profound roots and will continue to be a problem.

On the other hand, we see the globalization of the economy and the recognition that problems like the environment can only be addressed if we unify our efforts worldwide.

So, we have to understand that even if the world is very contradictory, it is still an integrated world – and nations are nervous about this. They are fearful of losing their cultures, their languages, and their way of life. Is that bad, or is that good? I think it is quite noble. At the same time we need global security and the economy for the future. Yet, globalization must not be a steamroller that creates total uniformity in the world, not paying attention to the diversity of cultures.

That is why we need to find a political mechanism within the United Nations and in the regional systems to harmonize these two tendencies. This is the number one issue today everywhere – from Spain to Belgium to China to Canada.

Recently, when a Canadian reporter asked me what I thought about Quebec's quest for independence, I told him that, of course, it was up to them to decide but they ought to think about the consequences. In the former Soviet republics today you can see the hardships that people must go through, how families are currently separated by living in five or six republics and cannot really be in touch. A son cannot help his mother because it is very difficult to transfer money from Russia to the Ukraine.

Having lived through this epic drama of the Soviet breakup and its continuing consequences, I think we should warn people against making sovereignty an absolute thing. If we just start dividing up all these countries it will be dangerous. It would only create chaos and confusion.

That is not what we ended the Cold War for. We wanted a new set of international relationships that would make it possible to address global issues.

The dismantling of the Soviet Union was a good thing. You **BUSH**
can't deny a people that want self-determination. I don't
think you can put it back together.

Let me ask Mikhail a question. In January of 1991, the
Soviet army used force in Vilnius, and I think also in Riga.
Did it worry you that, as your people came to you and said
you had to use force, you were jeopardizing our relationship? We were worried.

There is no doubt I was worried, but I was first of all **GORBACHEV**
worried about the reaction in my own country – a country
where more than 200 languages and dialects were spoken
and in which the way I acted in addressing ethnic issues
resonated far and wide, in the various capitals and cities
throughout the country. That was my main concern.

Certainly the use of troops was no credit to me. Probably
I was too weak as president then. But, definitely, those
troops were not used on my instructions. I refused to
declare an emergency, to declare presidential rule. I wanted
to avoid force and address problems politically – that was
my credo. But they wanted to tie me up and make me a co-
participant in the bloodshed. Unfortunately, it was not
possible to totally avoid bloodshed.

My conviction still, as a general principle, is that we
should not try to put everyone's house in order. We must
not become policemen instead of coping with situations
through politics. We should not take the big stick immediately to make order. I made this view clear to President
Bush during the Gulf War, always emphasizing that we
should not exceed the UN mandate to reverse aggression.
This is why I am concerned about the way the Yugoslav
crisis is being handled (with NATO). And this is why I have
been categorically against what President Yeltsin did in
Chechnya.

We too wanted to avoid the military test in the Baltics **MITTERRAND**
because this would jeopardize the position of Mikhail
Gorbachev. At the same time, for him to accept the uncon-
ditional independence of revolting nations was to accept
dislocation of the whole . . .

I believe that in the next century a new synthesis must be found between the two requirements stressed by President Gorbachev – the need for integration, as well as the need to affirm individual personality, sovereignty, and rights in different areas. And this is by no means a done deal.

The separation of the Czechs and Slovaks is a good example, but there will be other less harmonious separations in Europe. And let us hope it is not contagious and spreads to the American continent.

The aspiration for national identity is clearly understandable after what Mrs Thatcher called the fallen empires – certainly the main feature of the twentieth century. The end of empire releases ethnic and tribal groups. Each goes it alone, wanting to enjoy all the trappings of sovereignty. But that is not possible. It clashes with the other basic trend of globalization.

So, a synthesis is necessary. Though Lady Thatcher does not agree, that is what we are doing within the European community. Shall we succeed in effecting a synthesis between this need for great aggregates and this incipient need of each small community to affirm itself as such?

Absurd, would it not be, to encourage each splinter of a truth to lead to an independent international life? And yet, it is injustice to prevent anyone from doing so.

So, in the next century the world must create the rule of law that protects minorities, enabling them to live freely with most of the attributes that makes it possible to meet their national aspirations. At the same time national organizations must be created so that each country can maintain its cohesiveness.

If we do not do this, we shall see a tremendous scattering and breaking away. No one will be immune. The need for decentralization in the US or Canada will prevail over a federal state. And it will be the same in Brazil, in Spain, in Belgium. There would be no end, no way out.

Will we have political leaders capable of conceiving the organization of this huge world with a few major coordination centers obeying international laws set by the international community, and at the same time making minority rules that enable each to live according to his or her yearning?

Enough said. A new generation is rising. They will have to answer this question.

16 / The Great Criminal Revolution

Anatoly Lukyanov, whom Russian Communist leader Gennady Zyuganov refers to as "our Deng Xiao Ping," is Zyuganov's senior adviser. A one-time Politburo member when the Communist Party ruled the Soviet Union and now Chairman of the Legal Commission of the Duma, Lukyanov spent 18 months in prison for his role in the attempted coup against Mikhail Gorbachev in 1991.

I met him in Moscow in June 1995 at the offices of the State Duma across from the Kremlin.

NATHAN GARDELS Democracy seems to have resuscitated communism. Former communists have come back to power through elections all over the former East bloc, except in the Czech Republic. Why?

ANATOLY LUKYANOV In Eastern Europe we are already witnessing a new spiral of the law of development of the world. The "red Atlantis" will rise once more in Russia as well. You can win or lose elections, but you cannot defeat history. And the law of history is that we have reached a new stage where capitalism has exhausted itself. It must yield to a new system that takes the best from both socialism and the market.

This will not only mean more entrepreneurs and participatory democracy, but also an increasing role for the state in regulating the market so it doesn't destroy the environment or the well-being of a society.

This is not just an old Communist talking. This was the very message of the United Nations' conference on

the environment at Rio de Janeiro a few years back, and the
one on social issues in Copenhagen last year.

But isn't the market a better way of improving well-being **GARDELS**
for Russians than the Soviet central planning system, which
only led to stagnation?

Who has the market benefited? Who can buy all those **LUKYANOV**
plentiful consumer goods you see now all over Moscow?
Who are they for? Just a pinch of people in a vast sea of the
poor.

The correlation between the richest 10 percent in a
society and the poorest 10 percent is known as the "decile
coefficient." It is well known among social scientists that
instability sets in if a society surpasses a 10/1 ratio.

The late [French president François] Mitterrand told
me this ratio was 7/1 in France. [British Prime Minister]
John Major told me it was 7.5/1 in England. It is 6.5/1 in
Germany and 9.6/1 in the United States.

For 40 years in Russia it was 4/1. When I worked with
Khrushchev, Brezhnev, and Andropov we always made
sure it never was greater than this. We either increased
taxes or raised salaries to keep this ratio in balance. Though
not at all affluent by Western standards, we had as a result
a very large middle class in our society.

You know what the ratio has become under Yeltsin?
Thirty to one and getting worse. Thirty-nine million live
beneath the poverty line and another 21 million cower on
the precipice.

But the shops are full. **GARDELS**

Shops are all full of food products, but agricultural produc- **LUKYANOV**
tion has decreased by 49 percent while imports of foodstuffs
has increased to 52 percent overall and as high as 70 percent
in Moscow! A country that is reliant on food imports has
lost its independence.

At the same time, industrial production in Russia has
fallen by 52 percent. It only dropped by 23 percent during
the war with the Germans! It is no wonder that alcohol

consumption has increased to 18 liters per capita – a level that begins to damage the gene pool. Half of that alcohol is imported. We've actually lost control of the vodka monopoly that has existed in Russia since Peter the Great – and that monopoly provided as much as a third of the budget of the country.

Oh yes, shops are full, all right, but the price is too high. Yeltsin and his team have vandalized Russia, doing more damage in peace time than we suffered during the war.

GARDELS Who is the culprit behind all this?

LUKYANOV World capital, just as in the old days. An old Russian saying asks "where do the legs come from?" meaning where the root of the problem lies.

World capital today has Bill Clinton's legs – chicken legs from the state of Arkansas. In America you eat the white meat of the breast and dump the frozen chicken legs in Russia at a very low price. Because they are cheap, Russians buy them enthusiastically.

Due to this fact, the chicken industry in Russia has gone completely under and half a million people are jobless. The market has been won by the Americans. Competition has been destroyed. And now, with monopoly control, they are increasing the price.

No sooner did the Russian government squawk about this than the former governor of Arkansas got on the phone to Yeltsin. Our people surrendered without a fight.

The same thing has happened in our plants that produced precision calibrators. They were bought by two foreign firms, who pay the workers $150 a month as long as the plant doesn't operate. Once the foreign firms have captured the market with their imports, they will close the Russian plants.

There is nothing new here. World capital has worked this way for 200 years. It is just that when Russia was a great country, we resisted that.

GARDELS Speaking of surrender, looking out your window here, all those neon signs from Sanyo, Gillette, and Marlboro that have sprouted up around the Kremlin must seem to you like flags of occupation.

The great Russia of Tolstoy and Tchaikovsky is now the poor cousin begging to tag along at the G7 summits. Popular culture has become a pale imitation of trends already out of fashion in California.

As much as Russians like Big Macs, surely, at the same time, the sudden fall from empire must be deeply humiliating?

LUKYANOV We have to go through this childish ailment, this gorging. But it will lead later on to a hatred toward America.

Russia is not part of the West, it is a Euro-Asian country. Our political rights have always been less than those in the West, but the individual was compensated for that by the knowledge he belonged to a great nation, a great society that was taking care of human beings. As in the Orthodox religion, individual rights here have always been less than those of the collective, of society. The individual can only reach spiritual illumination if everyone does. It can't be done apart.

Today, the Russian man has been robbed of this feeling of being part of something great. He is only alone with his rights and a few kopeks, humiliated.

Russia deserves this greatness. The Communists want to preserve it. Above all, we are patriots. For 1,000 years we Russians were never fragmented. And then literally overnight, the Soviet Union was ended by the signing of some document and 25 million Russians were cut off from each other, beyond our borders. For the first time in Russian history, the nation has been broken. We will put it back together.

GARDELS At a pro-Zyuganov rally in Karl Marx Square during the presidential election I saw an old woman carrying a red flag with the face of an Orthodox Christ on it. This kind of sums up your whole program, doesn't it?

LUKYANOV Yes, you are right. That red flag with an image of Christ was first used in Russia in a battle in 1380. It meant then what it means today – the fight for uniting all Russians. This flag was also used in 1612 when Russia was liberated from the Poles.

The white, blue, and red tri-color flag of the Russian Federation that flies over the Kremlin was once just a trading symbol. It was also the flag of the Russian Liberation Army of Vlasov, which fought with the Nazis against the Soviet Union in the Second World War. In my own constituency, one out of three people died at the hands of the Vlasov traitors. Today, the tri-color is the flag of selling off Russia.

GARDELS If you had the power, what would the Communists do to restore Russia's greatness?

LUKYANOV First, we would put an immediate end to the Great Criminal Revolution that is robbing Russia blind. Yeltsin has transformed the great Russian nation into a raw-materials colony of the West. We sell off what we have cheaply to buy expensive finished goods from abroad.

Second, we would restore Russia's industrial and agricultural production. We were once second in industrial production and now are 40th. Textiles, light industry, and agriculture are all stagnant today, defeated by imports. That will require some measures of protectionism. I'm for competition with the West. But you can't compete if your country has been destroyed by dumping with cheap prices.

Once these industries are working again, that would improve revenues to the national budget by 25 percent. Once we recover the monopoly on vodka and tobacco – the Marlboro Man will have to ride out of town – we will improve budget revenues by another 30 percent. We will close the rest of the budget gap by ensuring that taxes, only about 40 percent of which today are collected, are paid. All this would lift the economy out of its collapsed state.

Third, our banks must support Russia by investing at home. The IMF is giving us $10 billion over three years, but each year $20 billion flows out of Russia to the West. When that money flows back, we can restore our industry without the IMF requiring us to throw people out of work because its economists are worried about inflation. If they had their way, we wouldn't pay any wage or pensions. Then there would be zero inflation. The operation would be a success, but the patient would be dead.

Isn't it humiliating to someone who sat proudly on the **GARDELS** Politburo of the Communist Party of the Soviet Union to have your country dealt with by the IMF on the same terms as Jamaica?

It didn't have to be this way. The term *perestroika*, first **LUKYANOV** uttered by [former KGB head and General Secretary] Yuri Andropov in 1982, was aimed at bringing Russia to the technologically advanced stage of a post-industrial society, into Alvin Toffler's "third wave." Andropov's *perestroika* meant strengthening socialism and Soviet power.

At the beginning of 1988, I and several other Politburo colleagues argued that the Soviet Union should follow the "Chinese path" to the "third wave" wherein the market was only a means to improve conditions in the country. Gorbachev refused and wanted to take another path: The market itself was to be the goal, not the means.

Not many people know that at the Plenum of the Central Committee in 1990 I refused, for this reason, to become a member of the Politburo which was set to take Russia off in this disastrous direction where we have now arrived.

In short, the program of the Communist Party of Russia **GARDELS** today could be described as "Andropov's *Perestroika*"?

Yes, but also political pluralism and freedom of religion. **LUKYANOV** We envision the use of market mechanisms, but also state regulation. Like the Chinese, we envision a mix of economic forms – the private, the cooperative, the state – that compete with each other. The state gives up its monopoly over property and only retains a precise place: strong regulation or ownership of energy, transportation, space exploration, communications, environmental preservation, and defense. All else is open to competition and the market.

GARDELS Yeltsin's campaign manager charged during the presidential election that the Communist Party was rebuilding secret cells in the workplace, which is banned by the Constitution.

LUKYANOV We were not and are not doing that at all. If we were, it would ignite a civil war. And that would be a catastrophe in a country loaded with atomic weapons, nuclear power stations, the world's largest chemical plants and a vast, dangerously run down system of gas and oil pipelines. Mines are collapsing, trains crashing and planes falling from the sky because all the infrastructure is old and decayed.

God forbid. We would do nothing that could bring that closer. If we had civil war under these conditions, we would perish. If a civil war starts it will be by those who robbed Russia, stole the property of the state, and won't give it back without a fight, believing the changes to be irreversible.

GARDELS Privatization is not irreversible?

LUKYANOV What if a thief stole 986 of every 1,000 rubles from you and then said, "OK, let us keep things the way they are starting today, and no one can ask any questions. I'm a thief, but what I've done is irreversible"?

Yegor Gaidar, the former prime minister and leading market reformer, said once that we Russians have a choice – to be with the thieves or the Communists.

Gaidar, with his "market Bolsheviks" who wanted to privatize Russia in 500 days, and Yeltsin chose the thieves. Now that we have regained a measure of power in Russian society, we will try to put an end this Great Criminal Revolution.

17 / Russia's Pink Clouds of Utopia

Yevgeny Yevtushenko, Russia's most well-known poet, is also an essayist and filmaker. His most recent book is *Don't Die Before You Are Dead* (1995) and his most recent film is *Stalin's Funeral* (1992).

Our situation today looks like a great tragedy. The **MOSCOW** Soviet Union was a kind of Tower of Babel. And when it collapsed some people were wounded, some crushed, in the ruins. Many illusions and false ideas were buried in the rubble.

All of us are hostages in these ruins of our own creation. And, as always, it is the children who will pay for the crimes of their parents. They are the most tragic victims in any kind of transition.

But there is hope in the ruins. Sometimes the most beautiful flowers grow in the graveyard.

Despite the economic disaster, the land of Sputnik and Bratsk Station hasn't lost its faith in the future. The time ahead has greater potential than the time we had, which was always pregnant with the danger of nuclear holocaust.

And what of our discredited utopia? All of us, when we think about the future, are more or less utopian. Indeed, the seeds of the present were planted in yesterday's utopias. Certainly, life without utopia would be horizonless.

What we must guard against is not the idea of a better time ahead. But our collective imagination must dismiss professional optimists as well as professional pessimists. Both of them push humanity into the abyss.

The professional optimists, under whom we have suffered in Russia more than anywhere else, pushed us into an abyss of the pink clouds of social and political deception. But after we dove into these pink clouds of Communism, it was very difficult to pick up the butchered remains of our illusions.

Equally disastrous, the dark prophecies of professional pessimists push humanity into the abyss of disbelief, of mistrust in ourselves.

It is time now to climb out of the abyss. It is time to trust ourselves without illusion, to face our disagreements without losing our hopes.

POST-COLD WAR PURGATORY

So what do we have now? We are no longer clouded in the pink mists but seem to be stalled in a kind of post-Cold War purgatory.

I like the Boris Yeltsin of the barricades in 1991, but not the Yeltsin of the Chechen War, the Yeltsin who totters between indecisiveness and unpredictability. Boris Yeltsin was wrong in dissolving the USSR because our republics didn't get the opportunity to make reforms without dictatorship at the center and because it led, in some cases, to bloody ethnic conflicts. But he is right in condemning its potential "forced resurrection" (which is unrealistic anyway).

So what is Yeltsin? He is just a Communist who has half-stifled the Communist in himself. This is not so much an accusation as a fact. He could not be any other man because of his long party career. And what is Gennady Zyuganov, leader of the opposition and head of Russia's revived Communist Party? He is just a half-Communist trying to look like a Communist in the eyes of pensioners with party cards.

The gentleman capitalists looking for investment opportunities can relax. The elite of today's Russian Communists have acquired a nice taste for private property. They are certainly not going to ban it if ever they return to power. This elite likes having bank accounts in Liechtenstein and, instead of state-owned dachas, their own personal villas, not just in the country near Moscow, but in Cyprus, Mallorca, and Miami.

Especially after Boris Yeltsin's victory in the election of 1996, it is clear we will have capitalism. The question is, "what kind?" We never managed to accomplish social-ism with a human face. Will we be able to manage capitalism with a human face? By present indications, capitalism in Russia could just be a hidden form of czarism, or even another dictatorship, just as socialism had been.

Why have we forgotten the bold alternative of Andrei Sakharov's, the idea of convergence between capitalism and socialism, a third way? Having been deceived by old false ideas and afraid to be twisted around the finger by new ones, we seem to have chosen only wingless, crawling pragmatism.

It is out of this vacuum of philosophy that all the infectious microbes – nationalism, tribalism, inferiority complexes, megalomania, and the hysterical nostalgia for lost grandeur – have arisen to dance on the corpse of the Soviet Empire. We should know by now that the empty soul is always more dangerous than empty pockets.

In Russia, as elsewhere, we need people in power who are both philosophical and who have a talent for management. But in Russia, as elsewhere, elections are becoming a national championship of mediocrities. And then, mis-takenly, the world judges a country by its politicians.

On election day in July 1996, my hand voted for Yeltsin, but my heart was with a future generation not on the list.

As much as Russia needs it, the time is not ripe for the new generation to come to power. First, we must finish this last battle between the old Communists, the final skirmish of this riven clan that will vanish along with the twentieth century. In four years they will all leave the stage.

Once the debris of mediocrity is cleared away, the younger generation born after the cold war will be able to take wing. Not only will they be partners with the West in business, but also in the creation of a new philosophy that provides the moral vision to challenge aggressive tribalism in the twenty-first century. And I'm certain that, even in

Russia, great leaders will emerge who are equal to their times. Not to hope for this would mean accepting Thomas Carlyle's lament, "No sadder proof can be given by a man of his own littleness than disbelief in great men."

18 / MTV and NATO Under Postcommunism

Aleksandr Kwasniewski, who ousted post-Cold War icon Lech Walesa as president of Poland, was founder of the Social Democracy of the Republic of Poland Party, which was formerly the Communist Party. After introducing his real-estate agent wife and plying me with (very smooth) Polish Chopin vodka, paté and sausages that his staff carried along for display at the World Economic Forum in Davos, Switzerland in February 1996, Kwasniewski reigned in his overdrive energy for a few focused moments to explain himself, his party, and his views on post-communism in Europe.

NATHAN GARDELS Like you, many former communists proclaim a belief in free markets and privatization, but the pain of reaching those goals has prompted most leaders across the former East Bloc to want to slow things down. Do you want to slow down or speed up?

KWASNIEWSKI Economic growth is the means to stem unemployment. Growth, growth, growth – that is the necessary condition to solve social problems. And growth comes from privatization and free markets. So we need to speed up, not slow down.

GARDELS Is there anything worthwhile left of the communist idea?

KWASNIEWSKI Social justice. A lot of groups in Poland are still expecting some real assistance from the state. The lack of security is a problem for many, especially older people. They understand values in a very conservative way. But for younger people social justice is redefined. It does not mean that we all should have the same salaries or that the state should take care of us. Not egalitarianism, but equality of opportunity. That means an equal chance to education, for access to culture and for a career, no matter where you are from, city or village, rich family or poor.

GARDELS   As the Cold War was ending, Willy Brandt once predicted that, as East joined West in Europe, all of Europe would tilt left. Do you agree with that prognosis?

KWASNIEWSKI   I appreciate Willy Brandt very much, but in my opinion he was not right. We are in a very special time in history. It is a time of the crisis of the big ideologies. We are in a situation today where no one ideology, even Christianity, no less socialism or liberalism or conservatism, can explain all the new phenomena around us and give adequate answers. This exhaustion of the old answers is a significant element of our *fin-de-siècle* period.

At the same time, we are in a world that is in much closer contact than only 10 or 20 years ago. We bump into each other all the time, and rubbing elbows rubs off. We all live practically in our daily lives with such pluralism, such a mixture of values.

The new century is much more than a slogan. It means real connection, as never before, between people and values from all over. There is a kind of convergence that is taking place as a result of contact. Without the old ideological barriers, today we are very practical in taking the good things that work from many ideologies. Social democrats now accept many liberal concepts, especially in the economy, and vice versa. This new pragmatism is the reason I can easily relate to Vaclav Klaus, Helmut Kohl, or Jacques Chirac – all from parties of the so-called right.

The important thing, as politicians, is that we all keep the main values in our head – democracy, openness to the outside world and cultural flows, friendship, a multilateral approach to European problems. But, to be efficient, we need to be pragmatic. Brandt was one of the last great visionary leaders in Europe. Now is the time of pragmatists.

How does what the Russians regard as a divisive plan for **GARDELS** enlargement of NATO fit into your idea of an open and connected world?

Let us look at what all this talk of "NATO vs. Russia, **KWASNIEWSKI** historical alliances and blah, blah" means to the younger generation. I'm in my early forties. My daughters, for example, are 15, 17, and 20. They have a lot of contacts; they have a lot of friends around Europe and around the world. They have traveled. They speak very fluent English. They use computers. They surf the Net. They watch CNN and Eurosport. They love MTV.

They ask me, "What is all this talk of enlarging NATO or not enlarging NATO? We have enlarged many times over, we are united around the world. What are all you politicians yakking about? Dad," they say, "you guys are just a bunch of bureaucrats. You are all politicians without imagination."

That is our challenge now, and our responsibility. We have to realize that the generations already coming up see far wider than us politicians; that MTV is more important than NATO.

For us old fogeys, though, why not a non-aggression pact **GARDELS** between Russia and an enlarged NATO that includes the former Warsaw Pact countries? Won't that defuse the mounting tension on this issue?

The most difficult stereotype to erase in the minds of the **KWASNIEWSKI** Russians is that NATO is against Russia; that NATO is a Cold War baby, an element of the past. Well, to some extent, that is true.

Our task is to explain that NATO is the most practical place to start with a mutual security organization for Europe. It is up and running. No one has the money to start up a new one. Step by step, carefully and with patience, we need to explain this to the Russians.

We then need some kind of agreement – perhaps a non-aggression pact or something along those lines as you suggest – to confirm this new role with Russia. I have told the Russians that, if they want another NATO different from the old one, they must enlarge it to include us in Central Europe. That will transform the Cold War baby into an organization that proves by its existence that we no longer live in a divided Europe.

GARDELS By cooperating closely with NATO in Bosnia in 1996, didn't the Russians legitimize this new idea of NATO you are espousing?

KWASNIEWSKI That is a crucial point. Neutral countries, Poland *and* the Russians, participated in this action. This is the best argument for the future: The deployment of forces in the former Yugoslavia shows what is possible in the rest of Europe. The best way to get rid of the old stereotypes is to show how we can work together practically under a new set of rules.

19 / Victorious West, Humiliated Russia

Alexander Lebed, the former Russian general and National Security Advisor to President Boris Yeltsin, is now the president's main political opponent.

In an exclusive arrangement with *Izvestia*, *NPQ*'s weekly Global Viewpoint service distributed the article in March 1997.

Translated from the Russian by Mikhail Bruk.

We have been hearing more and more often of late that **MOSCOW** Russia suffered a crushing defeat in the Cold War. Apparently, this is true. More than that, the present state of our economy demonstrates a complete defeat in carrying out reforms.

New dangers will arise, however, if this thesis of defeat is implanted too deeply in the minds of Russians and in the approach of the West toward Russia.

One gets the impression in the West that an "historic victory" has been won over world communism, and it is therefore permissible to behave like victors. And in behaving as victors, no difference is made between Russia and defeated communism. This is a serious mistake.

If the sense of loss and humiliation that comes with defeat is allowed to fester in the Russian mentality, it may lead to an inferiority complex that can only be overcome by gaining new victories, preferably over old rivals. That is also a big mistake.

Unfortunately, the political and military expansion of NATO to the East makes it probable that both of these mistakes will be committed.

My meetings with NATO leaders and politicians in the West have convinced me that the Russian saying "measure seven times and cut once" is not well-known there. The euphoria resulting from the crash of the Eastern Bloc, which they awaited for so long, has made them press forward incautiously toward the simplest solutions, seemingly unaware of the consequences.

NATO's leaders still seek strategic advantage so they can have a "dialogue" with Russia from a position of strength. Apparently, when the Cold War generation of politicians and military planners, who were so used to the lengthy "struggle of position" against the USSR and the Warsaw Pact, found themselves in a very favorable position, it proved too difficult to give up the temptation of finally, at long last, implementing their former plans – even though there is no longer any need for them because the Soviet threat has disappeared.

I doubt very much that pushing Russia in this way to the political back yard of Europe will increase the sense of stability and certainty, or make Russia more democratic and predictable. This approach of the West is destined, at best, to place both sides peering at each other suspiciously from across the fence, fists in our pockets.

Such is the logic of relations between the victors and the losers that seems to be unfolding.

In following this logic, one should not forget two lessons from history.

First, in everything, including politics, a sense of balanced measure is the basis of harmony and stability. It is a well-established principle that exceeding the limits of self-defense becomes an offense, an attack. Exceeding a balanced measure is a blow to justice which makes conflicts deeper and creates the basis for a certain "delayed" reaction at some future time.

Second, the victor should never humiliate the loser because it is dangerous, mainly for the victor.

The sense of measure failed the victors who imposed the

Versailles Treaty on a defeated Germany in 1919. The degree of this humiliation was so great that it completely eclipsed the sense of guilt. It injected the virus of vengeance into the defeated nation. Not long before these events, Russia had her own "Versailles" in the Treaty of Brest-Litovsk.

Territories and armies come and go. But humiliation of a nation's dignity remains in the minds of its people.

NATO: THE NEW EMPIRE

There is no doubt that the new regional conflicts in Europe are a danger that must be dealt with through joint efforts, as in Bosnia. However, there is no other universal instrument, apart from force, to help solve problems where everything is mixed in, from the special beliefs of the Serbian Orthodox religions to the seemingly genetic spirit of freedom of the Chechens, which resists any way of life imposed from the outside.

With this universal method of "force alone," NATO will have to take upon itself a number of fundamental, state-forming functions (which is already happening in Bosnia) because that is the only way to set certain legal parameters and minimize internal conflicts. In this way, whether it wants it or not, NATO will acquire the traits of a new type of "empire" with its own autonomous governing structure. This "empire" will necessarily live and develop according to the same laws which led all empires in history to collapse.

The recent internal transformations in the NATO apparatus itself confirm this course. After the demise of the Warsaw Pact, NATO had to find a new way to survive under radically changed conditions. The way out was found in broadening the mission and opening the structure of the Alliance so that it could absorb new members. But this imperial "over reach" will inexorably increase the costs, and the internal contradictions, of the system. Inevitably, the nucleus of the "traditional NATO" will one day implode under the burden of empire.

The consequences of this eventuality will be even more grave than the collapse of the USSR and the Warsaw Pact. Is this not understood in the European capitals? Most likely, it is indeed understood, which is why the search is on for an external threat that will protect the entire system from disintegration like some outer carcass.

The "South" and the "East" are said to cause the greatest apprehensions to the Alliance. But I do not think that for NATO the East means, first and foremost, Iraq, Iran, or China. Only Russia fits the official description of a potential external threat thanks to the efforts of our home-grown politicians, who want to rapidly knock together something "formidable" on the territory of the Commonwealth of Independent States, re-target nuclear missiles at the future members of the Alliance, and spare no effort in frightening Ukraine.

It is becoming obvious that we are being drawn into a process of mutual provocations. Once again, the old principles of relations and the terminology describing them – balance of power, the correlation of forces, etc. – are being used. This is not surprising given that no other criteria but the tired "external threat" has again been trotted out as the working concepts of geopolitics.

This reversion to old ways threatens the system of agreements which until recently have provided stability in Europe and in the world. The treaty concerning the conventional weapons in Europe, measures of trust in the military field, treaties on cutting nuclear arsenals – all face the threat of being reconsidered. Is it really worth undoing all that has been achieved so far only to start everything over again, from the very beginning?

AMERICAN OBLIGATION TO DEFEND EUROPE One of the most frequently used arguments in favor of preserving and expanding the Alliance is "defining NATO as the necessary form of American obligations to defend Europe." In simpler terms, this means Europe is interested in America paying for Europe's defense.

Apparently, it is this desire to get access to "American obligations" that explains the strong desire of certain countries of Central and Eastern Europe to become members of NATO as quickly as possible. "Defense" is a sufficiently abstract notion. American money is quite concrete.

Nevertheless, such a position taken by the member

countries of Central and Eastern Europe, provides the NATO leaders with another pretext to talk about the impossibility of acting against the wishes of "new democracies." This is a thesis intended for simpletons.

When we take everything into account, it is possible to understand the real situation: The United States needs NATO to keep Europe under control. NATO is important for Europe because it can "milk the US" for the sake of its own security. And for the United States and Europe together, NATO is necessary to keep Russia on the periphery of world politics.

The consequences of NATO expansion cannot help but influence the internal situation in Russia. I do not mean the reaction of the Russian leadership, which is now so widely discussed but not taken too seriously because of their in-effectiveness in practical matters. What I mean is a change in the attitudes which had formed in Russian society during the period of "new thinking," and "strategic partnership," attitudes quite divorced from the wishes or actions of the powers that be.

RUSSIA WILL WAKE UP

Having found no comfort among idealists who preach economic liberalism and praise democratic values, present-day Russia is clearly returning to the historic patterns of "community," to the principles of totalitarianism, and to the priority of national state principles. And Russia today is slowly overcoming the *diffidence* of the post-Soviet period as it gradually acquires an identity as a Euro-Asian power. In time, this process will determine the natural allies of Russia whose social and historical development has been similar to ours. In such a moment, Russian politicians should not seek to impose their will, but understand the social and economic fears that drive the public.

The feeling of total insecurity which exists in the society today sometimes compels people to act senselessly and with hostility toward everything in their path. Even the politicians who never agreed among themselves on anything now share ranks as severe critics of the West. Despite the sincerity of some, this environment can easily be manipulated by other politicians. They will attempt to divert attention from their own failings by blaming the West for all sins.

This dynamic may well come into play the next time the threat of a national general strike hangs over the government. It will be a strange sight indeed to see the crowds of half-starving Russians who do not get their pensions and salaries marching under the slogan – "NATO – Not A Step Forward." This is not only quite possible, but likely. Will the rulers of Russia then be able to explain the nonpayment of salaries by the necessity of creating new airplanes and submarines as an answer to NATO expansion?

As in the past, the forces that are pushing for the division of Europe exist on both sides. This time, our answer should be a typically Russian one, not swinging the nuclear club but turning to our own resources to realize the true foundations of national security. In this, the current offensive of the West is proving a great help.

20 / (Very Recent) History Has Absolved Socialism

Fidel Castro is the president of Cuba. *NPQ* Founding Publisher Stanley K. Sheinbaum and I met with President Castro twice for this interview, first for three hours at the president's office in Havana and then in New York during Castro's visit there for ceremonies marking the 50th anniversary of the United Nations.

Let us imagine that the United States lifts its trade embargo **NATHAN** against Cuba. What would Cuba look like then? Would **GARDELS &** Cubans now in Miami be able to own their own companies **STANLEY** in a mixed economy? Wouldn't it be good for the Cuban **SHEINBAUM** economy to bring back all that capital and entrepreneurial expertise from Florida?

Cuban businessmen living outside our country are not prevented from investing, not even those living in Miami – provided they are serious people willing to abide by the **FIDEL** Cuban laws. They are not being kept out while the blockade **CASTRO** is in force, nor will they be after it has been lifted. While the blockade stands, it is the US government, not us, that is preventing them, as well as other businessmen living in the United States, from investing in Cuba.

We are not excluding anyone, not even while the blockade stands. Cuba's open policy to foreign capital investment is aimed at finding solutions to our problems –

the need for capital, technologies, and markets. Any investment is possible that contributes one or more of these elements and complies with the new regulations set forth in our legislation.

[Cuba's revamped foreign investment law, passed on September 5, 1995 by the National Assembly, allows 100 percent foreign ownership of enterprises in all areas except education, health and defense. The law says foreigners will be able to own their own homes and offices, and that repatriation of profits is guaranteed. Although "exceptional cases" will be allowed, employers must hire workers through a state agency. – ed.]

GARDELS & SHEINBAUM   What about opposition parties, newspapers, TV stations or radio? Would they be allowed?

CASTRO   Mass media in the hands of the opposition? It is a widely known fact that, in the framework of Cuba's political system, the mass media do not respond to private interests – economic or political – but to the interests of society as a whole. I still do not know of a country where the private possession of the mass media has been translated into greater democracy and real freedom of expression.

GARDELS & SHEINBAUM   As long as the bottom-line gains of "the Revolution" are kept – the universal health care and education system – why put limits on other developments?

CASTRO   We are legitimately proud of health and education as basic achievements of the Cuban Revolution, but what is as essential as these is the preservation of our independence, our sovereignty, and Cuba's system of social justice and equality. In Cuba, no one is left helpless or abandoned.

GARDELS & SHEINBAUM   All the enthusiasm for the triumph of capitalism after the collapse of the Soviet Union has now become muted. Millions in the former East bloc, from Poland to Russia, have fallen into deprivation as a result of market shock therapy. In the past two years the former Communist parties in places such as Poland have seen a resurgence. In the United States, the gap between the rich and the under-class has grown to the highest level in the OECD countries. Thirty million people in Brazil alone live in marginal impoverishment. Does all this suggest to you that, in history's judgment, socialism still has a future?

Socialism as a system that promotes social solidarity **CASTRO** remains fully valid. Of that I shelter no doubt whatsoever. The collapse of socialism in certain countries does not at all mean it has failed. Due to several factors – treason included – socialism lost one battle. But I reject the notion that the future of mankind might depend on a system like capitalism that is based on inequality, selfishness, a ferocious com-petition among men, the most absolute irrationality and the most criminal waste of limited resources. In these respects capitalism as a system has not proven its efficiency anywhere in the world, least of all in the underdeveloped nations.

Do you see any models out there? **GARDELS & SHEINBAUM**

The Chinese have obtained remarkable economic success **CASTRO** while preserving their political system. In Cuba we thus watch and study with interest the Chinese experience, though obviously our conditions – that is, our history, our culture, our real features – do not bear similarities. Likewise, Vietnam is going through an experience which keenly interests us.

If not a model, perhaps elements of a model can be found **GARDELS &** in Chile where, along with high growth, there is a **SHEINBAUM** narrowing of the gap between rich and poor?

From what I know, your assertion that the gap between the **CASTRO** rich and the poor in Chile has been reduced doesn't seem justified. Anyway, it should be borne in mind that all those countries with a certain degree of economic success – for example, the countries from South-East Asia or even Chile – have received economic aid for their development programs. And you also can't ignore the fact that a ferocious repression against the workers in the stages of accumulation (of profits) and accelerated growth has not been lacking in these places. And there have been no blockades against these successful countries. Quite the opposite.

Cuba, however, far from receiving aid or cooperation, is still subjected to a tight economic blockade and constant harassment, which not only prevents the development of normal trade relations but also blocks access to the usual sources of credit needed for economic growth.

GARDELS & The late Michael Manley, another Caribbean leader of the **SHEINBAUM** left, said upon his retirement as Jamaica's prime minister that "our nationalist and statist approach didn't work . . . It is now clear to me that an unfettered market, not the imposition of political controls, can be the most effective instrument of opportunity for the poor . . . There is no way to eradicate poverty if one resists the logic of capitalism."

As for the international economic system, Manley concluded that "each of us has to find our niche in the global economy and pull ourselves up by our bootstraps. In the dispersed world economy, poor little Jamaica has only one choice: to find a foothold for its goods somewhere in the European Community or the Eastern seaboard of the United States, and put massive resources into educating and training its people to produce competitively for those markets. And we can make common cause with the transnational companies in our country through joint ventures. That will get us into the world economy."

Do you see validity in Manley's analysis? In today's global economy, mustn't Cuba's solution ultimately be the same as the one Manley lays out for neighboring Jamaica?

CASTRO I respect all well-meaning views and constructive approaches, as Manley's surely are. However, there is an indisputable reality: The present international economic order is unfair and it is necessary to keep on struggling to amend it. The Third World nations do not have any possibility to compete with those that have a monopoly over the most advanced technologies, the research centers and the financial resources to seize markets. The countries that only yesterday were colonies have even been deprived of their best talents, so nothing will be left to them except for the production of raw materials and cheap commodities with high use of the lowest cost labor.

As for the possible implementation in Cuba of the solutions proposed for Jamaica by Manley, I can only answer what every national leader must: Each country has its own characteristics and therefore should seek its own solutions.

Fernando Enrique Cardoso, now the president of Brazil, **GARDELS &** was once a leading theorist of the "dependencia" school of **SHEINBAUM** thought that said Latin American underdevelopment was due to its exploitative integration in the world market system. Cardoso now argues that "shared prosperity" in the hemisphere is the best way to eradicate poverty.

"We now identify integration and participation in the international system as the solution of our problems, not the cause of our difficulties," he says.

Do you agree with his change of mind on the idea of "dependencia"?

The forms of dependency may have changed, but certain **CASTRO** elements of subordination persist that jeopardize access to the means for development. Identifying dependency with economic integration in this day and age sounds absurd to me. Obviously, in the contemporary world there is a growing degree of economic interdependence among countries and regions. However, the point here is that there must be a struggle for a fair and equitable international economic system in which the big obstacles faced by underdeveloped countries – unequal terms of trade, financial and monetary manipulations by the rich countries, and the unbearable burden of the external debt – do not prevail.

21 / Why UN Peacekeeping Failed in Bosnia

Kofi Annan, now Secretary General of the United Nations, was formerly Undersecretary General of the UN for Peacekeeping Operations. We talked at the UN in 1994.

NATHAN GARDELS "Fiasco," "humiliation," "failure" – those are the words used to describe UN peacekeeping operations in Bosnia. Many say the UN operation there has not protected the Muslim civilians, but has instead provided a shield for the Serbs. What is your response?

KOFI ANNAN It is absolutely unfair to come to those conclusions. We have gotten a bum rap. It is extremely convenient for politicians trying to escape blame to point fingers at the United Nations. We can't hit back, we have no votes among their constituents, we cannot withhold our support of member states. So, we become an easy alibi.

First, look at the mandate of the UN force. They went in there to escort humanitarian assistance to the needy. And, during the last two winters, they saw several million people through a difficult situation, providing them with food and medical assistance. UN peacekeepers were also placed in the safe-havens to deter aggression. And there is no doubt that the presence of the peacekeeping troops has prevented an extension of the conflict beyond the boundaries of the former Yugoslavia. These are no small achievements.

When the safe-haven concept arose, our military commanders originally said we would need 34,000 troops to be effective. They also recommended that the size of the safe-havens be wide enough – about 30 kilometers in diameter – so as to allow the people in those safe-havens to have a normal economic and social life and to be outside the range of artillery and shells. It was also proposed that the safe-areas should be demilitarized. If we had stuck to those recommendations, the situation today would be different.

But the Security Council decided that 34,000 troops were too much. Instead, we were offered 7,600 troops for all six safe-areas and the diameter of the safe-areas was also limited. The Security Council also allowed that the government of the safe-areas need not give up their arms.

It is important to understand the word "deter." Peacekeepers were placed in Sarajevo and the safe-havens not to defend those havens, but to deter the factions from shooting, in particular shelling with tanks and heavy weapons, into those areas. It was thought that warring factions would not shoot and attack UN peacekeepers. If they did, airpower would be used in appropriate circumstances to take out the heavy weapons or tanks – targets they can effectively hit.

If the safe enclave is attacked by infantry, however, through a sudden and rapid advance, as it was in Bihac, it is difficult to use airpower to stop them. Then, everyone turns on the peacekeepers and say they have failed, that the UN has not done its work.

In other international situations, such as the Gulf War, where it was felt that aggression needed to be rolled back, Desert Storm was organized, with all the financing and forces commensurate to the task. This was not done in the former Yugoslavia. The lightly armed, outgunned and outnumbered peacekeeping force the UN decided to send there, beginning in 1991, cannot suddenly be transformed into a combat force to enforce an end to the war.

GARDELS   In a sense, then, the UN peacekeeping troops on the ground in Bosnia are hostages of the Security Council? In other words, the UN cannot fail, only its member states can fail, because the UN can only do what its member states mandate?

ANNAN   The UN can be as strong as the member states want it to be. We reflect the collective will and might of the member states. In situations like Desert Storm, massive resources were mounted in a very short period of time. If the Security Council decides to put in peacekeeping troops of limited number, with considerably reduced levels of armaments than recommended by our commanders, they cannot suddenly be expected to do anything more. If more is expected, then the mandate must be changed. Peacekeepers should either be pulled out, or reinforced with a new mandate.

GARDELS   What is the lesson you take away from the UN peace-keeping experience in Bosnia?

ANNAN   The international community has to have a better analysis of the situation that it plans to get into, and then go in with a force that is prepared for all eventualities. For financial reasons, we have tried to do peacekeeping on the cheap; putting in troops that are not adequate and without a collective will to sustain them. We have often been penny-wise and pound-foolish.

We saw this in Rwanda. We put in very limited resources and now we have to spend millions of dollars feeding the refugees on the ground and helping restore a state that is on the verge of failure. When the genocide was taking place in Rwanda, the UN had less than 500 troops on the ground, later expanded to 5,500, while the combined force of the government there was 50,000. Now we see the consequences. We were hopelessly outnumbered.

Alternatively, in Haiti, 20,000 US troops, with UN blessing, went into that situation to face 7,000 Haitian troops. In terms of firepower, the ratio may be a million to one. You can see the different results, just as we saw it in Desert Storm.

In sum, the resources and the will must be commensurate to the task the international community expects from the peacekeepers. Where that has happened, the operations have been a success. Where it hasn't, the result has been very bad.

In the future, do you expect the international community **GARDELS** will have learned from Bosnia, and take into consideration your suggestions for better peacekeeping?

I am not optimistic. We have been constantly required to **ANNAN** do too much with too little. And that will not change quickly.

PART III

POPULATION, MIGRANTS, AND MEGACITIES

Too many people are consuming too much, running down the resources of the planet. As Jacques Cousteau laments, more damage has been done to the environment in this century alone than in all of previous human history.

This growth of population is not even, but tilted toward the poor, largely unwired societies of the southern hemisphere. While they have all the people, as Paul Kennedy and James Gustave Speth point out, we in the North have not only most of the wealth, but also the cables, satellites, and personal computers.

When there is not enough room, people move. And they move anywhere there is hope of making it – to the already bloated city, to another country, to the north.

In this mania of movement, migrants and megacities are blurring all the old boundaries and bypassing the nation-state as the main political entity. By the year 2050, Asia alone is expected to have another billion people populating 50 post-urban settlements with 20 million inhabitants each. This has prompted the Dutch architect Rem Koolhaas' summary declaration that "the past is too small to inhabit," thus giving rise to a new phenomenon in the history of civilizations: the Generic City.

Will these great megacities of the future be more efficient nodes of the global order, such as Singapore, or sprawling Bladerunner-type zones of overflowing humanity and global culture?

Part III addresses how the global trends of the next century will affect the quality of our daily lives in the places where we live.

22 / Full House:
the Shadow of Global Scarcity

Lester R. Brown is president of the Worldwatch Institute and author of *Tough Choices: Facing the Challenge of Food Scarcity* (1996). This article was prepared for *NPQ's* weekly column Global Viewpoint, at the time of the Rome Food Summit in November, 1996.

Nearly 90 million people per year are being added to the **WASHINGTON** planet. Those of us born before 1950 are members of the first generation to witness a doubling of world population. Stated otherwise, there has been more population growth since 1950 than during the 4 million years since humans first stood upright. We are still struggling to understand the long-term consequences of such growth.

As our numbers multiply, our demand for food is beginning to press against some of the earth's natural limits. Marine biologists report that all 17 oceanic fisheries are now being fished at or beyond capacity. Thirteen are in a state of decline.

The oceanic fish catch went from 19 million tons in 1950 to 89 million tons in 1989. This 4.5-fold increase more than doubled seafood consumption per person worldwide, boosting it from 8 kilograms to 17 kilograms. Since 1989, however, there has been no growth in the oceanic catch. Nor is any expected. For the first time in history, the world's farmers can no longer expect help from fishermen in expanding the food supply.

Farmers are also struggling in the 1990s. After boosting the grain harvest from 631 million tons in 1950 to 1.78 million tons in 1990, they have managed to raise it to only 1.83 million tons in 1996. The growth of nearly 3 percent per year from 1950 to 1990 has dropped to only 3 percent during the past six years!

One reason for this slower growth is that there is little fertile land anywhere waiting to be plowed. After peaking in 1981, the world area planted in grain has declined as grain land has been converted to nonfarm uses and shifted to other crops in strong demand, such as soybeans.

Several Asian countries that are industrializing rapidly are suffering heavy cropland loses. For instance, industrialization in China has claimed millions of hectares of land for factories and roads. In Indonesia, the island of Java is losing 20,000 hectares of rice land per year, enough to supply rice to 320,000 Indonesians. Worldwide, cropland losses are offsetting land reclamation, preventing any meaningful growth in cropland area.

The growth in irrigation may also be coming to an end. From 1950 to 1993, the irrigated area expanded from 94 million hectares to 248 million hectares, but here, too, farmers are now pushing against the limits and beyond. Water tables are falling in major food-producing regions, including the southern Great Plains of the United States; the Punjab of India, the country's breadbasket; and throughout much of northern China.

As the demand for water begins to press against the limits of available supplies, the growth in demand in cities can be satisfied only by taking irrigation water from farmers. As water is diverted from the countryside to the cities, countries most often import grain to offset the loss. To import a ton of wheat is to import a thousand tons of water. In effect, grain becomes the currency with which countries balance their water books.

The key to raising land productivity since mid-century has been the growing use of fertilizer, which climbed from 14 million tons in 1950 to more than 140 million tons in

1990, a 10-fold increase. During the 1990s, however, world fertilizer use has dropped as farmers in many countries discovered they were using more fertilizer than some crops could effectively use.

The old formula of combining ever-higher-yielding varieties with more fertilizer that contributed to the near tripling of the world grain harvest from 1950 to 1990 is no longer working very well. And there is no new formula to take its place.

Meanwhile, the world's farmers, who are now struggling to feed nearly 90 million more people each year, must also respond to the extraordinary rise in affluence in Asia, a region with 3.1 billion people. The Asian economy, excluding Japan, has been growing at 8 percent a year for the past four years, raising incomes and consumption of livestock products throughout the region. There is no precedent for so many people moving up the food chain so fast, eating more pork, poultry, eggs, and beef – all grain-intensive products.

As the food situation has tightened, the cropland idled under US commodity programs has been returned to use. Meanwhile, world carry-over stocks of grain in 1995 dropped to some 50 days of consumption, the lowest level on record. Even with the idled US cropland back in production, the 1996 harvest will not be sufficient to rebuild depleted world grain stocks to a secure level.

There are still many steps that can be taken to expand output, but they are mostly small ones. There are no new technologies on the horizon that can match the quantum jumps in output that came from the growth in fertilizer use or the spread of hybrid corn.

It thus comes as no surprise that during early 1996, world wheat and corn prices set record highs. Wheat traded at over $7 a bushel, more than double the price in early 1995. In mid-July, corn traded at an all-time high of $5.54 a bushel, also more than double the year earlier price.

The world is in transition from a half-century dominated by surpluses to an era dominated by scarcity. Indeed, food scarcity could become the defining issue of the new era now unfolding, much as ideological conflict was the defining issue of the historical era that recently ended.

Third World urban dwellers who are trapped between low incomes and rising food prices will hold their governments responsible, taking to the streets. For the 1.2 billion people in the world who live on a dollar a day and who spend 70 cents of that on food, a doubling of grain prices is life threatening.

The resulting political instability could threaten economic progress in many countries and even the stability of the world economy. For the world's affluent, this potential political instability could affect the earnings of multinational corporations, the performance of stock markets, and the earnings of pension funds.

Historically, the world has relied on fishermen and farmers to achieve an acceptable balance between food and people by expanding production as needed, but now achieving such a balance depends heavily on family planners. Reversing the fall in grain supply per person may not be possible if population growth is not slowed quickly.

23 / Consumer Society is the Enemy

Jacques Cousteau is the famed oceanographer and environmental activist. I interviewed the energetic but reed thin Cousteau at the Paris offices of the Cousteau Society in January, 1996.

At 85 years of age, your life has spanned most of this century. During most of that time you have been concerned with exploring the sea and understanding the Earth's environment. **NATHAN GARDELS**

From this point of view, what have been the main developments of the twentieth century?

Mankind has probably done more damage to the Earth in the twentieth century than in all of previous human history. **JACQUES COUSTEAU**

Overwhelmingly, the damage has come from two sources – the exploding growth of population combined with the abuse of economics.

Today, there are 5.6 billion people on Earth. In less than 60 years – by 2050 – there will be 10 billion. This is the key fact of our time.

The radical increase in consumption that will attend this growth will place near-fatal stress on the Earth's resources. Even though the fertility rate is beginning to drop in some very crowded places like Indonesia, this only provides hope for the second half of the twenty-first century. Nothing will change before 2050 because 60 percent of the non-European population in the world today are under 16 years of age. As they have children they will double their presence.

For 50 years, we lived with the fight between communism and capitalism. When communism collapsed the reason was obvious: a planned, centralized system was no match for the market. In the West there was exhilaration over this fact. That is a big mistake.

A liberal economy is fine, but there is a big difference between a liberal economy – or free enterprise that relies on the law of supply and demand – and a market system. The market system, as we are living it today, is doing more damage to the planet than anything else because everything has a price, but nothing has value. Since the long term has no price in today's market, the fate of future generations is not considered in the economic equation.

Because of this formidable confusion between price and value, there is a fundamental unreality about economic life today; it has become an abstraction. The market system is becoming ever more concerned with things that don't exist than with things that do exist. Financial "derivatives" – essentially speculation on speculation – epitomize the distance of the market from reality. Real value gets lost in the game. Reality doesn't count anymore.

So not only are we destroying the diversity of species in the rain forest or the sea that took millennia to come into existence, we are selling off the future as well in the name of immediate gain.

The polar ice shelf, to take one example, is melting today as a consequence of global warming. That results from burning fossil fuels at a price that does not include the value of the iceshelf in maintaining a stable temperature and sea level, which is what makes living along the coasts of this water planet – where most population is concentrated – a viable proposition.

The list of the planet's pillage by the short-term calculus is very long: radioactive waste, nuclear proliferation and the black market of fissile material, building on flood plains, the consequences of projects like the Aswan dam on the rhythm of the seasons, the chemical catastrophes of Bhopal and Seveso. Soil erosion and widespread pollution of the seas are even more pernicious forms of environmental degradation.

Money is a wonderful tool of exchange, but it is a terrible danger for the planet. What the market today produces is retail sanity, but wholesale madness.

Ecological destruction comes not as part of some evil master **GARDELS** plan, but as the result of the banal practices of daily life, from driving a car down the freeway to using plastic bags at the supermarket to clearing trees to graze a few cattle. That's the retail sanity part.

Can these daily habits be altered without a revolutionary change of mind that accepts self-limitation almost as a religious principle?

How can an individual control himself when he is pushed **COUSTEAU** from morning until evening to buy things he doesn't need?

I did an experiment myself. One day in Paris, in winter, I went out at 7a.m. in the morning and came back home at 7p.m. I had a counter. Every time I was solicited by any kind of advertising for something I didn't need, I clicked it each time – 183 times in all by the end of the day.

How do you control yourself when at every moment you are pounded with the message, "Buy this, and women will fall into your arms"? I excuse the poor guy who buys all that stuff he doesn't need. How can he resist?

It is the job of society, not of the individual person, to control this destructive consumerism. I am not for some kind of ecological statism. No. But when you are driving in the street and see a red light, you stop. You don't think the red light is an attempt to curb your freedom. On the contrary, you know it is there to protect you. Why not have the same thing in economics? We don't.

Responsibility lies with the institutions of society, not in the virtues of the individual.

Democracy, the market and the consumer society are all **GARDELS** about giving people what they want when they want it – which is now. By definition, the future has no political constituency in such a system, and thus no voice.

The failure of communism made us distrust the future. But now that democracy and the market are triumphant, we need to find a way to remember the future. How can we do that?

COUSTEAU   In the aftermath of the Cold War, we need another kind of revolution, a cultural revolution, a fundamental change in the way of thinking.

That is why our hope rests with the youth – and with education. The survival of this planet depends ultimately on finding a way to incorporate the long-term perspective – the consequences for future generations – into present decisions by those who will come to power in business or government.

Today, no one seems to take responsibility for the future. Why? People lack objective information. Governments are subjected to short-term electoral concerns. Businesses are beholden to quarterly examinations of their financial health. The United Nations, which ought to be caring for the future, can only make recommendations, not take effective decisions. And, unfortunately, the universities, reflecting the ethos of the market, are not producing better citizens but instilling in them a kind of ferocious competition aimed only at success, fortune, more money. Young people today are being pushed into the social trap of the short-term mentality.

Addressing these major weaknesses of our contemporary society seems to me the highest priority. To this end, the Cousteau Society has joined up with UNESCO to create a worldwide network of programs within already established universities – from Belgium to Brazil, from India to China to the United States – that will adopt what we call the "ecotechnie approach." The main effort here is to promote an interdisciplinary approach to environmental management so that its concerns are reflected in the training for all professions, from business and economics to engineering and natural sciences.

This kind of long march through the institutions to change the mindset of our coming generation is the key thing.

It is also important to reach the youngest generation that is so influenced by the media. Like many others, the Cousteau Society publishes books and videos for children so that thinking about future generations becomes part of their everyday view of the world. For example, we now publish an illustrated magazine series called Cousteau Junior in French. Ted Turner's cartoon network has Captain Planet and so on.

The sole ray of hope we have is the imagination of young people and their awareness of the stress this planet will face as a result of the demographic upheaval of the next 50 years.

GARDELS | Because of the bias in our democratic consumer system toward short-term immediate interests, French President François Mitterrand once created a "council of elders" as one way of giving voice to the long-term.

Is that kind of approach useful on a global scale?

COUSTEAU | Mitterrand set up a commission in 1993 for "defending the rights of future generations," of which I was chair. I resigned from that post, though, in 1995 when President Jacques Chirac announced the resumption of French nuclear testing.

My view was that defending the future our descendants can only be done in a climate of tolerance, which is incompatible with the nuclear threat. Maintaining a nuclear capability in the post-Cold War period, when there is no enemy, is nothing more than a competition in arrogance.

As useful as this idea of some wise body – a kind of supreme court that stands above the market – might be, what we really need is not a council of elders, but a "council of youngers."

The idea of a group of elders is that, in past civilizations, they have linked worlds; the other world was also present in this one. There is also the argument that elders have "experience." The problem is that experience teaches fear of change. Experience kills imagination. Experience makes people conservative. What we are facing tomorrow requires the force of imagination, not wisdom from yesterday.

GARDELS So, what you are trying to do with your educational efforts is to create a counterculture to the market where enduring value reigns over short-term price, where the rights of future generations are integrated into present decisions?

COUSTEAU It is the market that is the counterculture! What we are talking about is building a culture where everything is not subject to the abuse of economics.

GARDELS Most people in the G7 countries have cars and refrigerators. What happens to the world when one billion Chinese become consumers just like us – if only with improved diets of meat and fish, no less consumer goods?

COUSTEAU If the Chinese diet improved to the point where they were all eating fish regularly, the ocean would not be able to feed them.

In my lifetime, we have already depleted the sea. When I began diving, all marine food – shellfish as well as saltwater and freshwater fish – represented one-tenth of the protein consumption of the world. And we were at that time only 1.7 billion people. Today the fishing industry has become very sophisticated and efficient. Schools of fish can be tracked electronically; we know when and where fish are spawning year in and year out. But there are now more than 5 billion people to feed.

The result is that the percentage of all the catch of the world is only 3 percent of protein consumption of humankind. And it will go to 2 percent, then one percent and then disappear altogether as we move toward the 10 billion mark. We will have exhausted the production capacity of the sea.

At the moment, virtually all the fish of the world are caught by the West. The fish that used to feed the primitive peoples along the coasts are taken out of their markets and sold to the rich urban consumers of the West. Is that a culture, or a counterculture?

That is the truth about fish. So, there is no way that the Chinese can survive thanks to the sea. No way. And, as you indicate, there is no way the atmospheric gases of the planet will remain stable if even half of the Chinese start driving cars or use refrigerators that operate with CFCs.

We talk about China because it is among the places where population growth will be most concentrated. The underlying implication of your question is this: In a world with 10 billion people, will everyone have the same chances? No way.

Will there be enough food and energy or living space? There will be severe scarcity in some places, but, yes, I do believe life on the planet can be bearable if we can bring down the inequalities.

I don't mean "equality." People are not equal. Some can jump higher than others, but not 20 times higher. In a society, people will understand a 10/1 ratio of difference, but not 2,000/1. They will not forever tolerate a situation, such as we have today, where only 60 human beings possess more wealth than all of Africa and a large chunk of Asia combined.

But what about the large animals, the giraffes and elephants? They will be the first to go because there will be no space for them to roam, to eat, to live. There will be too many people competing for the same habitat.

All that will be possible for them is a kind of Noah's Ark rescue – putting pairs of each in some high-rise zoo.

This, I think, offers an image of the kind of world future generations of humankind may be faced with.

Absent the triumph of culture over counterculture, your **GARDELS** vision of humankind's fate then resembles what happened to the people of Easter Island, the subject of one of your films?

Yes. Easter Island is the metaphor for Planet Earth unless **COUSTEAU** we can change course. The lesson of Easter Island was that inequity on top of resource scarcity leads to genocide and then to social collapse.

There is no mystery here. Some 50 people arrived on Easter Island in the seventh century and proliferated to more than 70,000 by the seventeenth century. Over these ten centuries, they cut down all the trees, the rains washed the soil away, and they couldn't feed themselves.

The society was divided into the priests, the sculptors of those large idols facing the sea, and the peasants. As a result of the scarcity on this small island, the social order broke down and total war broke out against the privileges of the priests and sculptors. Holed up in a fortress on one corner of the island, they were finally overwhelmed by the peasants and destroyed.

Most people were killed – and eaten – because there was so little food. After that, the population fell, and a second culture developed, but didn't flourish. They understood what happened as a warning from God: Overpopulation had destroyed the environment and the culture and led to genocide.

We can also take the experience of Easter Island as a warning from God not to commit the same folly at the scale of the planet.

24 / Overpopulation Tilts the Planet

Paul Kennedy is the historian and author of *The Rise and Fall of Great Powers* and *Preparing for the 21st Century*. Professor Kennedy, sometimes referred to as the "postmodern Malthus," has also been co-director of the Independent Working Group on the Future of the United Nations

Five years after the Berlin Wall fell and ended the division **NEW HAVEN** of the world into Cold War blocs, a new, more intractable cleavage masked by that conflict has become apparent: the demographic divide. Thomas Malthus, the overpopulation prophet, rather than Adam Smith, the champion of free markets, has become the more relevant thinker for the times ahead.

The 5.5 billion inhabitants of this globe are adding 95 million more people to this total every year. We add almost one billion people each decade. The World Health Organization and the United Nations Population Fund estimate that, by the year 2025, nearly nine billion people will live on the Earth, and 10–14 billion by 2050. The implications of this basic trend – for consumption, production, markets, education, services, the environment, investment, for war and peace – are fundamental.

This increase in population is not occurring evenly across our planet. In fact, 95 percent of the forecasted doubling of world population will take place in the poorer reaches of the globe – in India, China, Central America, and Africa. By contrast, in most richer societies, the populations are either slow-growing or even (as in Italy, France and Japan) in absolute decline.

Some societies are becoming increasingly adolsecent (60 percent of Kenya's population is under 15) while others are becoming increasingly geriatric (20 percent of Sweden's population is over 65). The Earth's demographic growth is dramatically lopsided. At the same time, the planet's wealth, and more importantly its capital, scientists, universities and research and development, are located in the demographically slow-growing or stagnant societies.

The impulses, ideas, cultural images, technology, and funds that shape the socioeconomic life of all humanity in these times emanate to the young and crowded world from the Silicon Valley, Atlanta, Hollywood, London, Zurich, and Tokyo. By contrast, capital, infrastructure, research and development, universities and health-care systems are disintegrating, and natural resources are being depleted most rapidly in those countries where populations are growing in leaps and bounds.

The anarchic collapse of Rwanda and Somalia offer, perhaps, a premonition of what is to come in places where the population is far larger and the infrastructure far worse than at the turn of the twentieth century.

In sum, there is today a vast demographic-technological faultline appearing across our planet. On one side of this line are the fast-growing, adolescent, under-resourced, undercapitalized, under-educated societies; on the other side are the rich, technologically inventive yet demographically moribund, aging populations.

Perhaps the most glaring cleavage today lies along the Mediterranean, between Southern Europe and North Africa. But there are also others – along the Rio Grande in North America, between the Slavic and non-Slavic people of Asia, between Australia and Indonesia.

The greatest challenge global society faces today is preventing this faultline from erupting into a world-shaking crisis. I agree with the Nobel scientist from MIT, Dr Henry Kendall, who argues that "if we do not stabilize

population with justice, with humanity and mercy, then it
will be done for us by nature, and it will be done brutally
and without pity."

25 / Women as the Earth's Last Hope

Nafiz Sadik, Executive Director of the United Nations Population Fund, was Secretary-General of the International Conference on Population and Development held in Cairo in September 1994. Her comments here are adapted from an interview conducted at the United Nations by NPQ Associate Editor Leila Conners.

CAIRO If we as a species are to be successful in controlling population growth, three conditions must exist simultaneously, and globally, to help reduce population:

- The education and empowerment of women that will give them the ability to participate in the decisions about family size and in the decisions about the shape and nature of society. Women are half the population of the world, half the population of every country. Because women are the only ones who become pregnant and bear children, population policy must be dealt with by them.
- The availability of family planning services and information. Women have always wanted to have some control over their fertility. Even if a woman wants four or five children, she should be allowed to space her pregnancies so she will be better able to care for her family.

  The needs of women should be addressed in consultation with them, not as a prescription imposed on them. Today, all too many women are still seen as, in effect, service providers on demand.

Family planning should occur at the individual level, not the institutional level. Maintaining control over women's lives at the institutional level is really the issue at stake in the Vatican's opposition to abortion, birth control and planning. Throughout history, cultural, social, and religious norms have been used to subjugate women.

Abortion should be made less necessary through the provision of family planning and medical services.

• The confidence by parents that their children will survive. One of the greatest reasons for large families in the impoverished world is the uncertainty that children will live through famine and disease.

CHANGING GENDER ROLES

In the next century, women will join national labor forces in immense numbers. Across the North and South, women are increasingly working outside of the home, admittedly first at the lowest paid jobs. In much of East Asia, women who are educated and become "breadwinners" are earning more respect from their husbands and families. Gradually, and begrudgingly, there will be more and more recognition of women's work, even within the household.

Alongside women's entry into the labor force, consideration should be taken that they are not pushed into overload – carrying the burden of work both inside and outside the home.

Feminism, as some have suggested, is not the cause of the breakdown of the family. The breakdown of the family is due to men having remained in their traditional roles. The woman should not be expected to take on double, triple loads; she must not be induced to sacrifice her professional career in order to look after the family because "it is her job alone." Fathering is also a job as much as mothering. Both parents should share the responsibilities of parenting and the household work.

If the status quo in fact was such that everybody was

equal and women and men were allowed to select their own roles, there would be no feminist movement.

There should be a changing of roles – a balancing of women's roles outside of the home with the man's role inside of the home. The Nordics are very good examples of this. The role of men and women in the parenting of children is quite equal there – especially in Sweden. In Sweden, it is not unusual for the father to take a leave from work to look after the children. Helping in the household is also very common. The division of responsibilities are such that sometimes the man cooks and the woman looks after the rest of the house. Sometimes it is the other way around.

Such role equality is not happening in the developing world to any important extent. Men remain pushed by what is expected of them, and they don't want to be laughed at by their peers for taking on some of the roles traditionally assigned to women.

Changing gender roles is threatening. Men and women are afraid of how these changes are going to affect them. Will they really be able to cope with the new circumstances? Women are also worried about a new role expected of them to be independent and fend for themselves. Change is always worrisome.

But these things can happen more rapidly than we might imagine. Major change could occur in a decade. If we can identify and engage key social groups to make changes – for example getting girls into school and literacy programs – then societies can be transformed in the space of a generation.

FAMILY Despite what some American conservatives or the Vatican may think, it is impossible to legislate family. I do not disagree that there should be a father, mother, and children in a "traditional family." But how do you make them stay together?

Women in fact don't leave their children and walk out; men do. Women keep their children. Most societies have condoned men having multiple sexual relationships. Societies don't frown on a man having mistresses, regardless of upholding marriage as sacred. In my part of the world, it is considered a great achievement for a man to have many women. It is power over women that confers on them their low status.

26 / Poor Girls

Benazir Bhutto, formerly the prime minister of Pakistan, wrote these reflections for *NPQ*'s Global Viewpoint service on the occasion of the Fourth United Nations Conference on Women, which was held in Beijing in September 1995.

ISLAMABAD In Pakistan, with our history of frequent martial law and the weight of a traditional, male-dominated culture, gender discrimination is an ever-present and often terrifying reality. But it is important to realize that these attitudes are frequently the direct results of crushing poverty: When a family can only afford to educate one child, it is invariably the son who goes to school because he will look after his parents in their old age, while the daughter will get married and go off to her new home.

For the same reason, the male child gets precedence over his sister in matters of food and medicine. Girls thus grow up in an environment where their worth is devalued in their own eyes and in the eyes of society. A basically economic decision has been converted over time into a social norm with all the weight of custom and tradition behind it.

As useful as grand convocations like the UN Conference on Women held in Beijing in 1995 may be in bringing global focus to the issue at the end of the day, it is still up to each country to address gender discrimination and get on with the tough battle to set half their population free.

Even with the best of intentions, transforming social

habits and attitudes is an uphill task, even in the prosperous and educated zones of the planet. The social issue of a woman's role in society still figures as one of the great emotional issues of American politics. Given the widespread prevalence of poverty and illiteracy in my country, our work is that much harder.

Ultimately, empowerment is attained through economic independence. As long as women are dependent on men, they will face discrimination in one form or another.

My government has made a small start by diverting scarce funds into vocational training programs and reserving seats for women while recruiting for the civil services. We have taken initiatives such as opening a women's bank to help women entrepreneurs. But I would be the first to recognize that these are only the first steps on the long, hard road to equality. Before we can bring about the political and social emancipation of women, we will first have to ensure that they can stand on their own feet.

We need to focus on tangible efforts to assist women. For instance, women are employed in the garment sector of the textile industry in large numbers. If importing nations increased their purchase of garments, this would directly benefit thousands of women. Grants designed to raise the literacy rates of women would have immense long-term benefits to the recipient nations. We need more tangible assistance and fewer seminars and workshops to analyze women's problems.

This is not to suggest that I am dismissive about the results of the Beijing Conference. On the contrary, I am confident that the discussions and resolutions that emerged from it will serve as a benchmark. If the next century is to witness the final emergence of women as equal partners to men, persistent pressure from the global to the most local level will need to be brought to bear on social habits that were centuries in the making.

27 / Global Inequality: *358 Billionaires versus 2.3 Billion People*

James Gustave Speth is administrator of the United Nations Development Program (UNDP). The 1996 annual Human Development Report of the UNDP profiled the growing income inequality globally, as well as within societies, since the end of the Cold War. The UNDP chief outlines below the key lessons that emerge from that report.

NEW YORK Two widespread and dangerous myths about the global economy have arisen to the status of conventional wisdom in the aftermath of the Cold War. These myths need to be dispelled with the harsh facts if the world at large is going to make any future progress on the path of "human" development.

The first myth is that most of the developing world is doing rather well, led by some 15 rapidly growing developing economies and spurred by the opportunities of market globalization.

As a result, the myth has it, the poor are catching up, and we are seeing a convergence of rich and poor. This is simply not the case. Unfortunately, we are living in a world that has become more polarized economically, both between countries and within them.

Today, we live on a planet which increasingly represents

not "one world" but "two worlds." Far from narrowing, the gap in per capita income between the industrial and developing worlds tripled between 1960 and 1993, from $5,700 to $15,400. Today, the net worth of the world's 358 richest people is equal to the combined income of the poorest 45 percent of the world's population – 2.3 billion people. If current trends continue and are not quickly corrected, economic disparities will move from inequitable to inhuman, from unacceptable to intolerable.

The second myth is that the early stages of economic growth are inevitably associated with growing inequality within a given country. But there is no iron law of development that makes this so.

Equitable growth is not only ideal in the abstract, it is efficient – and it is possible in the real world. Many economies in Asia – Japan, Hong Kong, Indonesia, Malaysia, the Republic of Korea, and Singapore – have had rapid growth and relatively low inequality.

Malaysia, for example, boosted its income more than 7 percent a year over the past decades. But it also took steps to achieve equity, reduce poverty and ethnic tensions. Malaysia reduced its incidence of poverty from 49 percent to 14 percent between 1970 and 1993, while raising life expectancy from 53 years to 71 years through investments in basic health. By 1993, every child was enrolled in primary school.

Since economic growth is the means and human development the end, the quality of growth is as important as its quantity. Otherwise, economic growth can be jobless, rather than employment-creating; ruthless, rather than equitable; voiceless, rather than participatory; rootless, rather than culturally rooted; and futureless, rather than environmentally sound.

The studies of the 1996 Annual Human Development report conducted by UNDP have demonstrated beyond question that economic growth and equitable human development must move together if both are to succeed in the long run.

Indeed, our study shows that, since 1960, no country has been able to follow a course of lopsided development –

where economic growth is not matched by human development or vice versa – for more than a decade without falling into crisis. During the past three decades, every country that was able to combine and sustain rapid growth did so by investing first in schools, skills and health while keeping the income gap from growing too wide.

There is no automatic link between growth and human development – a simple fact, often forgotten by growth advocates. Such a link must be deliberately forged by governments and regularly fortified by skillful and intelligent policies.

To successfully sustain development over the long term, equitable patterns of growth that translate the benefits of economic expansion into the lives of the average person must be pursued. Growth with equity combines the ideas of justice and equal opportunity, of people coming out of poverty to share in the world's bounty, of becoming integral members of our society.

The defining concerns of international affairs in the next century will revolve around this struggle for equity – equity among nations, equity within nations and equity between sexes. Equity for future generations, through protecting the environment in which they must also live, is also necessarily an integral part of the equation.

The script for human development in the twenty-first century is still unwritten. But we are beginning to write it by the choices we make today. Let it not be said of our time that we, who had the power to do better, allowed the world to get worse. Human destiny, after all, is not a matter of chance, but of choice.

28 / The Past is Too Small to Inhabit

Rem Koolhaas, author of *Delirious New York* and *S,M,L,XL*, is the most exciting thinker today on cities. The architect's Rotterdam-based Office of Metropolitan Architecture's many projects include the gigantic Lille convention center, equidistant from Brussels, Paris and London (thanks to the Chunnel).

I caught Rem on the run, literally, as he was commuting in May 1996 to Rotterdam, Los Angeles (where he is designing the new MCA headquarters at Universal Studios), Seoul, and London. In our conversation we covered a whole set of heavy subjects in the most generic of settings – the departure lounge of Los Angeles International Airport.

NATHAN GARDELS Octavio Paz, the Mexican poet, rejects the term "post-modern." He believes we have broken completely with modernity and now live in a "time without measure, or pure time."

What he means is that modernism was about trading in tradition for the future. Yet, after the failure of Communism and Progress, we no longer have faith in the future either. That leaves us abandoned in the permanently temporary present. There are neither ruins, nor utopia. This pure time is neither optimistic nor pessimistic. It is free. A tabula rasa.

Similarly, outside the central core of European cities, the rest of the cities on the planet are becoming a kind of "pure space" like Los Angeles, liberated from the captivity of the traditional center, and thus of a centering identity. Their

past history matters little as they become sprawling recep-
tacles of overflowing humanity and global culture.

It is in this pure space of the present that what you call
"the Generic City" arises. Singapore, the most successful
Generic City, you call "an ecology of the contemporary."

In your buildings and your writings, aren't you saying
"Let us embrace this tabula rasa and celebrate it. Regret
about history's absence is a tiresome reflex. History's
presence is not desirable"?

REM   No. I would never actively remove history. I like history.
KOOLHAAS What I dislike is the way a collective, free-floating anxiety
has been diagnosed as being about an absence of history,
center and place while, at the same time, a large part
of mankind seems happily capable of inhabiting
the "newnesses" that have been built from scratch, on the
tabula rasa.

The wallowing in anxiety over the lost past – even in
America, which, at the moment, is really gorging on
nostalgia at almost every level, from the populist to the
elitist – blinds us to the incipient emergence of another
world, another city, another way of being happy. We
somehow cannot imagine that anything contemporary –
made by us – can contribute to identity. But the fact that
human growth is exponential implies that the past will at
some point become too small to inhabit and be shared by
those who are alive.

Also, in a distressingly emotional and sentimental way,
this "other way" is simply rejected as if it smells bad. It is
never analyzed, described or investigated. Is the contemporary city like the contemporary airport – all the same? Is
it possible to theorize this convergence? And if so, to what
ultimate configuration is it aspiring? Convergence
is possible only at the price of shedding identity. That is
usually seen as a loss. But at the scale at which it occurs, it
must mean something. What are the disadvantages of
identity, and, conversely, what are the advantages of blank-
ness? What is left after identity is stripped? The generic?

That is why for my book *S,M,L,XL* I made myself go
and try to understand Singapore.

As I note in the book, I turned eight on a ship in the harbor of Singapore. We did not go ashore, but I remember the smell – sweetness and rot, both overwhelming.

Last year I went again. The smell was gone. In fact, Singapore was gone, scrapped, rebuilt. There was a completely new town there.

Almost all of Singapore is less than 30 years old; the city represents the ideological production of the past three decades in its pure form, uncontaminated by surviving contextual remnants. It is managed by a regime that has excluded accident and randomness. Even its nature is entirely remade. It is pure intention: If there is chaos, it is authored chaos; if it is ugly, it is designed ugliness; if it is absurd, it is willed absurdity.

By the way, I don't agree with Octavio Paz that we have broken with modernity. I see the present as a convulsive apotheosis of modernization. The postmodern vision is essentially a form of simplification that plays an important role in celebrating modernization. It removes qualms and resistance. It is lubrication for the modern.

Did the Generic City start in America?   **GARDELS**

Is it so profoundly unoriginal that it can only be imported? **KOOLHAAS**
The Generic City now also exists in Asia, Europe, Australia, Africa. The definitive move away from the countryside, from agriculture, to the city is not a move to the city as we knew it: It is a move to the Generic City, the city so pervasive that it has come to the country.

Some continents, like Asia, aspire to the Generic City; others are ashamed by it. Because it tends toward the tropical – converging around the equator where most people live – a large proportion of the Generic Cities are Asian. One day this discarded product of Western civilization will be absolutely exotic again, through the resemanticization that its very dissemination brings in its wake.

Your attitude toward Singapore seems ambivalent.   **GARDELS**
You have written that Singapore "is a city without qualities," a "Potemkin metropolis." Yet, you speak

with begrudging admiration about "the new norm being synthesized in Singapore – a hard-core Confucian shamelessness, a kind of ultimate power of efficiency that will fuel Asian modernization."

The rest of Asia, where there will be 50 megacities with more than 20 million inhabitants each, wants to emulate Singapore, leading you to remark that "two billion people can't be wrong."

The impression one gets is that there are only two alternatives for Asia: ordered Singapore or chaotic Bladerunner-type cities which can already be glimpsed in Calcutta or even Shanghai. Isn't Singapore the most prepared of any Asian city to enter the twenty-first century?

KOOLHAAS Another way to look at Singapore is that it is (a corporate) Bladerunner. I also don't think Singapore is the place most prepared to enter the twenty-first century. It is at the same time entirely new and incredibly old-fashioned in the sense that it has been completely planned. It is the opposite of flexible. It is a "real" city where absolutes have become encumbrances. It is serious, and therefore seriously vulnerable; by definition on-its-way-to-obsolescence. It is built to last, and thus will age. It will be viable as long as everybody knows their place, but that will not be forever.

Recently, I was on an island in Thailand and found an even more compelling model: a minimum of electronics and a minimum of substance – bamboo, palm leaves, corrugated iron. The fluorescent tube is the minimum increment of modernity. Sometimes two restaurants share a single light through switches on palm trees that suddenly illuminate a clearing in the jungle.

That kind of "liteness" seems supremely capable of dealing with anything bound to come along in the twenty-first century.

GARDELS What, then, might the Asian city look like?

KOOLHAAS It has been precisely in order to find answers to this question that I am working on Harvard's "Project On The

City" where each year we research clusters of interrelated theses on a different subject.

The subject this year is the Pearl River Delta, a region that includes an extreme diversity of cities, some of which are well known: Hong Kong, Macao, Guangzhou; some of them less known, such as Shenzen, Zuhai, and DongGuang.

We are trying to extract from our research – which incorporates subjects such as architecture, infrastructure, landscape, ideology, demographics – a new conceptual apparatus to discuss new urban phenomenon.

This cluster of cities in the Pearl River Delta is destined to become one of the world's megacities. The area already has more than 25 million inhabitants.

But what do we call this at first unrelated group of cities, each with its own history? We suggest the name of "City of Exacerbated Differences." It is undeniably a future metropolis, but each component defines itself in terms of maximum difference from all the others. We also call it "Bastard Metropolis©" because one component is overly dense, one is a garden city, one is expensive and therefore another cheap.

It is therefore likely that the Asian City of the future will have all conditions within its space – lite and heavy, intense and sparse, lively and sedate – rather than one overriding characteristic. If there is an advantage to being a megacity, with "impossible" demographics like 20–30 million inhabitants – then that multiplicity has to be one of them.

Another concept that will help us define the supercities of tomorrow is "Scape©." Scape© is neither city nor landscape, but a post-urban condition. It is obvious that the world of 2050, with its 10 billion people, will be covered by a lot of Scape©. This will be the pervasive, generic condition, punctuated by an event here or there, possibly architecture.

You have said "the street is dead." What do you mean? **GARDELS**

The street is dead mostly because it appears that all the new **KOOLHAAS** cities are less and less dense and more and more sprawling and sparse. But the vitality of the street depends on density.

From time to time it seems that people like density. They feel the apparent need for something eventful. But not too much. Not every day.

What is interesting about City Walk [a contrived main street of shops where people gather and stroll – ed.] at Universal City in Los Angeles is that it creates density in a city of sprawl. And it is a success! This suggests that only the dead can be resuscitated.

GARDELS   What about the widely heralded hope that cyberspace will be the new street, the piazza in our sprawling cities of connected isolation; that cyberflaneurs will promenade around the Net like Baudelaire taking a stroll around Paris?

KOOLHAAS   It is true that the Net has established an incredible, seething community, connected and bubbling. It is true that you can be a flaneur in cyberspace. But can you be more than a flaneur? Since people exist as bodies, they have to be "parked" somewhere.

Maybe the tumultuous richness of cyberspace reveals something about the apparent paucity, the minimalism of the new urban condition. Maybe the Generic City triumphs because cyberspace provides the complementary excess? The Generic City is what is left after large sections of urban life have crossed over to cyberspace. It is a place of weak and distended sensations, few and far between emotions.

But I am, and remain, an architect. I continue to bet, so to speak, on the continuing desire for intercourse of whatever kind. The point now is whether we can imagine hybrids of real and cyberspace.

GARDELS   Won't Generic Cities be redundant with the same global culture? Mickey Mouse, Madonna, and Baywatch will be seen everywhere?

As Maxim Gorky once said of Coney Island, cities of "varied boredom"?

Yet, at the same time, these tabula rasa Generic Cities will be the home of La Raza Cosmica – the cosmic race, a multicultural mosaic – anything but homogeneous.

In each time zone, there are at least three performances of **KOOLHAAS**
the musical *Cats*. The world seems surrounded by a
Saturn's ring of meowing.

Yet, I think the "threat" of homogeneity is grotesquely
exaggerated. For those with eyes, it is becoming very clear
that globalization implies, also, an explosion of difference.

The Generic City is, as you suggest, seriously multiracial, on average 8 percent black, 12 percent white, 27
percent Hispanic, 37 percent Chinese/Asian, 6 percent
indeterminate and 10 percent other.

Great odes to trade and finance are rising to the skies in **GARDELS**
Kuala Lumpur and Shanghai, taking the lead as the world's
tallest buildings; in Arab Islam mosques and monu-
ments are still built to faith and martyrdom. Yet, the most
interesting architects in the West today are building
cathedrals of the great entertainment empires. You are
building for Universal Studios, and Frank Gehry, Michael
Graves, and Arata Isozaki for Disney.

What is going on?

What makes Universal Studios different than Disneyland **KOOLHAAS**
is that it is a place of authentic production. Films and television are made there. There is also a place of consumption,
the theme park. City Walk is strange, a place of simulation
that has almost become authentic.

So we are definitely not involved in making cathedrals.
We have to organize and exploit for maximum social benefit
the coexistence on a single site of so many conditions and
realities, of which landscape is only one.

EuroDisney was said by one French critic to be a "cultural **GARDELS**
Chernobyl." Can a Disney park be a Chernobyl in Europe,
but not in America?

EuroDisney can only be considered a cultural Chernobyl **KOOLHAAS**
because the Europeans themselves are in massive denial.
They have refused the take the issue of mass culture
seriously, in spite of the overwhelming evidence that
Beaujolais, cappuccino, or the Roman Colosseum have

been unable to ward it off. Mass culture is the dirty secret of the European intellectual. They abhor the hordes that go there, but EuroDisney is the only institution that can receive them with a minimum of dignity.

GARDELS   Arata Isozaki says he wants to build "architecture without irony." He likes to build in America, he says, because there is no irony, no distance or conflict with the ancestral territory. "Ruins are the pathetic sentiment about what was lost," he says.

Is your Universal Studios project architecture without irony?

KOOLHAAS   Can anyone outrun irony today?

There are large ironies in America, one of them is that a culture which was about newness has abandoned its role in its further definition and development.

What concerns me, and what may be the result of a collective "flight backward," is that New York, which, if anything, used to be a real city, a city without selection, without exclusive morality, is now expelling, as in some kind of Biblical farce, the entire sector of sin. A cabal of well-meaning people has caused the death of 42nd Street. A last domain of randomness, possibility and, most importantly, urbanity – the Metropolitan – is eliminated in the name of rehabilitation and Disney.

By not understanding cities, urban life, we kill them. And when they are dead, we wring our hands and begin mouth-to-mouth resuscitation.

29 / Asia's Urban Century

George Yeo, Singapore's minister for information and the arts, is one of the most innovative new thinkers of Asia's governing class. His essay is followed by an interview we did in Yeo's sprawling office in the Port of Singapore Administration tower with floor to ceiling windows looking out over one of the busiest and most advanced container ports in the worlds. Through the humid haze caused by smoke floating across the straits from forest fires in Indonesia, the crush of ships in the harbor made it look like the D-Day invasion of Normandy.

Two big forces will shape the Asia Pacific in the next **SINGAPORE** century: information technology and urbanization.

Information technology will change the pattern of population concentration and social organization in the region. Political and economic power will become more decentralized. What was far can become near and what was once near can become relatively far. Thus we see new patterns of international trade and global manufacturing.

With the reopening of Asia and its rapid industrialization, hundred of millions of peasants will become urbanized in China, India, and South-East Asia. This urbanization process will have earth-shaking consequences. Just take China alone as a multiplier of trends. If all Chinese were to eat meat like Americans, there would not be enough agricultural land in the world; or if all Chinese were to eat fish the way Japanese do, there would not be enough fish in the oceans. Whether it is carbon dioxide in the atmosphere, energy consumption food production, the industrialization of China, India, and South-East Asia will alter the course of human civilization.

Information technology and urbanization will change the politics of Asia. It does not matter whether we are talking about democratic or authoritarian systems. In every country, the ability of national governments to tax and control resources is weakening. Factors of production have never been more mobile. Because of this, the devolution of political power is inexorable. Thus we see, for example, the phenomenon of weak central governments in big countries which, in turn, gives rise to problems of currency fluctuation.

All over Asia, managing the aspirations of large urban populations will become critical. Many of the major political parties in Asia today evolved their characters in response to the needs of strong agricultural constituencies. Japan's Liberal Democrat Party, China's Communist Party, Taiwan's Kuomintang, Vietnam's Communist Party, and Indonesia's Golkar all have strong party machines in the countryside. In contrast, their political bases in the cities are often weak. Cities like Tokyo, Osaka, Taipei, Bangkok, and Jakarta have a tendency to be less supportive of national governments.

As more and more people enter the cities, those political parties which are better able to solve urban problems will succeed. This is the fundamental change driving political development throughout Asia today.

The problems of the city are those of housing, crime, traffic, drugs, prostitution, pollution, and terrorism. All these problems are likely to become worse in the coming decades in many parts of Asia. Modern technology makes possible a concentration of population never seen before. But it also results in urban problems of terrifying magnitude.

Urban terrorism, for example, is bound to become more prevalent because of the freer flow of knowledge and the movement of peoples. The expertise to make bombs and other weapons of mass destruction is easily available, whether from Northern Ireland, the Middle East, the former Soviet Union, or elsewhere. The knowledge is available on the Internet. It is also easy to stay anonymous in large cities and be lost in the crowd, especially in places like airports, city centers, and train stations.

Unless cities as organic entities develop immune systems to protect their own life functions, urbanization can lead to misery and self-destruction. Thus the challenge for cities in the next century is the creation of internal systems which preserve them as warm and wholesome human habitats, despite the large number of human beings living and working in close proximity.

THE WEALTH OF CITIES

In the next century, the most relevant unit of economic production, social organization and knowledge generation will be the city or city regions. Nation states will still exist, but an increasing number of policy issues will have to be settled at the city level. This will create new patterns of competition and cooperation in the world, somewhat like the situation in Europe before the era of nation states. Dinosaurs thrived until their environment suddenly changed. Then their size became a disadvantage, leaving the way for domination by the small, sprightly mammals. It is a similar case with the nation state.

National authorities will not disappear, but become weaker. Their ability to tax, to impound property, to control capital flows and the movement of people will grow weaker and weaker.

The information revolution will not dissolve the world into an amorphous mass of weakened political entities. It will instead transform the world into more efficient units of power – in crossroad cities where people meet, interact culturally and stimulate each other.

We have seen this many times in history before with the big citystates in Europe and the large city states in China before the age of empire.

Human beings have options. Wandering scholars shopped for wise princes to serve. The cities which will prosper are those that will take a benign view toward businessmen and trade, that will have policies to attract talent, from administrators to artists, to their jurisdictions.

All this will change political thinking. The modern ideas of socialism and democracy arose in reaction to the industrial era of enormous concentration. Now that the world is breaking up into efficient units, democracy and socialism will also break up.

The era of big democracy and big socialism has passed. They will give way to small democracy and small socialism, to communities that can care for themselves and where each citizen has a clear and concrete – indeed touchable – vested interest in each other's well being. In other words on an efficient scale where accountability and relative equality can really work.

INFOHUBS In the competition among cities, those which are better at acquiring, processing, and making use of knowledge will prevail over those that are less able to. Thus, more and more, cities will become information hubs. Information efficiency will become a key factor determining the success of a city.

Cities also need to cooperate with one another. Thus, regionalism will be another trend in the next century. The creation of regional free trade areas is one aspect of it. The growth of ASEAN, the re-Asianization of Japan, and American and Chinese interest in APEC all express regional imperatives in different ways. Regionalism is in reality a sharing of markets and, at a deeper level, a sharing of knowledge and destiny.

When we talk about knowledge, we must make a clear conceptual distinction between public knowledge and private knowledge. In a competitive situation, it is important to have access to knowledge already available in the public domain, or else one will be at a disadvantage compared to one's competitors. But the key to competitive advantage is private knowledge which one's competitors do not possess. In a competitive situation, the basis of profit is private knowledge. Of course, once private knowledge is used to achieve an advantage, it becomes available to others. So there is an incentive all the time to generate new knowledge and keep it private for as long as possible.

In thinking about public and private knowledge,

there are two aspects to consider. One is the physical infrastructure – telecommunication systems, satellites, computers, switches, and multimedia facilities. This ensures the rapid movement of information. In the financial markets, even a fraction of a second can make a big difference.

The second aspect is what I call the culture of a city, by which I include civic society, the quality of administration, the legal framework, the immune systems to fight cultural infections of all kinds, and the ability to protect private knowledge.

In discussing information technology, we must not ignore the role of the cultural environment. Indeed the cultural environment may well be more important than the physical infrastructure. Satellites, optic fibers, and computers are commodities which can be easily bought and sold and therefore available to all players. What is decisive is the cultural environment which determines how efficiently and effectively knowledge is created, communicated and applied.

URBAN CULTURE

Take, for example, the quality of the city as a human habitat. Without a favorable environment, talented people from all over the world will not come and even home-grown talent will leave. In reality, all cities are in the game of attracting brains. The cities that will succeed the most are those which are best able to attract the most number of interesting and creative minds to work there.

This means good housing, excellent education, safety, smooth traffic, clean air, trees and flowers, music and opera, and an environment which is both wholesome for the family and interesting to individuals. Such an environment must be of human scale at the local level, however big the city. It must not be impersonal, and there must be a civic sense of human beings caring for each other.

Cities are complex systems, and the word "culture" is but a convenient way to describe this complexity. Urban politics and urban culture are both parts of one organic whole. That organic whole includes the immune systems which identify problems when they are still minute and react to them. Thus the difference in response between the population of Kobe and the population of Los Angeles to a major earthquake reflects the profound difference in the character of two complex systems. In one, there was quiet grief and social discipline. In the other, there was widespread looting.

The physical structures of a city can be repaired and rebuilt. The cultural system of a city, in contrast, is unique and not transferable.

*   *   *

NATHAN GARDELS You have said that different cultural systems will gradually create their own analogs in cyberspace and that the English-language Internet itself will become multicultural. Despite the fears of many, you have argued that the world will not go all Anglo-Saxon, dominated by Microsoft and Disney.

Do you then see the Internet as a kind of Tower of Babel destined to break down into many different discourses? If so, doesn't that deprive it of its main import, its universality?

GEORGE YEO In the physical world, we communicate through translators when we don't speak the same language. People who are bilingual or multilingual and multicultural bridge the gaps. The same thing will happen on the Internet.

Whether Microsoft or Disney can succeed and maintain their dominance in this multicultural, multilingual world depends on their ability to adapt. And they are doing so. Bill Gates is taking care to cultivate the leaders in Beijing. And he is negotiating with the Chinese government on how a Chinese-language version of Windows 95 can be introduced into China. The Disney channel, which broadcasts from here in Singapore, will soon be using Mandarin and Cantonese.

The fact that English is overwhelmingly dominant in cyberspace today is a temporary phenomenon due to the fact that American companies have led the way. The Internet will become increasingly multicultural and multi-

lingual. It may take another 10 or 20 years for this change
to take place, but it is inevitable and irreversible.

Perhaps English will dominate cyberspace as a broad, but   **GARDELS**
thin, top layer beneath which will flourish all kinds of
parochial, or niche, discourses of various cultures in their
own languages. The two will exist in tandem.

For example, Europe On-Line is in English, then
French, German, Italian, and so on. The link from
parochial to universal is English.

I don't see a breakup of the Internet as other languages and   **YEO**
cultures come in, but something more subtle with different
languages playing different roles.

For example, wherever you are flying on earth, including
over Siberia, the language of international air traffic control
is English. English will play a similar residual role in cyberspace much like the role played by French in the past in
international diplomacy, or before that, the role Latin
played in linking European cultures.

In the next century, other languages, like Chinese, will
become very important. The Internet will flourish in China
in Chinese. Chinese will be used for communication
between Chinese provinces, which are as populous as
European nations like France and Germany, and between
cities like Beijing, Shanghai, and Hong Kong. There is no
need for the Chinese to use an intermediate language like
English. Of course, of you want to communicate between
Shanghai and Los Angeles, you may need to use English.
But there the advantage will be with whoever is bilingual,
not with those who know only English.

Of course French was only a shared language of elites while   **GARDELS**
English is the language of mass, popular, global culture,
from McDonald's to Planet Hollywood. Won't its
popular omnipresence give it more staying power than
French?

It may, like Latin, but nothing is forever in history. In   **YEO**
relative terms, English will become less important, except

perhaps in its very basic form, almost mathematical in application, for writing basic software.

On the other hand, it has always struck me that the more higher software uses icons, the more similar it is to the iconographic structure of the Chinese language. If you look at icons on the computer screen in a casual way, they look like Chinese characters.

GARDELS Speaking of Bill Gates, he has said that Singapore is "trying to have its cake and eat it too" – it wants to be wired globally and linked to the world, but wants to censor information flows to protect its own community values.

Yet, Gates says, "Inexorably, with the revolution in communications the world becomes a smaller place. The ability to create islands and restrict things goes down dramatically."

How will you work out, as Gates put it, "this coexistence between colliding worlds?"

YEO Not only is there no necessary contradiction between the two, one is a condition for the other.

Take the example of cosmopolitan trading communities like the Jews or Armenians, or the Chinese diaspora in South-East Asia, or the Lebanese in Africa. They live in environments that are totally outside their control. They have to accept the world they live in for what it is.

For them to be effective and relevant, they must remain themselves. They must remain different with their own separate identities. The moment they cease to be different, whether as diamond traders or as spice merchants, they cease to be of use to the world.

Within the community, which is a cultural organization, they do things that sustain their sense of difference, by what they approve and disapprove of in the family or the clan, by the way they marry, by the way they raise their children, by ritual and tradition. This is true even if you are a Chinese laundryman living in a redlight district with children who are bombarded daily by influences you disapprove of.

So, the fact that we have today the Internet and cyberspace doesn't mean we must lose our sense of identity and the basis of our separate cultural existence.

To use another metaphor, cultural communities are like cells in a larger organism. All cells are part of a much larger system, but each keeps around itself a semi-permeable membrane through which it keeps in constant touch with the system outside but at the same time performing functions within that differentiate it from the outside. Similarly with cultures. There are semi-permeable boundaries that keep us what we are and immune systems that protect us from viruses that could destroy us.

Every culture functions in this way, including, for all its criticism of Singapore, liberal America. I was fascinated by the recent *contretemps* over the Calvin Klein ads for teen jeans that some thought were pornographic. Suddenly, there was a collective sense that things had gone too far, that a boundary of decency had been crossed.

All societies, whether American or Singaporean, practice censorship of one kind or another. Political correctness is a form of censorship. It is not possible anymore to effectively censor the flow of information. But, if you make a big fuss over an issue, you cause a dialogue in the community about what is good and what is bad. If you are a politician running for office, you are forced to take sides. In this way, values are upheld in society.

What is the point? The point of censorship is symbolic. It establishes a difference between what is right and what is wrong. It is what keeps a society together and aware of what it stands for. The fact that we sin every day is not a reason to abolish the Ten Commandments. Indeed, it is precisely because we sin every day that we need the Ten Commandments.

To continue your earlier analogy about cells and their **GARDELS** immune response, one can perhaps say that in liberal societies – both metaphorically and in some sense literally – we have acquired an immune deficiency. The boundaries of community have become so permeable that more often than not anything goes. In Singapore, at least you are trying to fortify your immunity.

YEO Yes. You put it well.

GARDELS In Singapore's many cases of press censorship, don't you worry that, as much as affirming community values, you are creating a chilling effect that will prevent the press from playing a check-and-balance role on nepotism, corruption or the purposeful manipulation of government statistics?

YEO If this were the case in Singapore, we would be destroying ourselves. All kinds of information flow through Singapore via the Internet, BBC, CNN, NHK, China Central TV, *The Economist*, the *Wall Street Journal*, Asahi Shimbun, capital market wire services. At any one time, tens of thousands of visitors are passing through. Ten percent of residents in Singapore are foreigners. One in two Singaporeans travel overseas every year. There is no way we can restrict the flow of information. Furthermore, Singapore is a small community, where word of mouth travels extremely fast even if there were no TV or newspaper.

We are a nation of arbitrageurs. We can't afford to be a nanosecond behind Tokyo, London, or New York. For us to try to limit information to a banker, a trader, or a journalist would sound the death knell for Singapore. It would be absurd and contrary to our entire economic strategy. In fact, we are doing what we can, not to control the flow of information, but to make that flow more efficient. We are putting every household in Singapore on the information highway. Every kid in Singapore will know how to operate the Internet before he gets out of high school.

That is why the government has to be fully accountable to the people of Singapore. That is why we insist on accurate reporting in the local and international media and the right of reply.

The cultural realm is different. While we provide easy access to information, we are determined to preserve our own value system and our own sense of self. For example, while Salman Rushdie's *Satanic Verses* may be available by fax or the Internet, we make a point of banning it and not allowing it to be sold in bookstores out of respect for the Muslims in our community. In this way, we affirm the religious and ethnic tolerance that undergirds multiracial and multireligious Singapore.

30 / Immigrants as Postmodern Prophets

Richard Rodriguez, the Mexican-American writer, is without doubt the most insightful observer of life in that zone where borders meet. He is author among other works, of *Days of Obligation* (1993), an editor at Pacific News Service, and a commentator on PBS. He wrote the following reflection for *NPQ* just after Proposition 187, which would deny health and education services to the children of illegal immigrants, was voted into law by the California public in 1994.

SAN FRANCISCO We might have expected it in France, in Germany, or in Japan. But is America, the land built and sustained by immigrants, also becoming intolerant of them? Let's face it: America has never really liked immigrants, at least not when the immigration is actually taking place. America ended up romanticizing the nineteenth-century immigrant, but only generations later.

Today, Americans insist that they are not anti-immigrant. "It is just the illegals we don't want," they say. American politicians warn that illegals are coming for our welfare dollars. But kids on the Mexican side of the border will tell you they are coming in search of a job. They are not coming because they have read Thomas Jefferson or because they know the Bill of Rights. They are coming because there is a rumor of work.

Illegals are an embarrassment to Mexico's government.

They are an outrage to suburbanites in San Diego who each night see the Third World running through their rose garden. They are often adolescent, often desperate or reckless. They are disrespectful of American custom and law. They are also among the most modern people in the world.

Decades before wealthy Mexicans decided to enroll their children in Ivy League colleges in the United States, Mexican peasants left their villages and trespassed across several centuries. They grew accustomed to thousands of miles of dirt roads and freeways, knew two currencies, and gathered a "working knowledge" of English to go along with their native Spanish.

Before professors in business schools were talking about global economics, the illegal knew all about it. Before fax machines punctured the Iron Curtain, coyotes [smugglers of illegal immigrants – ed.] knew the most efficient way to infiltrate Southern California. Before businessmen flew into Mexico City to sign big deals, the illegal was picking peaches in the fields of California or flipping pancakes at the roadside diner.

In 1994, we can say about them exactly what nativists a century ago said about the Ellis Island crowd: "They don't assimilate. They come to take, not to give. They are peasants who lower our national IQ."

The notion of the "legal immigrant" allows us to forget that all immigrants are outlaws. Immigrants violate customs; they assault convention. To be an immigrant is to turn your back on your father and your village. You break your mother's heart. The immigrant is as much a scandal to his ancient mountain village as to suburban Los Angeles.

Early in this century, Mexico passed paws to keep US business interests out. When Carlos Salinas de Gortari was Mexico's president, he began to denationalize Mexican business and open his country to US capital. Americans exclaimed, "At last, Mexico has a truly modern leader!" But the Harvard-educated President of Mexico was preceded to the United States by several generations of peasants.

In the 1920s, when Mexico was trying to seal itself off from the US, Mexican peasants were illegally making their way north. Every few months, illegal workers would return, by choice or by deportation. They returned to their sixteenth-century villages with seductive rumors of America. More than Pancho Villa, more than Zapata, the illegal immigrants became the great revolutionaries of Mexico. They Americanized the tiniest villages of Mexico.

Today, jets make the world convenient to US business executives and to middle-class tourists. We Americans assume our ability to roam where we will, making deals or taking pictures of each other in Bermuda shorts.

A Californian I know complains that a village in Ecuador is becoming more and more Americanized. Each year, he sees the change. I tell him, if he's so worried about the change, maybe he shouldn't travel so much.

We Americans have become like Shakespeare's dark lady of the sonnets. We stand at the window, we bat our eyelashes. We romance the world. We advertise our beauty and our sexy glamour. We display our happy white teeth. And then we wonder why the world is lined up at our door.

Although Californians voted for the anti-immigrant measure by a wide margin, it will not in the end decide illegal immigration. For the fact is that we all live in a world where economies overlap, where we no longer know where our automobiles are assembled, where billboards work their way into the adolescent imagination. We are headed for a century where the great question will be exactly this: What is a border?

The illegal immigrant is the bravest among us. The most modern among us. The prophet.

"The border, señor?" the illegal immigrant sighs. The border is an inconvenience, surely. A danger in the dark. But the border does not hold.

PART IV

GLOBALIZATION AND EMPIRES OF THE MIND

Globalization today is less a slogan of free-traders than a present reality. Capital, goods and labor move ever-more freely across borders. The sun never seems to set on the global financial markets or the new empires of the mind whose images, for better and for worse, occupy our awareness. The warblings of Michael Jackson and Madonna are the muzak of the new world disorder. The civilization of the satellite clashes with the civilization of the ancestral territory; its Planet Hollywood versus Hezbollah.

Can we expect then to see the reign of Disney *über alles?* Will Microsoft rule the alternative to the mass media, the Net? Or, as always before in history, will local Davids arise to challenge the global Goliaths? This is what the filmaker Costa-Gavras suggests.

As the Japanese management guru Kenichi Ohmae points out, it is no longer a dirt road across impassable mountains but satellite access that is the "silk route" to the riches of the world order. The wealth of the global consumer market – those who prefer Sony over the soil of traditional loyalties – lay within the footprint of their signal. If images rule dreams, dreams rule purchases.

Francis Fukuyama makes the point that not all cultures will fare equally under this global regime. Those that are cohesive socially and with high degrees of social trust are more likely to adapt well instead of break apart under the media-invasive and economically-competitive pressures of the new order.

31 / The Culture of Prosperity

Francis Fukuyama is the author of the most famous post-Cold War tract, *The End of History and the Last Man,* and was formerly an official of the US State Department's Policy Planning Staff. His latest book, *Trust,* is about community and "social capital."

Our wide-ranging discussion in Fukuyama's sparse office at the Rand Corporation's Washington office touched on topics from the end of the nation state to "bowling alone" in America's disintegrating communities.

NATHAN GARDELS Jacques Delors, who presided over the European Commission from 1985 until last December, argues that the American social model will explode because of "socially cruel" competitive individualism and the Japanese model will implode because excessive social guardianship over the individual suffocates all dynamism. For Delors, Europe alone, with its balance between the individual and society, will endure.

What do you think of this argument?

FRANCIS FUKUYAMA That is a typical but not very meaningful way of dividing the world regionally without much regard for the highly different cultural attributes within those regions, particularly within Asia and Europe. I think, for example, that the familistic cultures of Hong Kong or Taiwan have more in common with Italy than with Japan. Similarly, the cultural capacity of Germans to move beyond mere kinship ties to "self-organize" their society without at the same time relying on the initiative of the state makes them more akin to the Americans than to the French.

The problem with regional generalizations like the one Delors has offered is that they are too focused on the state as the primary locus of national and cultural identity. Advocates and critics alike of "the Asian model" or "the European model" all look to some industrial policy or other state policies as the chief means of identifying the model. Yet, the same industrial policy will work in one society and be an utter disaster in another. That is because it is the underlying cultural foundation, not the state policy, that is usually the critical factor in success or failure. Rather than pursue the essentially fruitless debate about state policies, it is thus more important to look at the intermediate layer of society, the cultural terrain between the individual and the state.

Accordingly, if we are looking for a mental map of the world I think it is far more useful to trace what I call the "distribution of social capital" than to track industrial strategies. Some societies – notably Japan, America, and Germany – are better able than others to generate new forms of voluntary association, what I call "spontaneous sociability."

The ability to organize into groups, from bowling leagues to large corporations, requires individuals to subordinate their individuality to common norms. On one level that means accepting the rule of law. But is also means the acceptance of informal moral habits such as honesty, dependability, reliability, reciprocal obligation and trust. This ability is not evenly distributed among all societies.

The primary form of sociability for the Chinese and the Italians, as I noted earlier, is through family and kinship ties. That is both good, and bad. Undoubtedly it is better to have strong families than not, but in certain societies, beyond a certain threshold, family ties can be too intensive and undermine broader social trust among people not related to each other.

The Chinese, who have very large and cohesive families, have a lot of trouble trusting non-kin. As a result there were and are very few large non-state organizations, such as private universities or hospitals in Taiwan or China, and very few large, world-scale private corporations. By contrast, the early phases of both Japanese and German industrialization were characterized by a remarkable communitarian impulse where unrelated people could come together very readily and work in large organizations.

On this score particularly, Americans misunderstand themselves as much as someone like Jacques Delors. Americans see themselves as individualistic Lone Rangers, defying authority and unable to merge themselves effectively in the group. But American social history tells us exactly the opposite: We have been an extremely cohesive society, raising barns for the neighbors, establishing hospitals, organizing community soccer or baseball matches, or setting up globe-spanning companies. Americans, in fact, have a very dense and strong layer of intermediate organization. Indeed, the chief characteristic noted by Alexis de Tocqueville was America's "art of association."

Such voluntary sociability bodes far better for the idea of citizenship than does a familistic way of organizing society. The problem of citizenship can be seen in Chinese culture from Singapore to Hong Kong. In Hong Kong the public spaces are not well maintained; people litter and spit on the street. If it doesn't concern their family, they don't care about it. In Singapore, the state has to enforce citizenship, going so far as to regulate personal manners as minor as chewing gum, because it can't rely on its subjects to be public-spirited. At least historically, that has never been true in America, or Germany.

Italy is a European case of weak voluntary association and strong family. Economic dynamism in Italy in recent times has sprouted mainly from small, family-owned businesses. Like Taiwan, Italy is a kind of familist-statist society. It has a dynamic lower layer of family business, and then the state or the Catholic Church. There is not much in between. In effect, the state compensates for the weak intermediate organizations and vibrant private sector through industrial policies and by setting up and running the big banks, steel or energy companies. Although efforts at privatization are now underway something like 30 percent of GNP in both

Taiwan and Italy is owned by the state, a far larger proportion than is seen in Germany or northern Europe where the intermediate civil society is much stronger.

We see a very different distribution of social capital in Japan, Germany and America. Both the small family business and the state are far less important than what comes in the middle – a large, strong, very cohesive network of private organizations from Mitsubishi to Ford Motor Company to Amway to the Sierra Club.

In the cultural settings of an Italy or Taiwan industrial policy can actually work well; in America it can just get in the way and make what works well already less efficient.

GARDELS   So the sociable cultures of Japan, Germany and America that can build large, efficient organizations are likely to be most competitive in the times ahead?

FUKUYAMA   That is a very complicated issue that depends on the overall direction of technology. During the period of industrialism in the first half of this century, steel, chemical and autos, for example, required very large, capital-intensive organizations for standardized production and distribution. The kind of sociability that existed in Germany, Japan, and the United States was critical for success in this kind of industry because of the high entry costs and substantial economies of scale. By contrast, the Hong Kongs, Taiwans, and Italys tended to dominate in apparel design, machine tools, furniture, toys, and other product areas where start-up costs are small and in which large scale is not particularly important.

It is obvious from this record that the distribution of social capital very much influences the global division of labor. The question of who gets richer now as a result of the distribution of social capital is complicated because the trend over the next fifty years fostered by information technologies is toward decentralization and smaller scale organization. Indeed, the Chinese family business has a lot of advantages over the large-scale Japanese corporation in certain types of hi-tech industries because they are more flexible and can respond more rapidly to market signals.

Certainly, the demise of IBM shows that large scale alone is no guarantor of competitiveness. At the same time, its eclipse by Microsoft shows how important the ability still is to move from small innovation to large-scale production.

Isn't the sociability you are talking about rooted, particularly in Germany or Japan, in the old idea of *volksgeist* or national spirit? In other words, in the tribe? **GARDELS**

Well, *volksgeist*, of course, has the bad connotation of some primordial, unchanging character of a particular people. And to be sure, culture changes less quickly than institutions or ideas. But all cultures adapt; their boundaries are constantly fuzzing and being shaped by mutual interaction with others. Also, there is a rational process that intervenes in cultural formation which the terms tribe or *volksgeist* don't capture. **FUKUYAMA**

What we are really talking about here is a certain pattern of moral habit that arises from different sources in different cultures. As I've noted, Chinese society is more familistic than Japanese society, which is more oriented to group association.

One small example is telling. Adoption of a non-biologically related heir is almost unheard of in China, but very easy in Japan where family outsiders from the larger social group are readily accepted. It was just this kind of moral habit that led to the widespread practices of professional management of family-owned firms in Japan well before the Meiji restoration. It led, in a sense, to a non-kinship-based civil society.

The cohesiveness of German society, I think, has to do with the survival of guilds that were smashed in France by liberal, modernizing reformers. To this day a form of those guilds survive in the apprenticeship system in Germany that is so admired by US Labor Secretary Robert Reich.

In the United States, sociability had many roots, one of them the sectarian character of the Protestant groups that settled this country. They created a very active space of association larger than the individual and the family, but autonomous from the state. In fact, by protecting their religious autonomy, the state nourished the growth of a vibrant civil society rather than acting as a sponsor of the given way of life of a particular sect.

Later, in the eighteenth and nineteenth centuries, the sociable habits of the Protestant sects persisted without the religious content.

GARDELS Yet, in America at least, aren't the moral habits upon which your vaunted social capital rests rapidly depreciating? Divorce and the breakdown of the family are ominous indicators. Crime and distrust are rampant. Aggressively disassociating gated communities are springing up along the outskirts of all major American cities.

FUKUYAMA Today, I would agree that the US faces a crisis of associational life. Unless we turn it around, it will have economic consequences *vis-à-vis* competition with those cultures like Germany and Japan that have been able to strongly maintain their social capital. The "art of associating" is an important economic virtue because it is not some rigid policy but an inherently flexible manner of facing challenges: People who trust each other and feel responsible to each other are good at adapting to new conditions with appropriate forms of organization. Such a society will prevail over one where there is generalized mistrust and where everyone looks to the legal system to mediate disputes, even within the family. When all that is left of the rich texture of society is a contract between individuals, then America will be in real trouble. Undeniably, that is where we seem headed.

The decline of sociability in America is first of all not just about the family. The American family has not been deteriorating because other forms of associational life are growing stronger; all are declining in tandem, and the importance of the family increases with the deterioration of other forms of sociability because it becomes the only remaining opportunity for moral community of any sort.

Robert Putnam at Harvard, for example, has published a study called "Bowling Alone," in which he documents the decline not only of bowling leagues, but of participation in all sorts of voluntary associations from Kiwanis Clubs to the Rotarians. A variety of reliable polls show a sharp increase in levels of distrust of others since the 1950s. The increase not only of crime but litigiousness is a further indicator.

People may be dropping out of bowling leagues, but aren't **GARDELS** they, in ever greater numbers, tapping into the chat lines on the Internet or electronic services like America Online?

Obviously, it is possible that the new technologies will **FUKUYAMA** enable people to create unprecedented forms of electronic community. However, community is not just the technological capacity to make contact. There is a moral dimension. What makes a cohesive community is shared norms, not modems. Without the bounded set of mutual obligations that arise from living in the same physical space, it is not clear to me that virtual communities can really develop a cohesive moral basis that will sustain them.

What are the sources of the breakdown of sociability in the **GARDELS** United States.

One is tempted to answer that America's dynamism and the **FUKUYAMA** sources of that dynamism – the suspicion of authority, cultural diversity and the rights of the individual – can be destructive when they go too far and come at the expense of traditional virtues and moral habits.

Surely, today's continuing capitalist revolution undermines local communities as jobs are moved overseas: Families are uprooted and loyal workers are laid off in the name of downsizing. Much of the American Midwest has been devastated in the last couple of generations.

As important an impact, however, has been the rights revolution in this country over the same period of time. This revolution had a justifiable and necessary origin – the civil rights movement, feminism, and gay rights. But it has led to the proliferation of a sense of individual rights and entitlement at the expense of forms of authority at every level. That balance that needs to be struck between the individual and group obligation has swung way too far in the direction of individuals.

Without doubt, much of America's competitive edge is due to the greater innovativeness and entrepreneurial energy of American companies, which in turn is fueled by American reluctance to obey traditional sources of authority. But when the old 1970s bumper sticker "Question Authority becomes the national ethos instead of a healthy attitude toward power, the American genius for organization can be seriously undermined. This is especially so when the bumper sticker on the competitor's car, say in Singapore, is "Respect Authority."

There is another related factor. It is possible to have too much diversity, to arrive at a situation in which people feel they have nothing in common besides the legal system, no shared values and consequently no basis for trust. Then there isn't even a common language of discourse to discuss our problems. Sometimes I feel we are very close to that state already.

In effect, modern institutions just won't work unless they are supported by pre-modern social structures like the community, religion and the family. Again, Tocqueville saw this very clearly. He understood that the tendency in a democracy was for people to lose their public spiritedness and retreat to their private lives. In an earlier America, Tocqueville saw the art of association as the counterbalance to the debilitating tendency of everyone to go private.

So, in a way, America's future depends very much on being able to revive the sociable spirit of the past.

GARDELS In effect, what you are saying is that Bill Bennett's *Book of Virtues* is a more important text for future American prosperity that Adam Smith's *The Wealth of Nations*?

FUKUYAMA I think that is right in the sense that we already accept to a great degree Adam Smith's view of the world. Not having enough free economic exchange is not our problem now; our problem is the unraveling moral cohesion of societies that were once bound by the habits of religion, community or family. These were bedrock social realities that all the liberal theorists thought would remain intact no matter what. We can no longer make that assumption.

It is now becoming clear that the most successful modern societies are those, like Japan, that are not completely modern; societies where there is a blend of new and old ways; a coexistence of the traditional and the modern, not the dominance of one over the other.

GARDELS | Your book *The End of History* was thought to say the liberal market model had triumphed globally in the wake of the Soviet collapse. Now you are talking about the need to revive traditional moral habits from within different cultures to coexist with modern technological society.

Can you explain how these two theses relate?

FUKUYAMA | First of all, in *The End of History* I emphasized that liberalism understood as a pure social contract between purely self-interested individuals is not a workable society. All the liberal theorists understood that the freedom they envisioned would be conditioned by religion, ethnicity or other forms of tradition. Two hundred years after the French Revolution, the unraveling of the religio-cultural underpinnings of liberalism, especially in America, have exposed that enlightened self-interest by itself is not enough to sustain a society.

What I did say in my earlier book was that the whole idea of social engineering by large centralized institutions guided by an overarching ideology has reached a dead end. No one believes in that anymore. There is no historical alternative to market structures and the liberal democratic state. There may be tinkering with this model, but there has been, globally speaking, a convergent belief that these institutional arrangements are the best that mankind has come up with. We have reached the end of history in the sense that we have exhausted the historical alternatives. There are no longer any artificial distinctions based on political structures such as monarchies, totalitarian states, and market democracies – all are striving for some form of the latter.

This does not mean, however, that all societies are going

to be uniform or that they will be equally successful. On the contrary, precisely because of this convergence, the differentiating factor among societies will be shaped chiefly by their cultural attributes.

I think Sam Huntington has hit on a real insight with his idea of a "clash of civilizations" becuse that highlights the extreme importance of culture as a determined factor in international social relations in the times ahead.

GARDELS   Your idea of the "end of history" and Sam Huntington's idea of a "clash of civilizations" have emerged as the most famous theses of the post-Cold War period. Both of you point out the importance of culture, but why can't civilizations at odds lead not to intransigent conflict, but positive influence of cultures on one another?

FUKUYAMA   Differences can obviously lead to conflict, such as with Islam, and that is what Huntington has focused on. Yet cross-cultural stimulation can also be an outcome of the heightened importance of culture.

American business has profited from being exposed to Asian ways of management. Not only has American manufacturing become more competitive in response to the Japanese, but in part it has become more competitive through adopting such Japanese ideas as quality circles and work teams.

More importantly, the whole debate over the Asian soft-authoritarian model and the Asian economy has actually been quite healthy for the United States. The Asian critique of Western society by someone like Lee Kuan Yew is much more penetrating and to the point than the Islamic or Bolshevik critique. It resonates because it speaks to our own doubts about a liberal society gone too far. The Asian critique resonates with us because it raises questions about how people take care of each other and about how to maintain a coherence of basic social structures.

The moralistic tone that an America versus Asia discussion quickly takes on is striking. American social critics can often most easily make their criticism of America through Asian mouths.

Stimulation can come from the other direction as well. **GARDELS**
Japan has always relied upon outside stimulation – from
Korea, from China and more lately from the West – for the
development of that island culture.

Let me cite the Japanese architect Arata Isozaki, who
designed the Museum of Contemporary Art in Los
Angeles: "In a book written in the 1950s, the Hegelian
philosopher Alex Kojeve described 'the end of history.' He
later added a chapter on Japan saying that it had reached its
'end of history' after the Hideyoshi shogunate. Kojeve
argued that after the 15th century Japan experienced a state
of internal and external peace for a period of several
hundred years, a period which very much resembled
Hegel's postulated 'end of history.' Conflict ceased, and the
Japanese boringly focused on endless repetition and refine-
ment of the formal arts. Today this condition is known as
Kojefu."

"I agree with Kojeve's analysis," says Isozaki, "and,
because I do, I fear for Japan. The end of history is the end
of conflict, of friction and the creative impulse. I want to
make another history."

For Isozaki, that history can only come from outside
stimulation.

I think that is a perfect case in point of how clashing **FUKUYAMA**
cultures can create new and unforeseen possibilities, not
merely lead to acrimony and war.

It seems to me that the relative ethnic unity of Germany and **GARDELS**
Japan can both support and counterbalance the institutions
of liberal market democracy without depleting their social
capital. Japan is very nearly a racially homogenous tribe.
Germany is less so, but there is still something about that
hike in the Black Forest that ties everyone together.

America, by contrast, is a land of immigrants not tied
together by tribe. As you pointed out, our moral habits and
patterns of sociability were formed in the crucible of the
early Protestant sects that settled this country.

That is all long gone. Can a non-tribal America replenish
its social capital and re-establish a cogent moral order

without a return to our religious foundations? Isn't there a limit beyond which moral habits can outlive their religious origins?

FUKUYAMA   That is, as they say, the $64,000 question. I don't have an answer, but I remain optimistic. American culture is sufficiently dynamic so that we will be able to work something out.

32 / Bypassing the State of Asia

Chai-Anan Samudavanija is renowned in the new Asia for his maps of that region's emerging "growth circles," Chai-Anan is director of the Chaiyong Limthonghul Foundation, a private think-tank, in Bangkok, Thailand.

No modern economy can any longer be limited to its **BANGKOK** country's borders. Much has been said in this regard about large firms spanning the planet and about instantaneous financial flows between Hong Kong, London, Frankfurt, and New York. But globalization has also enabled small communities and individuals in remote, undeveloped areas to have more opportunities and choices – "pathways from the periphery" – due to the free flow of information, better communications and lower costs of transportation.

Integration into the transnational economy necessarily implies a breakdown of the authority of the nation state because it opens up more room for non-state actors. Not only are transnational corporations exerting significant influence on national, sub-regional, regional, and international economic exchanges, but ordinary people who share similar ethnicity, languages and dialects have, increasingly, been able to move freely across borders. In consequence, today's borders have lost their impregnable definition and become rubbery.

The globalization process is essentially non-ideological in nature. It rests on cultural and economic interdependence rather than cultural and economic domination, on diversification and networking rather than integration and unification, on de-centralization rather than centralization, on participation rather than mobilization.

These changes wrought by globalization are now forcing their way beyond the old boundaries "mapped" by colonial powers in the nineteenth century. However boundary lines are not being erased the same way everywhere, but in different ways in different places.

The Soviet state did not "wither away" but disintegrated. The Chinese state is not going to wither away either, but its economic development also will not lead to a Western conception of the liberal-democratic state. Rather, a third Asian model is struggling to emerge that involves an activist bureaucracy, a "soft-authoritarian" political structure and a distinctive Asian conception of communitarian rights.

In Europe and North America, dynamic capitalist forces gave rise to an active civil society that forced the democratization of the state. In many countries in Asia such as Indonesia, China, Thailand, Myanmar, Vietnam, Laos and Cambodia the state has been able to resist being changed by "surrounding societal forces."

Transitions to industrialization and freer markets by Asian states have not led to democratization because of the one characteristic which sets them apart from Americans and Europeans: They strongly fear disorder. Thus, much of the "liberalization" that has taken place with privatization in these activist-bureaucratic states has not led to democratization, but to technocratization. Any purposeful shedding of state power is associated with the depoliticization of economic development.

However, even the "soft-authoritarian" states of Asia are finding their authority undermined by several significant developments in the region. Businesses are bypassing state boundaries as they become privatized and are building ties with counterparts in other states. The increased availability of telecommunications technology, such as mobile phones, fax machines, and cable televisions, is also undermining state attempts at social control. (Witness the mass social resistance to the miliary junta in Thailand in 1992).

The soft-authoritarian attempt in Asia to have globalization without democratization will, in my view, lead to a
generalized phenomenon of "bypassing the state," not just
by large businesses, but through traditional transnational
links by those marginalized grass-roots groups that could
not possibly change or effectively oppose state hegemony.

As this process develops, Asia needs new maps to replace
the nineteenth century style nation state map which is
becoming increasingly irrelevant. These new maps should
show the mass activity occurring along state borders in the
region as workers from one country migrate to work in
the factory of another to produce goods to be exported to
yet another state. While borders during the Cold War were
the site of danger and division, the borders between states
in Asia are now the locus of vibrant economic and cultural
transaction.

The "bypassing of the state" is affecting the Asian map
on two important levels. On the broader, macroeconomic
level, the weakening of the state is opening up the possibility of regional economic growth that follows trade
"flares" instead of artificial state boundaries. On the micro
level, people have been freed to follow jobs, or cultural ties,
and to build connections with neighbors in other states.

These trends suggest that rather than facing Professor
Sam Huntington's "clash of civilizations," an idea based on
the Western dialectical model that presumes opposing
forces must clash in order to eventually converge into one
model, the future in the Asia-Pacific region is more likely
to see dynamic "interactions over and under the state"
propelled by the coexistence of opposing and complementary forces. The combined forces of globalization, the
historical duration of distinct civilizations and ethnic
pluralism across Asia will, I believe, give birth to a "global-
ized communitarianism" as the alternative model to the
Western liberal–democratic model.

*   *   *

In May 1939 Colonel Joseph Stilwell, the American military attaché, left China traveling through Siam, Indochina,

Malaya, and Java. Two years earlier he witnessed the Japanese invasion of China and formed a strong opinion that the United States and Japan must inevitably come to war. By 1939, the Japanese already took control of Hankow and Canton, China's last access by sea to the outside world.

In the summer of 1939, Hia Kwong Iam, the president of the Thai Chinese Chamber of Commerce who had been organizing the anti-Japanese movement among Chinese in Thailand, went to Yunnan to help set up a defense line against the Japanese. At that time Yunnan became the main air base of Free China and the starting point of the Burma Road.

In 1994, Sondhi Limthongkul, the president of the M-Group Corporation, went to Yunnan by a private jet he rented from Thai Airways International to negotiate a joint venture with the Yunnan provincial government. Unlike Hia Kwong Iam or Joe Stilwell, his mission has nothing to do with the Japanese military; he is more concerned with how best to position his investment portfolio and satisfy his financial supporters which include Goldman Sachs, Nomura Securities and three other major Thai banking and financial institutions.

Yunnan's strategic position as the last defense line of China stems from its geopolitical location. The highland belt that separates China from mainland Southeast Asia stretches from Tibet to Assam, through northern Myanmar, the Chinese provinces of Sichuan, Yunnan, Guangxi, and Guizhou to northern Thailand and spills over into Laos and the hills of northern Vietnam.

These border zones had been the main trade routes for people of diverse ethnicities for several hundred years before the Anglo-French encroachment in the nineteenth century. In fact, prior to the establishment of British and French rule in mainland South–east Asia (with the exception of Siam), communities in these highland areas traded freely without any concern for state sovereignty.

Yunnan is the province of China inhabited by the largest number of minority nationalities (22), most of whom share common cultural, historical, linguistic and economic ties with ethnic minorities in Myanmar, Laos, Vietnam and northern Thailand. Eighty-four percent of its total land area is covered by mountains, 10 percent by plateaus, and 6 percent by basins and river valleys.

Today, Yunnan has returned to its historical role. It is no longer the backyard defense area of China, but a center for rapidly growing trade investment linking southwest China with the northern part of mainland South-east Asia.

Although the majority of the 220 million people in the five provinces of China are still very poor, they nevertheless make up a potential market of increasingly affluent consumers. Thailand, Burma, Vietnam, Cambodia, and Laos have a combined population of 215 million. This total market of 435 million rivals in size the European Community and the North American Free Trade Agreement region.

Geographically, much of southwest China is far closer to the ports of Myanmar and Thailand than to Guangzhou and Shanghai. Ruili, a small Chinese town near the Burmese border, is 4,000 kilometers from Beijing, but only 1,100 kilometers from Rangoon. Once the bridge on the Moei river connecting the Myanmar town of Myawaddy and Mae Sod district of Tak province in northwest Thailand is completed, the road network linking China, Myanmar and northern Thailand will serve as the main route for inland trade.

GROWTH CIRCLES

The end of the Cold War and the decisions of all socialist regimes in the region to speed up their "socialist market" reforms have resulted in the emergence of Asia's new "growth circles" encompassing such areas as the highland zones of southwest China, Myanmar, Laos, Thailand, and Vietnam.

In 1993 it was estimated that more than $5 million a week in goods were smuggled across the Vietnam–China border. Two-way trade between Myanmar and Yunnan was estimated around $800 million while the border trade between Myanmar and Thailand is estimated at $300 million.

Unlike in European and North American trading zones where modern transportation, communications and related services exist, most of the transactions in these areas have been made under pre-modern conditions. Mules, ox-carts, Second World War vintage roads and vehicles are normal sights in these budding trade routes.

Just imagine the new situation in the coming twenty first century when all the infrastructure projects, such as airports and new roads, are completed and the Mekong river, which runs through six countries, is fully utilized for water transport.

As trade becomes once again a purely economic activity in the wake of the Cold War, old trade routes which run through Yunnan, Myanmar, Laos, and northern Thailand are becoming reinvigorated. For over a century the traditional patterns of trade had been constrained by the restrictions imposed not only by the Western concept of the nation state – the British formalized trade in the region in the 1890s – but also later on by ideological conflicts. The fact that the old patterns have survived and flourished despite these limitations reflects strong traditional ties among communities forced by their common geographical factor to struggle for their survival.

LOCAL GLOBAL- IZATION The highland subregional zone I have described is a new "growth circle" in a different way than that conventionally conceived by economists and investment bankers.

Due to its geostrategic position, relative backwardness and cultural diversity, globalization has a different impact on this area than in Tokyo or Los Angeles.

Kenichi Ohmae, the Japanese management guru, has identified three primary forces reshaping the world: the globalization of consumers and corporations; the formation of region states as opposed to nation states; and the formation of economic blocs such as the European Union or NAFTA. But something different is going on here: The resumption of an age-old network of small communities which have survived the rise and decline of the nation state.

Globalization of these old networks has opened up new opportunities not only in the area of trade and investment liberalization within Asian countries in order to compete for international capital; they have also opened up new opportunities for interaction between the economic and non-economic factors that are becoming more and more important in regional and subregional cooperation. Culture, ethnicity, community belief and rituals, languages, dialect – all of which are not normally included in economic equations – have become more intertwined with patterns of migration, trade and investment, natural resource utilization, productivity, technological transfer, and human resource development.

In the age of globalization and de-ideologization, culture can fuel rather than limit rapidly-growing transnational economic transactions. This is the message of the rubbery borders in this part of Asia today.

33 / China's 600,000 Avon Ladies

Kenichi Ohmae Founder of Heisei ishin-no-kai (The Reform of Heisei political party), Kenichi Ohmae has been a closer adviser to Malaysian Prime Minister Mahathir bin Mohamad on his "Look East" strategy. This article for the Winter 1995 issue of *NPQ* was later expanded into a book entitled *End of the Nation State* (1995).

TOKYO On old economic maps, the most important cartographic facts had to do with things like the location of raw material deposits, energy sources, navigable rivers, deep-water ports, railroad lines, paved roads – and national borders. On today's maps, by contrast, the most salient facts are the footprints cast by TV satellites, the areas covered by radio signals and the geographic reach of newspapers and magazines. Information has replaced both propinquity and politics as the landscape feature most likely to shape the flows of economic activity. Physical terrain and political boundaries still matter, of course, but they – especially political boundaries – do not matter as much as what people know or want or value.

In a sense, the intangibles of local knowledge, taste, and preference have always played a critical shape-giving role. Long before nation states existed, long before the cities, towns and villages out of which they grew took recognizable form, groups of people linked by social and cultural ties regularly exchanged what they could hunt, fish, grow, gather, extract, or make. The meaningful horizons of their lives were cirumscribed not by the artifice of formal political institutions, but by the land on which they lived and by the social webs that enclosed them. Even in the modern world, with its crazy quilt of political borders, hundreds of millions of people – rural peasants, say, in remote areas of China – exist in much the same fashion. Political dividing lines got added late, indeed, to these venerable maps of local experience.

Though the ink is barely dry, it is already fading. Better information, made possible by better technology, is the reason. As the quality, range and availability of information improve, growing numbers of people – no matter what their geographical location – come to know in ever finer detail how other people in other places live. At the same time, they come to know what kinds of economic choices can be made and what levels of value attach to those choices. Such knowledge and awareness, in turn, inevitably work to undermine the tyranny of both physical distance and government edict. The larger the field of known possibilities, the harder it is for a central authority to limit that field arbitrarily – or to make those limitations stick.

Centuries ago, the first Western travelers to reach Asia returned with goods and spices and artwork that forever changed the universe of possibilities out of which tastes and preferences at home would later crystallize. On this road of discovery, there is no going back, or even going more slowly. Indeed, in recent years, when the Silk Road is no longer a dangerous route through uncharted terrain but merely a degree of access to global media, the time required for exposure to new dimensions of choice has shrunk to virtually nothing. And the barriers to such exposure have either disappeared or proven endlessly porous. Even given the irreducibly local portion in any mix of customs and preferences, a newly shared knowledge of what is possible cannot help but lead across geographies to at least a partial convergence – what I have elsewhere called "California-ization" – of taste. Global brands of blue jeans, colors, and stylish athletic shoes are as much on the mind of the taxi driver of Shanghai as they are in the kitchen or the closet of the schoolteacher in Stockholm or São Paulo.

For several decades now, this process of Californiaization has provided much of the market-driven support for the development of a genuinely borderless global economy. But this kind of convergence, important as it is, goes only so far. It overlays new tastes on an established, but largely unaffected base of social norms and values. It adds new elements to the local mix of goods and services, but leaves the world view of the people who purchase them unchanged. It expands the universe of what is desirable, but does nothing to shift the fundamental mindset of those who experience those pangs of desire. The contents of kitchens and closets may change, but the core mechanisms by which cultures maintain their identity and socialize their young remain untouched. Political borders may offer little meaningful resistance to invasion by new constellations of consumer taste, but social borders limit their scope and effectively quarantine them within the superficial layer of culture.

But this, too, is now beginning to change. Even social borders are starting to give way to the information and technology-driven processes of convergence that have already turned political borders into largely meaningless lines on economic maps. There are two reasons for this. First, as societies move up the economic ladder of development past the $5,000 per capita threshold, there is a notable upward ratcheting in the speed with which the lifestyles of their people – what they see and hear, what they buy, how they spend their time – grow more and more alike. The effects of this flywheel-like acceleration reach, to some extent, into the underlying nexus of culture. Some rough threshold of critical mass does exist beyond which changes in degree of shared lifestyle become changes in kind of attitude and orientation.

But second, and more important, this acceleration is taking place at a moment in history when the very nature of the media exposure driving it is itself undergoing radical change. The multimedia experiences increasingly made possible by new technology have consequences that go far beyond surface issues of taste (and their second-order implications for culture) to fundamental issues of thought process and mindset. In those societies open to the influence of multimedia, the critical balance is already beginning to shift: Children and teenagers are, at deep levels of sensibility and worldview, becoming much more like their counterparts in other societies than they are like the older generations in their own cultures. The essential continuity between generations, on which every society necessarily depends for its integrity and survival, has begun to fray.

This can be clearly seen in Japan where the global media **NINTENDO** has forged a deep rupture between generations, not some- **KIDS** thing shared between them. It cuts, at last, the already thinly stretched cord, severing both the vertical linkages across age groups and the relationships of authority that have long held Japanese society together. In their place, it weaves new connections – not, however, with older cohorts of Japanese, but with the tens of millions of "kids" everywhere else in the world who have learned to play the same sort of games and so have been exposed to the same implicit lessons. The web of culture used to get spun out of the stories a child heard at a grandparent's knee. In today's increasingly subnuclear families, it derives from that child's experience with interactive multimedia.

The social glue of intimate familiarity and shared experience once came only from participation in and with family. Now it comes from watching how a "kid" from another culture whom you've never seen before reveals character and mindset through programming style.

But it goes further, too. The "kids" in Japan or wherever who master a joy stick-driven environment have shown they can move, with unbelievable speed, to comparable mastery of a PC's alpha-numeric keyboard. This is especially important in Japan, where shared problems of writing and typing have long been a source of in-group social cohesion. Today, millions of "Nintendo Kids" have ready access to multiple avenues of external communication. This is even truer for their younger siblings and will be truer for their younger siblings and will be truer still for their children. The link among generations has been broken; a new link with those sharing similar experiences has been forged. This means that the "Nintendo Kids" will have more in common with similar youngsters outside Japan than with other generations within Japan, and as such will form a "civilization" of their own. First in the history of mankind, they will have more things in common across national borders during their upbringing than with their own families and tribes.

THE "BRUTAL FILTER" Reflecting on the huge waves of immigration from Europe that changed the demography of the United States during the nineteenth century, the historian Oscar Handlin described the process of upheaval triggered by such large-scale social movements as that of passing through a "brutal filter." Along the way, some – but not all – of the ties and allegiances that had long kept the members of particular old-world societies bound together snapped. Deeply entrenched connections between generations were uprooted. Inevitably, the elements and groupings so abruptly set free came together in the new country in countless new combinations and permutations. Some linkages entirely disappeared, some survived intact, some new ones formed; all were changed. America was born.

Worldwide, the experience of today's "Nintendo kids" is leading evidence that the societies from which they come, wherever they may be on the ladder of development, are beginning to move – if at different speeds and in different sequences – through a comparably brutal filter. This late twentieth century wave of immigration is being driven, on the surface by the development of global brands and shared tastes in popular culture and, at a much deeper level, by the infectious spread of new information-related digital technologies. What we are witnessing is the birth of a "New America," with a massive migration of the mind and cultural outlook. As in the old America, most immigrants are looking for freedom and a new haven, not bound by traditions, taboos and a rigid class, or social system.

The journey is still at a fairly early stage. Even so, it is possible to see its broad contours and general direction. The countries from which these uprooted people are independently setting out are traditional, politically defined nation states. The country to which they are all migrating is the global economy of the borderless world. The communities in which they hope to settle – and through which they hope to plug into that borderless economy, or New America – are region states. Their movements along the way will redraw the maps of our economic world, and the Declaration of Independence may be drafted by the "Nintendo Kids" to kiss goodbye to the old generation, narrowly defined civilization, restrictive governments and even the United Nations. Shall we pack up and go on the journey of Dragon Quest, the contemporary version of the Mayflower?

*   *   *

Girls in Guangzhou, the capital of the state of Guangdong in China, are eager to get hold of Avon lipstick. There is a reason for this. Avon ran a TV commercial called "Hong Kong Girls" about two years ago. It implied that Cantonese girls, if they become rich, could look as pretty as Hong Kong girls. The girls in the TV commercial, clad in mini skirts, dancing the go-go and wearing this American lipstick, looked very attractive indeed.

Today, after just three years in operation in Guangdong, Avon has mobilized more than 30,000 door-to-door Avon ladies in Guangdong alone. The Avon people thought door-to-door sales were necessary, but demand is so great that the ladies come right to the distribution points for more products. It is estimated that more than 600,000 Avon ladies will be needed in all of China by the turn of the century.

Although Avon just opened its Shanghai operation, it has already hired 6,000 Avon ladies. Those girls snatching up lipstick probably don't remember how to spell "communism" anymore. Nor do they care about it. The promise of prosperity has completely and irreversibly changed their priorities and agenda.

As a result of such influences from outside, China is going through a major transition from a centrally controlled nation state that was oriented toward Beijing to a commonwealth of (reasonably autonomous) region-states. Chinese people in Dalian, Tianjin, or Shanghai watch more world TV shows than the news from Beijing.

What is happening in China today is a case in point of how the power of information has become the key determinant of the future shape of the world. It has tumbled walls. It is erasing borders and undoing the traditional nineteenth century model of the nation state.

In such a world, Dalian has become just another region-state interacting with the rest of the world. The same is true of Tianjin, Guangzhou and Wuhan. I can count 28 such region-states in China.

Deng Xiaoping's March 1992 speech in Shanghai calling for full speed ahead in the regions spelled the end of the old regime. It is incredible for that vast country to have moved this far in just two years. Last year alone, more than $110 billion in investments were pledged for the future by foreign concerns. The only limitation facing China is its ability to digest that kind of massive inflow of capital.

In today's world, industry moves along with capital and information. Companies are certain to crisscross borders along with investment. Information, industry, individuals and investment; communication, corporations, consumers and capital – all cross national borders almost freely. As this happens, national governments are finding their ability to control the people's basic interests and their fate very, very limited. The fundamental fact is that states can no longer monopolize information; they cannot indoctrinate their citizens about what is happening around the world, what is good and not good for them, or what actions they are obliged to perform.

Japan, too, is going through a major psychological and spiritual transition. Its government has traditionally told the Japanese people what is good for them. And the Japanese people have pretty much put up with orders coming from the center. But not anymore.

The United States, of course, is a federation in which each state has a reasonable amount of autonomy. As a result, the country called the US has become a virtual collection of regions in varying stages of economic development. The

Midwest rust belt may be on the decline, and Manhattan may be experiencing a depression in the financial sector, but Texas, the Mountain States (Colorado, Utah, and Arizona), the Pacific Northwest region (Oregon, Washington) and Silicon Valley (Santa Clara around San Josè, California) are flourishing.

The American federation is today like a zebra. From a distance it looks "gray" – posting four percent annual growth overall. A closer look, however, shows distinct "black" and "white" stripes with over 10-15 percent growth in the Mountain States. Jobs are being created in Colorado, Utah, and Arizona. Yet at the same time, Southern California is suffering from cuts in defense spending. It is no longer a question of the country called the US picking up or sliding economically as a whole, depending on what Washington decides.

Canada is going through the same kind of process. A vast country like Canada will have an increasingly difficult time keeping itself together as a united country. Canada has vast borders with the United States, and as much as 90 percent of the Canadian population, 22 million people, live within 100 miles of the US. In other words, if the borders are gone, the Canadians will tend to look toward the south rather than look sideways.

In fact, the most recent general election in Canada served as a remarkable leading index for that country's future. Montreal (Quebec) was not the only province to vote for separatism. British Columbia's own political party won the majority there. And in Ontario, a totally independent party won the majority. The same is true in Alberta and Manitoba. In other words, no single political party emerged as a dominant party across the nation. Parties advocating regional interests won the majority in each location. A coalition of such parties is jointly operating the country called Canada at a time when the southern border with the United States is becoming fainter and fainter as NAFTA is implemented. Mexico is going through the same transformation. Once NAFTA goes into effect, the prosperous north will be further separated from the poor south.

Likewise in Italy. To win the election last year, Silvio

Berlusconi's Forza Italia organization had to form a coalition with the Milan-based Northern League. That particular party, in its more radical moments, is looking for independence from Italy! They would like to join the European Union without taking full responsibility for supporting Italy's poor south.

THE EMERGENCE OF THE REGION-STATES What we're witnessing as a result of the cross-border movement of information, investment, industry and individuals is the emergence of a more natural form of economy – region-states. They are optimally sized economies dictated by today's technologies, TV broadcasting coverage, physical distribution, and the ability of corporations to open stores and service networks within a reasonable reach.

A typical region-state has a population ranging from five million to about 20 million. Anything bigger than that will pose control problems for the central government. Anything smaller will have problems of economies of scale – the return on corporate investment will not be very attractive. Of course, there are exceptions. But this is the basic pattern that is emerging.

Region-states are very different from nineteenth-century nation states. Nation states get very upset if invaders set one foot within their borders and retaliate with military force. Nation states tend to protect their own industries, because they feel it is the responsibility of the government to protect indigenous industry. Region-states aren't concerned about such things, as long as the money – that is, investment and corporations – keeps flowing in. And they become the hub and spokes for the global flow of capital markets and corporate activities. All kind of information then flows generously, individuals will visit, and prosperity follows.

The city-region of Dalian on the Liaotung Peninsula of China is a good example of the emergent trend. As many as 2,500 of the 3,500 companies located there are foreign-affiliated. The mayor of Dalian has no choice but to become a most hospitable host to the foreigners. He cannot afford to specially protect Chinese indigenous companies. In fact, Chinese state-run companies are becoming a burden for

Dalian because their competitiveness has dwindled since the entry of the foreign companies and more than 50 percent of them are now losing money. It's a burden, rather than a source of national pride, to keep the old industries running.

Lech Walesa founded Solidarity in Gdansk in the name of **THE WALESA** the Polish national interest. And he was able to wrangle **SYNDROME** independence from the former Soviet Union. Yet, Poland's youngsters today insist that Walesa is the country's biggest problem. That is because he represents old industry interests. The very constituencies which supported him through Solidarity are linked to the uncompetitive national and state-run industries, for which modernization is politically difficult, if not impossible. At the same time, the market mechanisms Walesa has introduced have led to the entry of quite a few foreign companies, who pay wages more than twice what the national companies do. Therefore the younger people flock to work for the foreign companies.

When I asked these people on a recent visit, "Where is your Polish spirit? Where is your patriotism?" they answered, "We don't want to discuss that subject. We want to have a good life," to which Walesa, subsequently voted out of office, was an obstacle.

It was only four years ago that we became euphoric about the emergence of these market mechanism-oriented countries in the Eastern bloc. But the result is already very clear: Capital markets, global corporations, communications and informed consumers serve to discipline the sovereign governments. They act as a kind of score card: If the governments are very good, more investment will come. And if they are not good, global capital markets, corporations and consumers will turn away.

Such a situation also provides new opportunities. Central governments normally feel they have to find solutions for domestic problems within the country. But if you believe in the borderless global marketplace, the solution for domestic economic problems could come from without – from outside that economy.

As Dalian has found, billions of dollars from hundreds

of companies have come in from outside to support the growth of that regional economy. Nation states which fail to recognize these new forces at work are going to be a problem not only for their own people, but for the rest of the world too with the arrival of the real information era. That is because they tend to use taxpayers' money for the most inefficient things. They feel obliged to average out in the name of the civil minimum. They want to provide equal governmental services for everyone, prompting a focus on lowest common denominators.

Look at Japan. Eighty-five percent of the prosperity and wealth is created in the three regions around Tokyo, Osaka and Nagoya, yet urban residents are not getting their fair share of the wealth they create because less developed, poorer regions are more important politically. Politicians from poorer regions work hard to carry out their mission of bringing money back home.

Japan has spent $300 billion over the last three years in the name of stimulating its depressed economy, but to no avail. We haven't seen any signs of economic recovery because of this public spending. In fact, this illustrates the problem of Keynesian economists, who suggest that demand will rise by stimulating the economy, as supplies and jobs are created to meet the demand.

But that doesn't work in the borderless economy. Even if demand rises in Japan, Malaysia or the United States, supply might come from outside. In fact, that has been the case over the last decade of deficit spending in the US. Supply comes from Canada, Mexico, the ASEAN countries, China, Japan, and Korea.

In short, there is little relationship anymore in the borderless world between supply and job creation.

FEWER FARMERS, CHEAPER FOOD Despite these changes in the way the global economy works, national governments continue trying to implement averaging devices in the name of public interest. But very few bureaucratic organizations have ever successfully carried out these enterprises. Look anywhere in the world and you'll see that the projects they choose tend to be very inefficient and tend to lose money.

For example, food is cheaper in Singapore than in Japan. The reason is Singapore doesn't have farmers! We grew up in Japan learning from textbooks that our farmers are the most intelligent and work around the clock to fill our stomachs. Well, that may be true, but it certainly doesn't translate into fair prices for the Japanese consumer.

The region-states of 5 to 20 million people emerging in the world today don't try to average out a civil minimum because they tend to seek solutions from without instead of totally from within. The new role of the government after the nation state is to make the region attractive for capital markets, global companies, and consumers. They act as a catalyst in creating the prosperity of the region. Their role has changed from protecting their own industries to promoting prosperity through strengthening linkage with other regions.

34 / Planetized Entertainment

Michael Eisner, the President and CEO of The Walt Disney Company, is one of America's most powerful creators of culture. In this article, adapted from a conversation with *NPQ* in Fall 1991, Eisner discusses the global appeal of American pop culture.

LOS ANGELES The American entertainment industry plays a far more important role in international relations than many of our government leaders recognize.

It can be argued without exaggeration that Mickey Mouse is known by more people around the world than any other American. And it can also be argued without too much disagreement that Mickey is one of the best good-will ambassadors this country has ever had.

The fact is that Mickey achieves instant friendship with almost every child he meets. To Italian children he is Topolino, in Spain he is El Raton Miki. For many years he co-starred with Donald Duck in China, where he was seen by an estimated 200 million people a week. There he is known as Mee-La-Shoo.

More than 200 million people a year watch a Disney film or home video; 395 million watch a Disney TV show every week; 212 million listen or dance to Disney music, records, tapes or compact discs; 270 million buy Disney-licensed merchandise in 50 countries.

More than 50 million people a year from all lands pass through the turnstiles of Disney theme parks in California,

Florida and Tokyo, bringing the total since they opened to over half a billion people. And that is not even counting EuroDisney outside of Paris.

Such figures would mean little in themselves except that they are similar to the figures of other American entertainment companies, demonstrating the universal appeal of American culture. In fact, along with the aircraft industry, the American entertainment industry generates the largest American trade surplus with the rest of the world.

At present, motion pictures made in the United States account for less than one-tenth of the world's annual production of feature-length films. Yet these American films account for 65 percent of box office receipts worldwide.

Out of the top ten films showing in any European country, including along St. Germain des Pres in Paris, at least seven, and often more, will have been produced in the United States. Seventy percent of movie box-office receipts in Greece go to American films. That figure is 80 percent for the Netherlands and 92 percent for Britain.

India creates far more movies than any other country, and Brazil is the volume leader in television production. But in both countries, the majority of moviegoers, music listeners and TV-viewers prefer American entertainment. And I haven't even mentioned the explosion in home video, where the same pattern maintains.

Why is there such vast appeal? There are several reasons.

THE ECONOMIC EDGE

The massive, assured English-language market in America – and increasingly elsewhere – enables Hollywood studios to raise the necessary financing for production and marketing that is not possible for studios in a much smaller, say, French- or German-language, market. This has given the American entertainment industry the ability to pick up the stories, stars, songs and talent from across the world.

I would argue that because of this, the entertainment industry of this country is not so much Americanizing the world as planetizing entertainment.

EXPORTING THE AMERICAN DREAM For viewers around the world, America is the place where the individual has a chance to make a better life and to have political and economic freedom.

Diversity of individual opportunity, individual choice and individual expression is what American entertainment imparts – and that is what people everywhere want.

Our cultural product makes fun of the government and the establishment. Not once in my career have I had to give thought to what the government might think of something I was producing. Can you imagine trying to produce a farce like *Police Academy* in North Korea?

ORIGINALITY As a result of the unhindered freedom to create, the American entertainment industry generates originality unlike that seen any other place on earth. Originality attracts interest, and to me it is the essence of American pop culture. Madonna is so original she recreates herself every two years, as does Michael Jackson.

America's cultural diversity contributes in important ways to this phenomenon. In homogeneous societies, as in homogeneous companies, the grass never seems greener on the other side and every idea kind of blends into the next.

In a culture as ethnically heterogeneous as the United States – over 50 languages are spoken at Hollywood High School – something new is always emerging. Rap music is not the same as rock, which is not the same as jazz. Steven Spielberg is not the same as Walt Disney.

THE CONTAGION OF INNOCENCE The specific appeal of Disneyland, Disney films and products – family entertainment – comes from the contagious appeal of innocence. Obviously, Disney characters strike a universal chord with children, all of whom share an innocence and openness before they become completely molded by their respective societies. For the whole family, as anyone who has ever visited Disneyland or Walt Disney World knows, these places respond to the child within us.

I know that some intellectuals around the world fear that what they call "American cultural imperialism" will level distinct cultures into a kind of lowest-common-denominator amalgam of mass entertainment. On these grounds, one French avant-garde theater director, in fact, attacked EuroDisney as a "cultural Chernobyl." Although he probably shared the late French premier Georges Clemenceau's view that "America is one nation in history that has miraculously gone directly from barbarism to degeneration without the usual interval of civilization," the theater director was surely unaware of how Frenchified Disney has been from the beginning. Disney's first live-action feature was French science-fiction writer Jules Verne's *Twenty Thousand Leagues Under the Sea.* And while American classics like *Paul Bunyan* and *Johnny Appleseed* were mere short-subject films, the French fairy tales *Cinderella* and *Sleeping Beauty* received full-length feature film treatment.

In the first place, such a concern is technologically outdated. Least-objectionable-programming, to use the industry term, was a real concern in the United States when there were only three TV networks, but with the end of the telecommunications oligopoly, that went out the window.

Now that there are four networks, a plethora of cable channels, PBS and video to boot, virtually any opportunity for the viewer is possible, from the highest quality to the lowest. At any given moment, the viewer can tune in to a performance of *Candide,* end-to-end coverage of the Russian parliament deliberations or Mickey Mouse cartoons.

France has moved away from two government-regulated stations to five stations that are less regulated; Italy has scores of TV stations. In such a situation, if American entertainment still attracts the most viewers, it is far less a matter of imperialism than consumer choice. To be sure, when Saddam Hussein chose Frank Sinatra's globally recognized "My Way" as the theme song for his 54th birthday party, it wasn't as a result of American imperialist pressure.

"If they go to see one of my plays," Voltaire wrote, "it is probably a good play. If they don't go, it is probably not a very good play." The same is true for American entertainment in general, and for EuroDisney in particular.

Yes, EuroDisney will have the hallmark castle at its

center – a French castle, it should be noted – and Main Street and Frontierland.

But in place of Tomorrowland there will be Discovery-land, inspired by Jules Verne. In Fantasyland, the fairy tale characters will all be heard in their native tongues, with Snow White speaking German, Pinocchio speaking Italian, and Cinderella speaking French.

It would, of course, be an absurd exaggeration to say that EuroDisney could replace the Berlin Wall as an emblem of freedom and harmony instead of conflict and division. But it may not be such an exaggeration to appreciate the role of the American entertainment industry in helping to change history.

The Berlin Wall was destroyed not by the force of Western arms but by the force of Western ideas.

And what was the delivery system for those ideas? It has to be admitted that to an important degree it was by American entertainment. Inherent in the best and the worst of our movies and TV shows, books and records is a sense of individual freedom and the kind of life liberty can bring. It's in the movies of Steven Spielberg; it's in the songs of Madonna; it's in the humor of Bill Cosby.

The unspoken message to the world is, "We choose to make this product. And in a world where nationalist barriers are being resurrected, you should have the choice to watch it."

35 / Resisting the Colonels of Disney

Costa-Gavras is the Greek-born film-maker of such movies as *Z, State of Siege, Missing, Hannah* and *Betrayed* (about militias in America). A resident of France for decades, he is currently at work on a film about genetic engineering.

I sat down with Costa-Gavras at the end of the summer of 1995 at the Peninsula Hotel in Beverly Hills to discuss the then recent ABC–Disney merger and other issues.

Worries long expressed by the European film community, **NATHAN** particularly the French, that American mass culture and **GARDELS** the English language will dominate the planet, were no doubt furthered by the recent ABC–Disney merger into the world's largest media company.

Are you concerned that culture on a global scale is going to be flattened out and homogenized, that all cultures threaten to be in the image of Mickey Mouse?

Or, do you see the opposite: monopoly can't satisfy, leading to a process of mutation, competition and selection that will yield to a new diversity?

I see both happening. As a filmaker who has worked in **COSTA-** America as well as Europe I see this issue of American **GAVRAS** media concentration as one of David versus Goliath. I worry about the small guy – European filmakers like myself. Giants are large and trample all else in their path, but they are also inherently conservative because they have so much to lose. They stick to the formula that has worked in the past to make them so large. The small guy has nothing to lose, so he takes risks, he fights to change things, he is not afraid to try something different.

This spirit of difference, characteristic of France but also of the American independent filmakers, is what animates the resistance to Hollywood's growing concentration of power. In France we talk about the importance of "the cultural exception" – to keep alive the language, the memories and the imagination that makes France different.

The small guy will be heard sooner or later because people get bored with the same old recipe being offered for dinner every night.

So, let us see what will be exceptional about these new giants apart from raising the share values of their stockholders.

GARDELS   Your emotive use of the word "resistance" recalls your film *Z* about resistance to the Greek dictatorship. Do you see a common thread in your concerns now about the need to resist the rule of the colonels of Disney?

COSTA-   Yes, because this too concerns the problems of democracy.
GAVRAS   Anything so big and with so much power over the minds of men is dangerous to the democratic spirit. At the same time, as in Greece during the colonels, Goliaths necessarily call forth Davids.

GARDELS   Would you agree, then, with the poet Octavio Paz who says that in a world of "planetized entertainment," to use Disney head Michael Eisner's phrase, the most important things can only be said at the margin?

COSTA-   This is an extreme way to put it. Accidents do happen.
GAVRAS   Important things can be said in blockbuster films.

GARDELS   Democracy is also about choice. By and large Americans just find most French films boring, especially when compared to a *Jurassic Park*. By all box office accounts,

Jurassic Park was just as popular among Europeans as it was at home.

Of course we like American films. After all, American **COSTA-** cinema is truly international because it springs from a cul- **GAVRAS** ture of immigrants from everywhere. And there is also the attractive myth the American cinema propagates. The most political films I ever saw were those of Esther Williams, which I loved as a little boy. Why? She was beautiful. She had the biggest car and the thickest carpets I had ever seen. Everybody looked wonderful. This was America! Of course, the camera didn't show the other side.

Now *Jurassic Park*, was nice entertainment but what happens when it is shown in Europe?

When *Jurassic Park, The Fugitive* or any other big film comes to Paris, the American distributors dictate the terms: "You can have *Jurassic Park* for 10 or 15 weeks, but to have it you must take another four or five American films to run along with it for two weeks each. This is called a train – a locomotive film with cars that follow along. No matter how well the secondary films do, they stay for the number of weeks stipulated in the contract.

Of course, the exhibitor agrees because he won't be able to get another *Jurassic Park* to pull in the audiences. This means there is little room for French or other European titles in any given cinema.

So American films come in trains that combine an extraordinary feature with a lot of garbage. This kind of distributor power makes your garbage more important than ours. Sometimes the American market will accept the most extraordinary European film, but never our garbage.

As a result of this overwhelming American presence in **GARDELS** popular culture, haven't the sensibilities of audiences around the world become more attuned in their tastes to the rapid-rhythm, action-packed, flashy special effects of Hollywood blockbusters and less tolerant of those films that plod along like narrative literature from centuries past?

COSTA- It is true that audiences are today more visually attuned;
GAVRAS they can more easily follow the quick, shifting images
spliced together with no apparent narrative like on MTV.
In a film today you can jump from New York to China and
back without explanation.

But the popularity of American popular cinema is not
primarily a matter of rhythm. Most American popular films
are built on a simple recipe, a fixed formula of good lions
and bad hyenas, to which some nuance or attempt to make
the audience think is added.

Of course, I don't mean to suggest that no art is made in
American film. It is, by Francis Ford Coppola, Martin
Scorsese, most of the time Sydney Pollack, and a score of
others.

Simple recipes are sure to do well because they can be
understood by everybody. For Disney, everything since
Fantasia has been formula, up to and including *Lion King*.
By contrast, in France most of the time we do just the
opposite. Usually we think first of what we want to say in a
movie, and then use a recipe if it fits.

In Europe, by and large, drama still counts more than
visuals. We want to get to the emotions through the head,
not to the head through the emotions, or as is the case with
most action films, not to the head at all.

We have the tradition of tragedy from Greek times that
still resonates in the European imagination – it explains to
us how and why we live. That tradition doesn't travel easily,
especially to America.

The American popular cinema recipes, on the other
hand, travel far and wide because they are so light. When
this is combined with the extraordinary weight and
pressure of the American economy and marketing strategies, the very sense that makes us European and not
American is threatened.

This brings us back to the "cultural exception": Let us
preserve some space for our own culture! American films
already have 65 percent of the French market, 85 percent
of the Italian market, 90 percent of the German market and
nearly all of the British market. Enough is enough!

Therefore quotas that limit the exposure of American **GARDELS**
films?

Unfortunately, we need rules so that American occupation **COSTA-**
is not total. You impose rules on Japanese car imports. Why **GAVRAS**
is it then such a heinous act to impose rules on something
vastly more important – culture?

In France, quotas only apply to television. If we didn't
have quotas, we'd show nothing but syndicated American
programs, which cost about 10 times less to buy than it
would cost to produce an original show.

The result already – even with quotas – is that French
teenagers know more about the American justice system
than their own. They have probably never seen a French
living room, no less a French courtroom, on TV.

Now I'm talking about a relatively large country, France.
This same thing occurs to an even greater degree in smaller
countries. What about Albania, Portugal or Greece? They
will have lost their souls completely in 15 years' time if there
is no protection. It is not that they will become Americans.
They will become nothing, not even themselves. They will
be tourists in their own country.

This issue came to a head with the Americans, but was
not resolved, during the last round of negotiations to set up
the World Trade Organization. It is my view, and that of
most Europeans, as different as we are, that our souls are
not for sale. Culture, whether cinema or genetic information, should not be up for negotiation.

You have been around American film for 25 years. How is **GARDELS**
it different now than it used to be? What drives Hollywood
today?

The biggest difference is that the role of real producers has **COSTA-**
been eroded by the financiers, the bankers and the execu- **GAVRAS**
tives of the big companies that have bought up the studios.
It is imperative to them that each film bring in huge
amounts of money; each film must top the last blockbuster.
There is only one conversation in Hollywood on Mondays.
It is about what film had the largest gross ticket sales over

the weekend. The whole ethos of the place is more and more that of the financier than the creator.

My film *Missing,* about the disappearance of a young American in Chile during the coup, would be ten times more difficult to make today. One really feels the pressure these days to lower the level and the subject matter to the broadest possible audience.,

The worst thing is that, more and more, a few big stars – some of them great actors and actresses – are running the show. What does it mean that one human being receives $10 million or even $20 million for three months of work? And then his biggest fear is that his star will dim because he won't be able to draw as much for the next film? This creates a whole enterprise around a star that has little to do with the spirit of artistic performance. The actor here is no longer in service of the story; the story is in service to the actor! The story disappears!

Why does every film have to be a blockbuster and make as much money as *Jurassic Park?* Books are not like that. Some books are meant to be read by a few thousand people, others by tens of thousands. The book market is very diverse.

Does everyone have to be a champion? Why? Must everyone be a Steven Spielberg? Everyone can't be. What is wrong with a thriving market of small films like those by Woody Allen with only 2,000 prints in all of America?

We must accept and respect the small guys, too, in film and society.

GARDELS Michael Eisner offers this rationale for the worldwide appeal of American films: "Diversity of individual opportunity, individual choice and individual expression is what American entertainment imparts – and that is what people everywhere want."

COSTA- What individual? What diversity? At Disney, 10 or 15
GAVRAS people make the decisions and all the rest follow like an army. Eisner speaks like a politician, saying things that make people feel good and sleep better.

It is propaganda. Disney sells its products with nice

words and comforting formulas. Of course, everyone wants to be an individual and have opportunity. But not everyone can be president, and not everyone can be the champion. Perhaps it appeals because it is so far from the hard truth. We don't live in Disneyland. We live in blood and in time, not in Fantasyland. We live in a tragic world.

We can't just blame Disney for flattening culture with **GARDELS** milk-and-water concoctions. Because technology has homogenized time and space, hasn't experience itself flattened out?

In the eighteenth century, the German romantic Johann Gottfried Herder (who worried about French dominance of world culture) could still say that one couldn't understand a Scandinavian saga if one hadn't experienced a North Sea storm Now, we all drive the same cars, fly the same planes, shop in the same malls, listen to the same music, visit the same theme parks, drink the same wine and coffee, eat the same cheeses, and use the same credit cards.

Unless you are a pilgrim cleansing yourself in the Ganges or a fervent Muslim in the Sudan, daily life is just not all that different.

Hence the appeal of the other-worldly special effects of a *Jurassic Park* or the excessive violence of *Pulp Fiction*; they respond to the demand for something different, something new in a boring world.

With the advent of global companies, there is a kind of **COSTA-** worldwide imitation that produces the same buildings, the **GAVRAS** same planes, the same cars. But this conformity of technical backdrops itself inspires a certain resistance, in the arts and architecture, even in the punks with their green or red hair. More dangerously, perhaps, religious and ethnic resistance to homogeneity also arises. This is the so-called confrontation between "jihad" and "McWorld."

In the end, our cultural DNA – the language and a way of seeing the world rooted in a particular history, the spirit – is still what matters. Technology is an extension of our hands and our feet, not our spirit. It is the spirit that makes us different and offers plenty of material for interesting movies. That is why we need to preserve cultures.

Experience is not flat; American mass culture is closed, by and large, to the translation of experience not its own – in film, in books and even in newspaper commentary. France, as well, is, for example, too closed to the vast output of the Indian cinema. So, there needs to be access, and access invites curiosity.

GARDELS   Most of your films have been about politics and social injustice. The film you are working on now is about genetics. Why genetics?

COSTA-   Because developments in genetics – from the discovery and
GAVRAS   correction of hereditary diseases such as Alzheimer's to mapping of the human genome that will, eventually, enable the redesign of the species – will transform our lives radically. For the first time we can correct nature. Humankind thus has the potential of creating hell and paradise, of eliminating illness, but also, for example, of eliminating ethnic groups and creating master races. Parents will have the ability to design their dream child just like their dream house.

This kind of choice, which can tend toward elimination of differences, is very dangerous. Seventy-five percent of those seeking to adopt children in the United States prefer children with blue eyes and blond hair.

Already religious leaders have launched a jihad against genetic engineering. Genetics is God's work, they say. Admittedly, we may have had cause to correct God several times, but I would almost prefer the choices remain with Him. Yet, religion has always adjusted too late. The religious leaders cannot stop advances in genetic science. They will happen. We must therefore search for an ethics that will allow the positive effects, but resist the negative potential of genetic science.

GARDELS   Here, too, as in cultural issues, the concern is about uniformity and homogenization over diversity. Here, too, the French are at odds with the Americans: The French disallow the patenting of DNA discoveries, believing them to be the heritage of all humanity. In America, every discovery can by copyrighted. Inevitably, then, genetic information will become part of negotiations on world commerce.

This is the logic of capitalism. The discussion in the corporate laboratories is not about how many women can be saved from breast cancer, but rather about the $5 billion market out there if the genetic cure can be packaged and sold.

COSTA-GAVRAS

At the expense of human life, this mentality already retards the sharing of scientific discoveries for fear that someone else will register the patent – and thus reap the profits – before the other guy.

As in cinema and TV, there must be rules that protect what is essential about humanity – our diversity. It is the same issue, really. Would we really want a world without homosexuals or those with brown eyes? Recently, I took a trip to Northern California to see the sequoia trees. They were fantastic. Beautiful. But would we want all trees to be sequoias? I think we need the palm trees, too, the maples, oaks and maybe even some weeds.

36 / A Democratic Media Market

Bill Gates is the chairman of the board and CEO of Microsoft Corporation, the largest software producer in the world. We spoke in the Spring of 1995.

NATHAN GARDELS The Republican leader Newt Gingrich and the futurist Alvin Toffler have declared we are in the midst of a "third wave" revolution where the new information technologies will enable the decentralization of power and dispense with the need for big government.

Gingrich also sees that the new interactive networks will enable the overthrow of the liberal, secular media class that dominates and, in his view, subverts the traditional values of American culture through broadcasting from Hollywood and New York.

What do you think of all this?

GATES It is a very strange notion that in a capitalist economy that the media somehow distorts the message. People on every end of the political spectrum can certainly feel that way. But it is hard to understand why there would be a systematic bias. After all, the owners of the media have the sole aim of seeking to give their audience what they want in a relatively competitive environment.

To be sure, with broadband multimedia capacity people's access to information will be broader than ever before. So, you won't have just one or two newspapers and a few broadcast networks. With all those choices I do think it will become far clearer what people like and don't like.

One can say that it will make the market mechanism for culture work much more efficiently than it does now. The match between buyers and sellers – what you want to read, what you want to learn, whom you want to spend time with – will be far more precise and customized.

I'm not sure what is meant exactly by the term "media class," but one thing that will happen is that the editorial premium – the level of guidance in the information networks – will increase. Who is doing a good job? Whom can you trust? Who has the equivalent of the Michelin restaurant guide "five stars" for quality information? Who will give you an index of all the deluge of information that will direct you toward your interests?

We already have this kind of function with books. Nobody reads all the books that are published or watches all the movies that come out or buys all the cars that are made; people are guided by reviews, by Consumer Reports, by word of mouth or by the recommendation of friends. It is all indirect.

No one know how this editorial or guidance function will work exactly, but the whole effort is to make the match of need or desire and available information more efficient. So, in the future, if someone doesn't like some liberal-minded commentator he will readily find a whole other world of like-minded opinions elsewhere.

Having said that, I may be that the current media set-up is not as inefficient in terms of delivering information as some people claim it is.

GARDELS In films, the French are pushing for quotas against American movies to ensure that at least 50 percent of films viewed in Europe come from there.

It seems this whole issue will be exacerbated by the development of cyberspace, which eludes territorial jurisdiction. I'm thinking of the case where a San Francisco pornographer was sued in a Memphis court because someone downloaded his porno program that was legal in California but illegal in Tennessee.

How will we cope in the future with a community's right to protect its own values?

GATES You know, we are not facing a black–and–white situation here where one day everything was done within some territorial jurisdiction and the next day in cyberspace. For some time now, most new financial transactions have been conducted in cyberspace.

So, I don't think there is some conundrum that will hold things back. In culture, as in finance, the jurisdictional issues will be worked out and a new legal regime will be established.

One of the trickiest issues right now on this score concerns bulletin boards on the Internet. Who is liable for what people put up if it is not edited in advance? Or, like a newspaper, are you liable for what is said on your space?

I think what will happen in the future is that a set of rules will be established that indicates in advance whether a service is edited or not, thus protecting the network if someone, uncensored, says something libelous.

GARDELS The government of Singapore just sued the *International Herald Tribune*, a global circulation newspaper, and one of its op–ed contributors because he alluded in an article to a prosperous Asian country with a pliable judiciary, which the authorities in Singapore took to be their country.

What would happen if some official in Singapore accessed an on–line bulletin board where someone questioned what many in the West believe to be Lee Kuan Yew's authoritarian proclivities?

GATES I recently had dinner with Lee Kuan Yew and his son, who, as the number two man at Singapore Telecom, is putting in the Internet infrastructure there. We talked about this very subject: How can you enforce local community values in a world of cyberspace? Undoubtedly there are some tough issues if you believe strongly in preserving community values . . .

... and the Singaporean leaders have made clear often **GARDELS**
enough that they value social discipline at home above free
speech. ...

That is true. Yet, inexorably, with the revolution in **GATES**
communications, the world becomes a smaller place. The
ability to create islands and restrict things goes down
dramatically. This has already been true with the phone,
video and the fax. The new interactive technologies take it
a step further by allowing people to find common interests
with others outside their local community.

But these issues will not hold them back in Singapore.
They are going to try to have their cake and eat it too
because joining cyberspace is essential to the role they
play as a major hub in new commerce. They want to be
connected globally, but maintain local values. I admire
Lee Kuan Yew and will watch keenly how he and his
compatriots work out this coexistence of two colliding
worlds.

Democratic governments have expressed concerns about a **GARDELS**
growing gap between the information rich and information
poor; some also worry that an information superhighway
will have eight lanes rushing one way into the home
dominated by the same old entertainment and news giants,
but without comparable on ramps or off ramps. They worry
that only a narrow two-way footpath will lead back out to
service greater diversity. Do you share those concerns?

The normal course of any new technology is that not **GATES**
everyone will get it on the first day. And that undeniably
gives some an advantage over others. This is especially so
in capitalist societies that allow private corporations to price
their products and let consumers decide what they want to
buy. So, there are valid questions that arise about rich vs.
poor, rural vs. urban, and old vs. young.

Where the market fails to achieve certain societal goals a
government may choose a variety of public policy tools to
attain them. Each society must decide the balance it wants
to strike.

Similarly, not every country will have a new technology in equal proportion at a given point in time. Most people look at the United States as having such a focus on developing the new information technologies that, when combined with its continental size and linguistic homogeneity, will allow it to get out in front of the rest of the world.

New applications are making business and education so much more efficient that everyone will be required to compete effectively or fall behind. It would be like a country trying to compete in the new marketplace with a terrible phone or road system. Too vast a gap of this kind is probably not such a good thing. Governments have had to correct infrastructure deficiencies before where the market doesn't do the job, and I expect they will have to address this new gap as well.

I don't worry inordinately about on ramps and off ramps. The highway metaphor is in many ways a bad one. People are going to be able to send mail and submit their own creations to others through the network. That is in the very nature of the technology we are discussing. We're not talking here about cable or television and radio broadcast, we are talking about broadband which is the greatest advance in two-way communication since the invention of the telephone. I wonder is such critics ever used an on-line service? I suspect this is just some kind of political punching bag.

Believe me, when you are spending tens of billions of dollars to build these networks you are going to allow every application that can generate revenue, including enabling any individual to offer home videos to the world at large.

GARDELS   Nicholas Negroponte of the MIT Media Lab expects broadband, interactive multimedia to pervade the United States within two decades. Within ten years, he projects, people will spend more time on the Internet that watching network television. Is your timeline the same as his?

GATES   Technologists are not famous for predicting the date on which things will occur. I basically agree with what he says, and my company is certainly investing at a level in accord with his projections, but what does it matter if it is 2010 or 2015? It is on the way. In less than 25 years, we'll be there.

37 / Singapore:
Post-Liberal City of the Future

Nathan Gardels wrote this article for *The Washington Post.*

SINGAPORE Fashionable though it may be to vilify Singapore as just one more historically outmoded dictatorship, a case can be made that it ought to be extolled as a model for the future when the center of gravity of human civilization shifts to Asia. Probably no place on the planet is as prepared to enter the twenty-first century as this orderly high-tech, middle-class, multiculturally tolerant – but post-liberal – city state.

By the middle of the next century, Singapore's far-sighted (and highly paid) governing class will be remembered as one of the first to recognize that the small size of a city-state, once thought to be a disadvantage, is the most efficient scale for any stable polity in a perpetually shifting global economy.

As Singapore's young and impressive minister of information and the arts, George Yeo, says, "The information revolution will not dissolve the world into an amorphous mass of weakened political entities, but transform it into more efficient units of power – crossroads cities like the big city-states in Europe or in China before the age of empire."

Singapore's governing class will also be remembered as among the first to see that nurturing the "cultural infrastructure" is every bit as important to the survival of a community as its physical infrastructure: that cultural self-determination for their small swatch of destiny is a postmodern virtue, that, indeed, it is the right of a community not to surrender supinely to whatever the entertainers, newsroom editors, executives and marketing wizards of the great Western media empires think is best for them.

Thus Singapore's leaders have not only built an air-tropolis and container port that are among the most advanced in the world, they are also hard at work wiring their society into cyberspace as a matter of policy. (Singapore has its own home page on the World Wide Web and a program to ensure that all high school graduates have the skills to navigate the Net.) At the same time, however, they are making a point of standing up to an "anything goes" world of information flows.

Lee Kuan Yew, still the eminence behind power in Singapore, made the point passionately during a long conversation recently at Istana, the former British governor's residence in Singapore: "Good governance, even today, requires a balance between competing claims by upholding fundamental truths: that there is right and wrong, good and evil . . . If everyone gets pornography on a satellite dish the size of a saucer, then governments around the world will have to do something about it, or we will destroy our young and with them human civilization."

This explicit willingness to meddle in the media has rankled the West no end and tarnished Singapore's reputation. *New York Times* columnist William Safire has made a regular practice of trashing the tyranny he sees in Singapore. Microsoft's Bill Gates told me after a visit to Singapore that "they want to have their cake and eat it too" – they want cyberspace and control – but "no place is an island anymore."

But there is another perspective. Is it really so heretical to suggest in the wake of the O.J. media circus, Calvin Klein's proto-porn teen ads, hyperviolent films, gangsta rap, and the descent of the mainstream press into tabloidism that the Singapore authorities are not behind the times, but ahead of them?

Is it so outrageous to believe that those societies that actively monitor what their children are exposed to and how it affects them, that have no qualms about drawing the line between what is appropriate and inappropriate, are going to hang together better in the social squalls ahead than those that don't?

Perhaps it is time to consider the possibility that the Western attitude that has all but cast away the notion of appropriate social authority might be outmoded. After all, the key problem of Western civilization now is not the absence of tolerance, it is how to cope with so much freedom. Anyone who watches Jerry Springer, Ricki Lake or Sally Jessy Raphael has to know in their gut that the issue of our time is no longer which limits to erase, but where to draw the boundaries.

AN AVANT-GARDE TOO FAR It is this context that makes Singapore's leaders post-liberal rather than merely reactionary authoritarians. Their stance arises not so much out of fear of what liberalism might mean to their hold on power but from the demonstrated failures of the permissive society carried to extremes. In America they have seen what for most of the postwar era was touted as the future, and it doesn't work.

I asked Lee if he agreed with Zbigniew Brzezinski's worry that "America's own cultural self-corruption – its permissive cornucopia – may undercut America's capacity, not just to sustain its position in the world as a political leader, but even as a systemic model for others."

"That has already happened," Lee responded. "The ideas of individual supremacy and the right to free expression, when carried to excess, have not worked. They have made it difficult to keep American society cohesive. Asia can see it is not working. Those who want a wholesome society where young girls and old ladies can walk in the streets at night, where the young are not preyed upon by drug peddlers, will not follow the American model." In other words, extremism in the name of liberty is a vice.

As always in our conversations, however, Lee was careful to praise America's innovative edge – the genius of innovation and the ability to recover manufacturing productivity in the face of Japanese auto competition. But isn't that innovation and capacity for initiative linked to the very unfettered freedom he so condemns, I asked?

No so, says the senior minister in a revealing insight that echoes those who have argued that America went wrong with the extremism of the "rights revolution" of the 1960s and 1970s. Lee similarly argues that when the lifestyle experiments of the cultural avant-garde are democratized, society subverts itself.

"The top three to five percent of a society can handle this free-for-all, this clash of ideas," he says. "If you do this with the whole mass . . . you'll have a mess. In this vein, I say, let them have the Internet. How many Singaporeans will be exposed to all these ideas, including some crazy ones, which we hope they won't absorb? Five percent? Okay. That is intellectual stimulation that can provide an edge for society as a whole. But to have, day to day, images of violence and raw sex on the picture tube, the whole society exposed to it, it will ruin a whole community."

Neither Lee nor Yeo, however, has any illusions that censorship can be effective. Rather, as Yeo put it, "censorship is a symbolic act, an affirmation to young and old alike of the values held by a community."

But ought this kind of power be in the hands of the state?

"What is the power of the state in local Singapore, a city-state with less than three million people?" asks Yeo in response. It is not, after all, a Leviathan like the old Soviet Empire or even the French State or the American Federal State. "We are really what in America is a local community. What we do is not so different from the people of Omaha or some other community saying, "We don't want the Playboy channel to play here because it is offensive and contrary to what we believe in."

Fair enough, but in the name of a wholesome and trusting society the Singapore government never hesitates to drag *The Economist*, the *International Herald Tribune* or even the local *Business Times* to court for libel or for publishing leaked information.

Isn't there a chilling effect, I asked, that will prevent the press from playing its critical check-and-balance role on corruption, nepotism or the manipulation of government information?

"If this were the case in Singapore," Yeo answers not wholly convincingly, "we would be destroying ourselves. . .We are a nation of arbitrageurs. We can't afford to be a nanosecond behind Tokyo, London or New York. For us to try to limit information to a banker, a trader or a journalist would sound the death knell for Singapore. It would be contrary to or entire economic strategy."

SINGAPORE WORKS Whatever one's doubts, this balancing act of good governance that guards the integrity of the cultural infrastructure in an efficient city-state of manageable administrative scale has been highly successful.

Anyone arriving in Singapore from the poverty and chaos of Calcutta or even Bangkok will readily acknowledge that it is a social model that works. Though it can be seen as one huge, immaculate shopping mall that is comparatively boring on the evening entertainment front, it is undeniably a very decent place. Indeed, the indices of social decency in this island nation of just under three million people are a reverse mirror image of the indices of American social decay.

Drugs are nonexistent as a result of one of the toughest polices in the world. On your immigration card you cannot miss the bold warning in red ink that drug smuggling carries a mandatory penalty of death. The boulevards, landscaped with palms and orchids, are spotless. Graffiti, penalized by caning as we know from the Michael Fay case, is nonexistent. Famously, women can safely walk the street alone, late and in the dark.

The standard of living in Singapore is as high as in many European countries, and more egalitarian. Fifteen years ago, the average income of the top 20 percent was 14.4 times that of the bottom 20 percent, the average income of the top 20 percent fell 3 percent while the average income of the middle 60 percent rose more than 4 percent. Savings rates are as high as they get in any society.

Chinese (who dominate ethnically) and Malays, Hindus, and Muslims live and work together side by side as harmoniously as anywhere else. English is the dominant language to reach the outside world. Mandarin the inside. English is the language of the important newspapers; Mandarin the language of the most popular television channel. There are also Hindi and Malay TV stations.

Any businessman will tell you that Singapore is one of the few places in Asia where you can trust the rule of law not to be wholly corrupted. In a region where the notoriously blurry line between connections (*guanxi*) and corruption pervades all commerce, Singapore stands out. Late last year *Fortune* magazine named Singapore the best place in the world to do business.

At a time when so many societies are decaying or growing out of control, Singapore is going to make it. It is a place where I would feel comfortable raising my children but, admittedly, would hesitate to live as an adult. That I, like so many others, sometimes arrive at just the opposite conclusion about the United States assures that the Singapore model will continue to resonate as a critique of permissive societies run amok well into the next century.

PART V

TERROR, DEMOCRACY, AND PEACE AFTER THE COLD WAR

With the end of the Cold War, the prospect for peace finally opened up in the Middle East, only to remain imperiled, as elsewhere, by the old conflicting dreams of land and nationhood. Israeli prime minister Benjamin Netanyahu here explicitly rejects the notion of Palestinian statehood – the very condition for peace in the Arab view.

The practice of democracy, once a rhetorical pawn in the power play of ideological conflict, came to be judged more on its own terms in the post-Cold War years. The focus on freedom turned to an ascendant Asia instead of the Soviet bloc, and to the Arab world, which lost its Moscow leverage and recovered its religion. The most famous Chinese dissident, Fang Lizhi and his counterpart in Burma, Aung San Suu Kyi, ring the lonely bell of human rights in their part of the world. King Hussein talks about the legacy of democracy he wants to leave behind as his greatest accomplishment.

As the anxiety over nuclear war between the Soviet Union and the United States calmed down, a new, more pervasive anxiety less susceptible to rational games of deterrence took its place. Loose nukes and freelance terrorists are the focus of our nervous attention now. Teheran more than Moscow is the object of our security concerns. And, these days, we are always looking for suspicious packages on the Paris or Tokyo subway.

Shimon Peres, the former prime minister and shepherd of the Israeli bomb, talks about the new threat of old religious fanaticism coupled with modern weapons. Alvin Toffler and Jacques Attali address the challenge of the next century when, for the first time in history, the state no longer has the monopoly over mass-destruction weapons.

38 / Old Fanaticism, Modern Weapons

Shimon Peres is the former prime minister of Israel. In this wide-ranging interview in the summer of 1995, Peres talked about the Iranian bomb, the role of Israel's nuclear capability in the Middle-East, and how "the global television culture" threatens Judaism more than the Arab states.

The United States has launched a campaign for international sanctions against Iran because it is considered "an outlaw state" trying to obtain a nuclear bomb and to wreck the Middle East peace process with terrorism. Is Iran the main state actively trying to undermine peace? **NATHAN GARDELS**

Yes. Iran has adopted the Machiavellian dogma that communism did: The goals justify any means. So they kill, they cheat, they subvert. They finance and train Hamas and Hezbollah in an effort to export their fanatic ideology. We know it, yet they deny it at the same time as they publicly proclaim the need to destroy Israel. For them, Israel is a kind of collective Salman Rushdie. **SHIMON PERES**

And now they want a nuclear bomb. If there is one country in the world that does not need the civilian nuclear power they claim they want only for energy, it is Iran. They have all the cheap oil they need and nuclear power is expensive.

If there is one lesson to be learned from the Second World War it is that danger arises not from the possession of military arms, but from the state of mind of a man like Hitler and the weakness of the West in not comprehending the intentions that flow from such a state of mind. Aside from the United States at the moment, the rest of the West is making the same mistake about Iran.

It is not an overstatement to say that after the collapse of communism, the kind of fundamentalism coming from Iran is the greatest danger in our time. It has a ready audience – 1.3 billion Muslims spread around the world, mostly mired in poverty and illiteracy.

For the first time in history, a fanatic movement can get hold of modern weapons, including the kind of chemical weapons of mass destruction used by a small group in the Tokyo subway. The Inquisition didn't have chemical or biological weapons; Hitler didn't have the atom bomb. I can imagine no greater danger than the combination of old fanaticism and modern weapons. Let's handle this storm before it breaks.

GARDELS The Khomeini revolution is old and ailing. So many people in Iran seem to be living double lives: Teenage girls may listen to American heavy-metal rock music at home, but, in fear of the religious police, wear the chador out on the street. As with the Soviet Union, systems in which the whole society must live a lie can collapse overnight. Is Iran really a threat the world does not comprehend, or a hollow revolution destined for history's dustbin?

PERES A race is on between self-destruction and the destruction of others. We don't know which will win first. That is what makes Iran so dangerous.

GARDELS It is estimated by some of the more alarmed analysts that Iran could possess a nuclear capability within five years. As a man closely associated with building Israel's own nuclear capability, do you see signs they are that close to building the bomb?

PERES It depends on three things: how many scientists and engineers they can obtain formally and informally; how much nuclear material and equipment they can smuggle; and when they can build the reactors. When they build a gas-centrifuge (necessary to enrich uranium), they will have established capability.

So the time frame depends on how quickly and how successfully the Iranians can obtain the necessary experts, know-how and material from abroad. Already 150 Russian scientists and engineers who are highly sophisticated in the nuclear field are working in Iran. This, Russian President Boris Yeltsin did not know until presented with the facts (by outside powers). It is also unclear what China's real policy is in assisting Iran. We also have hard evidence of Iranian attempts to buy radioactive material, and they are offering a very high price.

GARDELS Are the scientists the Iranians have hired at the level of Ernst Bergmann, the father of Israel's nuclear capacity?

PERES Ernst Bergmann was a scientist. Scientists have knowledge and information, which today are much more widespread. So building a nuclear capacity is now more an engineering than a scientific problem. And the Iranians have the engineers they need.

GARDELS You are in some sense the shepherd of Israel's nuclear capability, going back to your 1956 visit to Paris with David Ben-Gurion and Moshe Dayan to secure French help in building reactors at Dimona. How does your career-long effort to build an Israeli nuclear capability square with the new realities of the peace process in the Middle East?

PERES They are complementary. First, it enables us to be more flexible on the territorial side because of the deterrent, or because we are considered to have a deterrent. Second, we can now say clearly that we can have a Middle East free of nuclear weapons provided we have a belligerent-free Middle East. It is like a two-storey building. The first storey is the end of belligerence, the second storey is de-nuclearization. You cannot build the second storey until you finish constructing the first.

GARDELS   Reportedly, Israeli nuclear missiles were aimed to deter the Soviet Union so that it would constrain its Arab clients from going too far in a military assault on Israel. Since the Soviet Union no longer exists, where is the aim of your deterrent?

PERES   Today, non-conventional arms are not only nuclear, but chemical and biological. We don't see any reason to tell a country that might attack Israel with chemical and biological weapons that "don't you worry, you can attack us and nothing will happen." Their suspicion is our deterrent.

GARDELS   Though the peace process may end belligerence with Israel's Arab neighbors, Iran will still be out there. When and if they obtain a nuclear bomb and long-range missiles from China, won't you need the deterrent against them?

PERES   Yes. And for many Arab states, though they wouldn't admit it, our deterrent is the only guarantee of their security against Iran.

GARDELS   At the end of your memoirs, *Battling for Peace*, you make the surprising observation that as peace settles into the Middle East, Judaism faces a new threat: Global television culture is undermining the Hebrew language that ties Judaism together. In a strange sort of way, will mass American culture spun out of Hollywood be a greater danger to Judaism than hostile Arab states? Already, you can hardly tell teens in Tel Aviv apart from their cousins in the suburbs of Los Angeles. Without the Hebrew language, won't Israel become a cultural suburb of America?

PERES   I agree. Today there are five million Hebrew-speaking people. Never in history have we had so many. In the past, the cultural boundaries were smaller and reading and writing could hold together the people of the Book. Never before have we had to sustain the culture for such vast numbers of people – who are at the same time an audience for global television.

           So, we would like to do two things. First, all Jewish

people should adopt Hebrew as their second language. Second, in spite of the influence of television, we need to make an effort to translate more books into Hebrew. True, this may only concern an elite, but a "deciding elite."

Economically, these days, there is no national sovereignty. Strategically, borders are becoming meaningless. Scientifically, only the globe and the universe matter.

What is left that is ours? Culture and historical memories expressed in our language. A country is not just some land within borders, it must have a spiritual and moral identity. Just as we have concentrated so much on defending our borders, we must concentrate on defending our heritage.

39 / Third Wave Terrorism rides the Tokyo Subway

Alvin Toffler is author with Heidi Toffler of *Future Shock, The Third Wave, Powershift* and, most recently, *War and Anti-War,* a study of the effects of the information age on warfare. This interview, which took place just after the sarin gas attack in the Tokyo subway, was conducted for *O Estado de São Paulo* in Brazil.

NATHAN GARDELS The nuclear Non-Proliferation Treaty (NPT) was renewed in 1994, yet, as the sarin chemical attack in the Tokyo subway has shown, weapons of mass destruction are no longer just the province of state-versus-state war or subject to regulation by treaty.

Has a new form of warfare arisen in the information age that eludes control by the state? Soon, any apocalyptic nut or sect with a laboratory will be able to access a lethal formula through the Internet, build a weapon and hold entire societies hostage.

ALVIN TOFFLER What we've seen in Japan is the ultimate devolution of power: the demassification of mass-destruction weapons. No longer is it only the state that can possess such weapons on behalf of the "masses" in its territory; now a mere individual or small group can possess the means of mass destruction – if he or she has the information to make them. And that information is increasingly available.

The sarin attack in Japan was qualitatively different from the old forms of terrorism that cause havoc but kill or maim only 30 or 50 people. Remember that this Japanese attack was very crude – a briefcase, bag, or box left on the subway train. When a greater sophistication evolves on the part of terrorists in the use of chemical and biological weapons, including remote detonation devices for binary weapons, thousands upon thousands of people can be felled in one blow.

This is a momentous development because it signals, as you suggest, the failure of the state system itself, which was founded on the ability of the governing elite, or the gang in power as the case may be, to enforce its authority with organized violence and to control alternative means of violence, no less mass violence, in its own territory.

This doesn't mean the end of the nation state, as some suggest, but that it will become just one player among many others of relatively comparative power in varying realms. As the power of the state fragments, the number of players is multiplying – all of whom are potentially capable of laying their hands on weaponry.

In addition to commanding the means of violence, historically the state had fiscal command and control over its currency and market. It also controlled knowledge – whether through religion, ideology or mythology.

A state may well have all or some of these attributes today, but there are counterforces that also have these attributes that are outside the control of any state. These stateless counterforces range from the global currency and bond markets to the Internet and CNN or MTV, from the Catholic Church to worldwide religious sects, narco-traffickers, international civilian organizations like Greenpeace and globe-spanning ethnic networks.

If you lose control of violence, wealth and knowledge, you've lost power. That is the power shift that has diminished the state and to which the sarin attack in Japan adds yet another blow.

But the state will still have importance – particularly in providing socially necessary order against the kind of attack we saw in the Tokyo subway.

GARDELS So, here are the components of "third wave" warfare, or terrorism in the information age – scientific prowess in the form of development of deadly chemical and biological warfare as well as the unlocked secrets of the atom; a broad, global pool of people with graduate-level eduction in the sciences; access to lethal knowledge and free societies organized to defend against enemy or rogue states, but not rogue individuals or small groups among their own population.

TOFFLER Yes, and this emergent reality poses a particular problem for democratic societies. If a state can use overwhelming force and repression, it can probably crush any threat within its territory, at least for a certain period of time. But democratic societies limit that kind of use of power by the state.

The rise of stateless violence threatens not just repressive states but the socially necessary order of democratic societies. I have no doubt that there will arise in response to these acts of violence a great deal of sympathy among the average population to monitor anyone considered potentially dangerous.

Will democratic states then begin monitoring cults, or for that matter religions in general, or other organizations like Greenpeace or any ethnic group that hails from a troubled homeland? What will that mean for freedom and pluralism?

GARDELS Something else you have written about makes us more vulnerable than in the past to terrorist attacks like the one in the Tokyo subway, or with ordinary bombs, at the World Trade Center in New York or the federal building in Oklahoma City: In complex, interdependent systems – with airports, 747s, Eurotunnels, skyscrapers and subway systems – a small intervention can be leveraged into a mass disaster.

TOFFLER As the scientist Ilya Prigogine has noted, when a system becomes what he describes as "far from equilibrium" it loses any linear relationship between cause and effect. In such a condition of disequilibrium, a small input can produce a disproportionately large effect.

This means politically that small groups or grouplets that choose to disrupt a society can do so massively, especially when their power is magnified through possession of lethal knowledge. To the extent that mass politics has seen its day, as I believe it has, there will be a proliferation of small congregations of people all trying to make their mark, some with violence. The Aum Supreme Truth sect in Japan has only something like 5,000 members in all of Japan.

GARDELS So, in the future, we must all live in the fear of some kook with a beef?

TOFFLER All of us today live with a kind of free-floating fear in the background of our lives. This makes me think of the way that Paleolithic humans lived in ancient times when they knew nothing about the external world. They had no reliable information, no scientific knowledge. Everything was uncertain. People were afraid of trees, stones and the sun.

Today, it seems, we are heading back toward living constantly with that kind of anxiety.

GARDELS Talk about a deep irony – our anxiety today about an insecure environment comes not from ignorance, but from the wide dispersion of information, including lethal knowledge!

What can be done?

TOFFLER First of all, everything will have its distinct signature and we will have tools that can monitor their use. In the future every product is going to be bar coded and identified. Every canister of chemicals will have an ID number that will be readable, perhaps even detectable from a satellite.

So, levels of surveillance – of goods as well as people – will rise, though you cannot, of course, see what is in the minds of people.

Moreover, as we move toward electronic money, we will be able to track all transactions. Even today your credit card record will reveal where you had dinner, breakfast, or lunch. In the future, it will take much more sophistication to hide the flow of money and the use of goods.

On the other hand, I believe, all communications are inevitably going to be encrypted. There is already a race on between the code-makers and the code-breakers.

The encryption issue also involves a re-evaluation of the way we have looked at freedom of information. Reasonable people who believe in freedom of information have recognized that a certain modicum of secrecy by the state, until now, slowed proliferation of nuclear weapons.

The question is: To what degree will it be possible to control information in the future in ways that will stop the spread of these chemical and biological weapons that are more easily manufactured? The answer is that it will be very, very difficult.

Though I lean toward a libertarian view on the free availability of information, I cannot simply brush aside the concerns of the FBI or Interpol that the inability to control the spread of certain information can lead to the mass murder of innocent people.

The stakes are larger than they have ever been. It is one thing to say we don't like big government and we don't want Big Brother looking over our shoulder. But do we like the alternative of a world where the most ruthless and most depraved can gain access to the means of mass destruction, apply them, and get away with it?

40 / Trading in the Apocalypse

Jacques Attali, founding president of the European Bank for Reconstruction and Development, was the top aide to François Mitterrand during the first ten years of his tenure as France's president. In 1994, Attali prepared a study on trafficking in nuclear materials and expertise for the United Nations renewal conference on the Non-Proliferation Treaty (NPT). His most recent book in English is *Millennium* (Times Books, 1993). The three volume memoirs of Attali's years at the Elysée are entitled *Verbatim*.

The 1994 conference at the United Nations that was **PARIS** convened to renew the nuclear Non-Proliferation Treaty (NPT) Conference provided an opportunity to reflect on the nature of the trade that takes place in the nuclear sector – trade that is illegal on a military level and broadly legal on a civilian level. Since the fall of the Berlin Wall, trafficking in nuclear materials and expertise has been growing at an alarming rate. This is true of all three factors of production in the armaments industry: the experts, the technology and the materials themselves.

This trafficking cannot be viewed separately from proliferation: It is illegal trade, and proliferation is the illegal production of the elements needed to make nuclear weapons. This form of trade is the instrument of proliferation, and proliferation is the object of this trade. The fight against proliferation means attacking the very roots of this trade. And the reverse is also true. That is why the extension of the NPT was so urgent and important.

Where do things stand now?

In spite of the NPT, about 20 countries already have nuclear weapons capability – or soon will have. Either they are able to make their own weapons and have decided to hold back, or they want this capability and are not far off because they have the necessary technology.

In spite of the NPT, the use of such arms is more likely today than it ever was: Fanatics do not fear death; drug cartels have no territory to defend. And for them, the conventional principles of nuclear deterrence, which presuppose the fear of reprisals, no longer have any meaning.

In spite of the NPT, technology continues to develop, and a rudimentary nuclear weapon is now within easy reach of any group that has a few hundred million dollars to spend. This is all the more true for tomorrow's most dangerous weapon – the "radioactive" weapon – which calls only for a few hundred grams of fissile materials. The shortest way to access fissile products is through trafficking, which is thus more of a temptation than ever.

Where can the products and the necessary know-how for proliferation be found? In the former Soviet Union. Fear has taken the place of the rule of law there, and the control of nuclear installations is further deteriorating each day, especially in the civilian sector, making it easier for those involved in trafficking. Because of lack of funding and inadequate international support, the situation is rapidly getting out of hand.

So far, the number of serious cases of trafficking that have been identified is small – and no foreign country has been caught flagrantly trying to buy. However, this trade is now falling into the hands of the organized mafia. It has been estimated that, to date, about 30 kilograms of fissile material has been stolen – enough in theory to make at least two or three nuclear bombs.

Furthermore, all countries are being encouraged to develop nuclear power plants and so, indirectly, to produce plutonium for reprocessing. Plutonium, a byproduct of nuclear fission, is one of the most toxic substances that man has ever produced – it is the supreme instrument of sovereignty and an object of fascination to scientists and politicians alike. Although today it is still viewed in a different category from radioactive fuel and dismantled weapons, its only current use is to make weapons because is can only be used to produce energy under conditions that make no economic sense and which would spell ecological disaster.

The international community has not yet found any scientific way to use this plutonium, nor to destroy it, nor even to destroy radioactive fuels – nor even to manage them in the long-term. This is clearly a major scandal in which the politicians have been misled by scientists.

In light of these threats, the international instruments created during the Cold War to contain trade and proliferation are now quite inadequate. The NPT, signed in 1968 by 172 countries, has worked only because the two superpowers were absolutely determined to prevent proliferation. The International Atomic Energy Agency (IAEA) is the body whose task it is to inspect nuclear installations, but it can inspect only those states that agree to inspection, and only then during times when they are willing. The IAEA has practically no resources of its own to conduct inquiries and to monitor, not even in the spheres of its own competence. Its budget is highly inadequate. It cannot uncover clandestine activity. It never carries out spot inspections, and it has no powers to sanction. Reprocessing radioactive fuel, movements of experts, non-fissile radioactive material and industrial activities that turn fissile material into a bomb are not controlled – or barely.

HELPING RUSSIA

Since 1992, the former Soviet Union has needed international support, but such help is still highly inadequate, even though the United States has contributed considerable resources to this end. There is no way for the UN Security Council to be certain that a clandestine program is not being developed somewhere, or that the international community will have the means to intervene if such a program is uncovered.

The worst-case scenario is right there before us: If

nothing is done, in ten years nuclear weapons and radio-active weapons will have become common currency.

A SECRET DOMAIN

One cannot speak of the illegal traffic of ideas. The free circulation of a multitude of scientific documents reduce the necessity for espionage in this area. However, there does remain a secret domain that is linked to weapons know-how that can only be found in a few places, and only in a few brains. The collapse of a certain lifestyle and the loss of social compensation once accorded to scientists and thinkers in the former USSR has created a particular migration: that of gray matter. Many Russian scientists and nuclear specialists have already emigrated to the United States, France, and Great Britain. They are also going to other "proliferating" countries, anywhere where they can obtain income for themselves, or for their laboratories.

Scientific nuclear collaboration between Russia and India is open and growing. China hires russian experts, even if they still are unable to pay that much. According to the Russian defense minister, more than 2,000 Russian scientists went to China in 1994, 300 of whom are working in military nuclear programs and missile programs. Other Russian experts sell their knowledge to the Chinese without even leaving their offices in Moscow via fax and modem and e-mail. Russian authorities also intercepted 36 scientists leaving for North Korea: They were promised $2,000 a month.

It is estimated that about 1,000 Russian specialists are now working for "proliferating" countries. With the Internet and with forthcoming virtual video-conferencing, it will be possible to participate from anywhere in the world in the development of nuclear bombs without any official control.

To impede all this, the two sacrosanct and mythological principles of international relations must be abandoned: equality of treatment for all countries and non-intervention in the domestic affairs of a country. This fight must rank countries in terms of proliferation and trafficking in nuclear materials and expertise. This fight must also consider that certain radioactive materials, both before and after irradiation, represent a danger to mankind and should not be left for individual countries to manage alone.

To reduce both supply of and demand for these different factors, it is important to go much further than this and attack the root of the evil: Sanctions against the protagonists in this illegal trade should be stepped up, and, in particular, dealers and experts working as mercenaries in countries that are producing weapons should be subject to extradition. It is also important to control the development of what in the civilian nuclear sector accelerates proliferation – enrichment and reprocessing.

In order to accomplish this, the IAEA must have more means of control and verification that would enable it to carry out special inspections on a routine basis and to control the process of military production. Greater agency resources could be generated by a worldwide tax imposed on nuclear energy.

But the last and most important thing is to reduce the quantity of nuclear materials that could be used for military purposes by halting the production of any new plutonium, whether for military or civilian purposes, and by eliminating any surplus plutonium. All surplus nuclear materials in the former Soviet Union should be purchased and the republics paid in the form of partial forgiveness of their public debt. The construction of any new reprocessing plants should be prohibited and the use of existing plants slowed down in any country considered to be unsafe.

Therefore, beyond the extension of the old NPT we need the negotiation of a real Civilian Nuclear NPT. Its comprehensive implementation and control would be exercised exclusively by countries whose nuclear scenario is safe – in other words, the democracies. Jointly, they would share the heavy responsibility of managing global stocks of nuclear waste.

41 / Deng's Legacy:
A China Consumed by Chaos

Fang Lizhi, one of China's most famous dissidents, is often referred to as "China's Sakharov." Fang, an astrophysicist, escaped arrest the night of the Tienanmen crackdown in 1989 by finding sanctuary at the United States Embassy in Beijing. He stayed within the walls of the Embassy compound for a year before being spirited secretly to the United States where he now lives in exile as a professor of astrophysics at the University of Arizona.

HONG KONG Most obituaries of Deng Xiaoping judge the legacy of China's paramount leader since the early 1980s in terms of his contribution to China's high rates of economic growth. Few, I'm afraid, focus on the costs of Deng's prosperity.

I am not referring just to the heavy price already paid by the Chinese people themselves, such as the 1989 Tienanmen massacre, the military crackdown on demonstrations in Tibet or the many thousands of political prisoners. The highest price is yet to be paid by China and the world: the eruption of widespread chaos in the wake of Deng's demise.

China's future is shadowed by chaos because the phantom stability Deng created through oppression, repression and massacre cannot hold. The apparent stability today in Beijing, Shanghai, and other large cities has been purchased through what might be called political deficit spending that bankrupts the future legitimacy of the central authorities. As with all political deficits, someday the bills will come due.

Everyone in China knows this, as evidenced, for example, by the growing trend among the sons and daughters of the current leadership to try to find some way to emigrate abroad.

These signs of lack of faith in China's future stability are often overlooked because of the view that the benefits of economic growth will overcome any discontent on a wide scale. Some people even believe that if China continues uninterrupted along the path of economic transformation, a stable and democratic society will emerge after a certain threshold. The unpleasant facts are the opposite: Despite a continually rising gross national product, China is closer to chaos and further from stability today than it was five years ago.

The Mafia-like trading in weapons, the violation of copyright and intellectual property laws and the black market in illegal emigration by boat are spreading by leaps and bounds. The theft and counterfeit production of CDs and computer software – repayment, perhaps, for the delinking of trade from human rights – reached such a scale that the US government had to take the drastic step of imposing trade sanctions on China before finally coming to terms.

This pervasive corruption is just the tip of the iceberg. In the past few years China has become submerged in a sea of corruption. It all has the same root cause: The violation of human rights and the absence of political reform that establishes a system of rule by law. Deng had little enthusiasm for the rule of law because that would have constrained his power. Even when he formally renounced his "retirement" he remained beyond accountability in the top position of power.

From this perspective, Deng indeed reformed political power in China. He changed it from the rule of one man under Mao to the rule of corrupted men. And for anyone who knows China's long history of collapsed dynasties and upheavals triggered by corruption, there can be little comfort in the belief that the most pervasive corruption in our history will somehow, this time, result in enduring stability. Deng and his autocratic comrades know China's history. That is why they have taken every glimmer of rebellion as an extremely dangerous threat to their power, whether in the form of the Tienanmen demonstrations in 1989 or, in the past year especially, the mounting number of workers' strikes throughout the country.

Belying their own rhetoric of stability, they are constantly tightening the grip of their repressive insecurity. On the fifth anniversary of the Tiananmen massacre the Communist government issued the "Detailed Implementation Regulations for State Security Law." According to this new set of laws, even contact with foreign non-government organizations, such as human rights groups, is a criminal offense. The "crimes" of political prisoners include such things as membership in political organizations or independent trade unions not sanctioned by the government; participation in strikes, demonstrations or independent study groups, and public expression of political opinions dissenting from those of the government.

Aside from outright repression, Deng's successors turned to nationalism as a replacement for Marxism in the absence of any other legitimation for holding power. Many people forget that the first decision made by Deng when he took power in 1979 was to start the war with Vietnam. The old slogan of "Communists will win all over the world" has been replaced with "The 21st century belongs to China."

Since 1989, military expenditure in China has grown 20 percent annually. Arms sales to radical regimes in the Near East continue to grow.

Those who thought Deng was on the right track because he was non-Maoist and non-Marxist now must think twice about what an economically strong but dictatorial regime that possesses nuclear weapons might mean for peace and stability in Asia. History has taught us, and the experience of Japan and Germany earlier in this century remind us, that nationalism combined with economic development will lead to chaos and conflict at home and abroad.

Finally, we should remember that the most typical

source of chaos in a monolithic, totalitarian state is the power struggle among top leaders for succession. It is a dangerous game without regulation.

The turmoil during the Cultural Revolution of the 1970s shows the depths to which China can sink in the course of such struggles for power. In the wake of Deng's death one cannot rule out the appearance once again of rogue gangs, regional warlords, and secret societies such as those that terrorized and plundered China in those sad years.

It is true that after the monstrous episode of the Cultural Revolution, most ordinary people in China desperately hope for peace and stability this time around. The average person had the same hopes in the 1970s, but it meant nothing because the military was controlled by those at the top engaged in the power struggle.

In recent years well-meaning politicians have spoken of a new world order. I wish them success. But from my part of the world, I can say than an order that intends to rest in Asia on Deng's legacy – an order built upon the belief that a market economy leads to political freedom; an order that exchanges human rights principles like bargaining chips for short-term trade interests – is an order destined to dissolve into chaos.

One of the most important lessons that the victims of the Tienanmen massacre have bequeathed to us is that human existence is a very fragile thing, and that any small loss of order can deprive individuals of their right to exist.

It is with lesson in mind that we must not treat any hidden dangers left by Deng lightly. Deng's era is over, but his regime continues. The stable China the world wants depends on whether the remains of Deng's day can be cleaned away.

42 / Democracy is Asian As Well

Aung San Suu Kyi was awarded the Nobel Peace Prize in 1991 for her efforts to bring democracy to Burma, now known as Myanamar. This article, which appeared in the Winter 1995 issue of *NPQ*, was adapted from an address Aung San Suu Kyi smuggled out of the country to a UNESCO Conference in Tokyo.

YANGON It is often in the name of cultural integrity as well as social stability and national security that democratic reforms based on human rights are resisted by authoritarian governments. It is insinuated that some of the worst ills of Western society are the result of democracy, which is seen as the progenitor of unbridled freedom and selfish individualism. It is claimed, usually without adequate evidence, that democratic values and human rights run counter to the national culture, and therefore to be beneficial they need to be modified – perhaps to the extent that they are barely recognizable. The people are said to be as yet unfit for democracy, therefore an indefinite length of time has to pass before democratic reforms can be instituted.

The first form of attack is often based on the premise, so universally accepted that it is seldom challenged or even noticed, that the United States is the supreme example of democratic culture. What tends to be overlooked is that although the US is certainly the most important representative of democratic culture, it also represents many other cultures, often intricately enmeshed. Among these are the "I-want-it-all" consumer culture, megacity culture, superpower culture, frontier culture, immigrant culture. There is also a strong media culture which constantly exposes the myriad problems of American society, from large issues such as street violence and drug abuse to the matrimonial difficulties of minor celebrities.

Many of the worst ills of American society, increasingly to be found in varying degrees in other developed countries, can be traced not to the democratic legacy but to the demands of modern materialism. Gross individualism and cut-throat morality arise when political and intellectual freedoms are devalued while fierce economic competitiveness is encouraged by making material success the measure of all prestige and progress. The result is a society where cultural and human values are set aside and money value reigns supreme.

No political or social system is perfect. But could such a powerful and powerfully diverse nation as the United States have been prevented form disintegrating if it had not been sustained by democratic institutions guaranteed by a constitution based on the assumption that man's capacity for reason and justice makes free government possible, and that his capacity for passion and injustice makes it necessary?

It is precisely because of the cultural diversity of the world that it is necessary for different nations and peoples to agree on those basic human values which will act as a unifying factor. When democracy and human rights are said to run counter to non-Western culture, such culture is usually defined narrowly and presented as monolithic. In fact the values that democracy and human rights seek to promote can be found in many cultures. Human beings the world over need freedom and security so that they may be able to realize their full potential. The longing for a form of governance that provides security without destroying freedom goes back a long way.

Support for the desirability of strong government and dictatorship can also be found in all cultures, both Eastern and Western: The desire to dominate and the tendency to adulate the powerful are also common human traits arising out of a desire for security. A nation may choose a system that leaves the protection of the freedom and security of the many dependent on the inclinations of the empowered few; or it may choose institutions and practices that will sufficiently empower individuals and organizations to protect their own freedom and security. This choice will decide how far a nation will progress along the road to peace and human development.

43 / A Pluralist Path in the Arab World

King Hussein, one of the most influential Arab leaders in the Middle East, is the leading proponent of democratization in the Arab world. The King sat down in late 1996 in the patio of the Hashemite palace in Amman to talk about Islam and democracy in the Arab world.

Now that the external foil of the "Zionist enemy" is being removed by the PLO–Israeli peace process, won't the Arab states be deprived of their reason for national unity and be forced to look inward? There is no longer any excuse for autocratic rulers not to open up their societies. **NATHAN GARDELS**

I hope this will happen. There is no doubt that the rug will be pulled from under the feet of many a leader in the region who used the confrontation with Israel to aspire to or justify his own power. Time and again that has been the root cause of instability in the region. **KING HUSSEIN**

I have been saying for a long time that this region should emulate the European model of integration, since there is so much complementarity. If relations can be based on mutual respect, we can move away from confrontation.

Our Palestinian brethren insist at this point that they want a confederation with Jordan. I insist we do nothing except work from the grass roots upward. And that requires an opening up of Arab society so that any coming together is something that is natural, normal and meaningful.

This same logic would apply to a broader integration of the region. We have seen so many efforts at unity, but they have all failed because they weren't built from the grass roots upward. Now, with the PLO settling their affairs with Israel, we may for the first time have this opportunity.

True unity can happen only when there is pluralism and freedom of expression so that we can deal with each other on a people-to-people basis. Then the relationships mean something and are not based on the whims or moods of unaccountable leaders.

GARDELS You are in the odd situation of being a monarch who is the leading proponent of democracy in the Arab world. What is behind this new democratic model you are promoting in Jordan?

HUSSEIN Some of the national movements succeeded in their early days in mobilizing public opinion around the issue of independence. But later, the political elites were not able to lead Arab societies in the quest for development and progress. They failed to maintain the bridges that linked them with their popular base. As a result of their obsession with security, and their view that they had a right of tutelage over others, the right to confiscate their freedom, and the right to think for them, they forgot that any objectives, proposed by any authority in today's world, cannot be valued higher than human rights. Instead, such objectives should be derived from human rights and they should be devoted to serve and further these rights.

My belief in my people is firm. My duty to them is to enable them to partake in shaping their future. Our democratization is not new. We have been trying to do it but have not been able to continue in a normal way for many years.

In 1956 we held free elections. But then people in Jordan, including myself, believed in Arab unity. Many did not believe that this country had anything distinct to offer. So, political pluralism did not really exist except insofar as parties were extensions of those elsewhere in the Arab world. The nation-building began after that and went through very difficult times – the 1967 war and beyond.

The resumption of elections was only possible after we disengaged with the West Bank in 1988, which enabled the PLO to accept (United Nations Resolutions) 242 and 338, and for all the developments now resulting in self-rule to occur. We couldn't have elections before that, with half of what was legally Jordanian jurisdiction under occupation.

So, at the first opportunity, in 1989, we took the first step of holding general elections and developed a National Charter through a Royal Commission, with representatives of all schools of political thought in this country. A new constitution was formulated and our path toward genuine pluralism was charted. Now, there is no turning back.

The charter defines our system of government as a parliamentary, hereditary monarchy where government decisions are subject to the approval of a freely elected parliament. While affirming that Islam is the religion of the state and Islamic law is the principle source of legislation, the charter guarantees tolerance and the right of citizens to hold varying opinions. It guarantees the right of political participation of all citizens and upholds the supremacy of the rule of law by rejecting violence as a means of effecting change. Jordanian men and women are equal under the law, and discrimination is forbidden on the basis of differences in race, language or religion.

GARDELS What is most interesting about Jordan's emergent political opening over the past few years is your experience with Islamic militants. At one point a few years back, 40 percent of the parliament and five ministers were from the Muslim Brotherhood. Once seen as a threat, in the November election they were seen as just another alternative among many.

HUSSEIN When popular movements are put to the test of government, people become aware of their limitations. And free people always tend toward pragmatism.

GARDELS   So the Islamic Action Front of Jordan today is competing for election against scores of other groups and individuals with the slogan "Islam is the solution." Meanwhile, Islamists are being executed weekly in Algeria and Egypt. Isn't democratic inclusion a better way to cope with the threat of militant Islam than repression?

HUSSEIN   Let me say this without reference to any other Arab state in particular: We are determined to make an example of something that can work, or something that the world can look at which reveals the true possibilities of Islamic society and defects from the image presented by intolerant extremists, or perceived in ignorance by those who know little of Islamic faith and tradition.

In the short and long term, stability has to be augmented by people sharing and shaping their future through democratic institutions; by people exercising their rights and seeking their hopes through direct involvement in political life. I hope that Jordan will be an example of something that works, including for those who have given themselves the name of the Islamic Front because, after all, the country is Muslim as well as Christian. We are all one family equal under the law.

GARDELS   So bringing people into the process breeds moderation; keeping them out through repression breeds extremism?

HUSSEIN   That ought to be obvious. There was a time when we were almost alone in this entire region, misunderstood and under tremendous pressure following the disaster of the Gulf War and the invasion of Kuwait by Iraq. I think, without our journey toward democracy and without the people forging the policies of this country, we wouldn't have survived. This is the kind of strength that is inherent in democratization. There is no substitute for it.

Individual rulers come and go. Only institutions founded in the will of the people live on. That is what I hope will be my legacy to the future generations of this troubled region.

Of course, there is no guarantee that more democracy in the **GARDELS** Arab world, as demonstrated by Jordanian public attitudes about the United States and the coalition states during the Gulf War, will mean a more pro-Western attitude. Wouldn't it be a mistake for the West to assume so?

What democracy means is that people are free to determine **HUSSEIN** their own sovereign decisions. Now let me be very clear about Jordan's position during the Gulf War. We were never in favor of Saddam Hussein and did not support Iraq's invasion and occupation of Kuwait. Jordan was worried, like every single Arab state, about fragmentation. We were worried about the human and material losses.

Jordan was not against the United States, but we were against the destruction of the Iraqi people made to suffer dearly for the policies of their leaders. We tried to resolve the problem in an Arab context and failed. I was pained during that war when we were told by Americans that "you are either with us or against us," because our friendship with the Americans is built on the principles and ideals on which that nation was founded and which we, in our own way in this moment, are embracing.

During the Cold War, Jordan was the only voice in this region standing up against the tide of communism that otherwise might have reached all the way to Africa.

You have stood with the West, but will a democratic public? **GARDELS**

I am sure. **HUSSEIN**

44 / Why Separate States?

Benjamin Netanyahu is the prime minister of Israel. Puffing a Davidoff cigar in the late afternoon of November 27, 1996, at his heavily guarded office in Jerusalem, we sat down and spoke contentiously and at length.

GARDELS   After redeployment out of Hebron, most of the Palestinian population will have autonomy, but they still won't have most of the "land for peace" they expected to get under Oslo, which was always a key goal of Arafat. That was to come as a result of further Israeli redeployment from the West Bank.

NETANYAHU   Well, there are no specifications of what that would include. The Oslo Accords leave open the final disposition of where the Palestinian Authority will be in geographic terms. It does not say that "such and such a percentage of the territory will be ceded to the Palestinians." It only says that at the end of the interim period, Israel will retain specific military locations and settlements to be defined.

Surely, there will be differing intepretations about what that means.

But the Oslo Accords also say that in the final status negotiations, all of this will be thrown wide open again. This means that everything that has been agreed to up until the point of the completion of the interim settlement is not binding on the final status. Thus, Oslo leaves open the question of what it would all look like, in both territorial and functional terms – what powers and responsibilities would accrue to the Palestinian authority and where it would reside.

GARDELS You have called for moving on quickly to the "final status" negotiations. Will you outline your opening position?

NETANYAHU We intend to resume the final status talks, and when we do, I think we should lay out a clear vision of how we see the final settlement. But first we must seek the agreement of as broad a segment of the Israeli public as we can.

This is important for two reasons. First, negotiations as pivotal as the final settlement with the Palestinians require the broadest possible public support. I take a different view from my predecessors. An agreement as critical as this – one that decides the fate of Israel – cannot be taken on a very narrow parliamentary base.

Now, my parliamentary base is already considerably broader than theirs. Even so, I will seek to further broaden the public agreement for the view of the final settlement I propose. Civic peace inside Israel depends on this.

Second, this broad consensus would help achieve a final settlement with the Palestinians. Their expectations are way out of line with the majority of Israelis – not only the right, but the center and the moderate left. The fact that they will see that a majority of Israelis have a united view will induce realism and compromise.

GARDELS Am I safe to assume that vision will not encompass a Palestinian state? You once said "the fledgling Palestinian state that Arafat and the PLO are trying to establish is not what the Israeli people want."

NETANYAHU That is right. In the final settlement we need to define a new model for Israel and the Palestinians. People seem caught in a bind that says either there will be military subjugation by Israel or complete unbridled self-determination for the Palestinians. We need to escape this bind and find a modus vivendi in between.

This is not only true in the case of Israel and the Palestinians, but in dozens of countries that are faced with the same problem. And it is seldom accepted anywhere any more that the solution is just to split up countries where national groups are embedded in the territory of a lager national group into separate and equal sovereign states.

Such a solution would be hugely problematic for us. Most Israelis shudder at this, not only because of their historical attachment to the heart of the Jewish homeland – the Judean and Samarian hills – but because of the threats that can emanate from such an open-ended, sovereign state. They could bring in a large army, rockets, missiles, control the air space above Israel and the water table beneath. Sovereignty usually implies the control of all these things. And that is an unacceptable risk for Israel. Even those Israelis who ostensibly agree to a Palestinian state will tell you they mean "as long as they don't enlarge their army or make pacts with other states like Iraq or Iran, as long as they don't control their air space, as long as they don't bring in millions of refugees" and so on.

For peace to endure, there must be a balance between Israeli needs and Palestinian needs.

GARDELS Why are you so insistent on building new settlements?

NETANYAHU What is all this noise about the settlements? Do people think there wasn't an election here? Even the previous government made it clear the settlements would stay. Rabin himself said under no circumstances did Oslo "preclude" the further expansions of existing settlements. And he was true to his word. Under his government, the existing settlements underwent an unprecedented expansion. I don't think you can expect me to do less.

I have to say that this conception that we have to make the heart of the Jewish homeland a Judenrein of some kind is inimical to peace. I am completely baffled that the world still somehow sees an "apartheid peace" as a prescription for harmony between Israelis and Palestinians.

If I had told you that we have to eliminate the Palestinian

settlements, or constrict the natural growth of their communities, you would be up in arms.

Yet people are telling us that those Jews living in areas that have been the Jewish homeland for 3,000 years can't get married, they can't have children, they can't have schools, it is verboten, they have to leave – this kind of monstrous human engineering we would never seek to apply to the other side.

We don't seek to control the natural growth of Palestinian communities. Why should that inhuman standard be applied toward us?

We've got to get beyond this mantra that "settlements are an obstacle to peace." Why are they an obstacle to peace? Why can't Jews live in Judea? Why can't they live anywhere?

Go into the West Bank. It is empty. It has 3 percent of the density of Israel's crowded coastal plain. And it would have remained empty if, because of what Mark Twain called the force of "life and circumstance," Jews hadn't come here.

There is no legal, moral or historical basis to deny the Jewish people the right to live in their ancient homeland. We are not trying to expel anyone who lives there. Why are they trying to expel us? We have to find a way to live with each other. The sooner we eliminate from the political lexicon the idea of uprooting settlements or expelling anyone – Arabs or Jews – the sooner we'll get to a genuine peace.

GARDELS The Arab nations making up with Israel have done so on the basis of "land for peace," which they take to mean the existence of a Palestinian state someday. As it becomes clear to them that this won't happen, what will happen to peace with the Arab states?

NETANYAHU Well, I don't think they had any thought that Menachem Begin or Yitzhak Shamir was going to create a Palestinian state. For that matter, Rabin, for most of his term, was quite adamant about this point as well.

It is de rigueur on the part of these Arab states to assail

any new government in Israel that doesn't accept their vision of a final settlement with the Palestinians as "anti-peace."

It also flies in the face of what negotiations mean. Of course, we have a different conception. They will present their views; we'll present ours. Then we will compromise. But to a priori accept their view of a final settlement means there would be no need for negotiations. But the Israel people won't accept any such dicta that they must accept the 22nd Arab state that could be a mortal danger to the one Jewish state. To have good people around the world gullibly accepting this formula as the way to good relations in the Middle East is not conducive to peace.

GARDELS Rabin and Peres relied on Arafat more than you do to control terrorism, saying the more trust there was between Israelis and Palestinians, the less terror there would be. Can that trust be rebuilt?

NETANYAHU It can be rebuilt if the Palestinians back it with actions. We intend to see a continuous battle against terrorism and an adherence to those provisions of the Oslo Accords that have been systematically violated by the Palestinian Authority.

Why has the covenant in the PLO charter not been annulled? Why has a new document recognizing Israel's right to exist in no unequivocal terms not been adopted? Why do they keep calling for the "right of return" of refugees, which every Israeli knows is a code word for the destruction of Israel?

As long as the mainstream elements of the PLO adhere to these positions, trust will not be built in the minds of most Israelis or their government.

No one here has a blank check. We have to see action, not words. I intend to keep the accord as promised. We are doing our part. But there must be reciprocity.

At the same time, words do matter. The concept of peace is incompatible with the daily calls for jihad and the elimination of Israel as the Zionist entity. This has to stop as well.

GARDELS What does Arafat say when you say that to him?

In one of our meetings I said, "This has to end." He **NETANYAHU** promised. It hasn't ended.

What I'm saying is we are seeking peace through both sides keeping their commitments and by effecting a psychological change. I have taken great efforts to convince the constituency that elected me that peace means "if we sign agreements, we keep them."

That hasn't been easy for me to do. I negotiated the Hebron redeployment, even though I did not sign that agreement and there are great risks involved. But I have followed through. I have told my people that agreements have to be kept. I have not seen a similar effort from the other side to habituate the Palestinian public to peace with Israel. And I have not seen that effort on the part of many of the Arab countries who have participated in the vague and not-so-vague threats toward Israel if we do not subscribe, in advance of the negotiations, to what their version of peace would look like. That kind of behavior will make the peace dissipate. Violence and even war will then ensue.

After the emergency Washington summit of October 1996, **GARDELS** Jordan's King Hussein told me he thought your decision to open the tourist tunnel under Jerusalem was a statement saying, in effect, that Jerusalem was nobody's business but Israel's. He said this was "unacceptable."

He also said that the Jordanian-Israeli peace treaty was at stake if you didn't press on with the Oslo peace process.

How are relations now with Jordan?

All Israeli governments have regarded Jerusalem as the **NETANYAHU** unified capital. No one in his right mind is going to re-erect a Berlin Wall to redivide the city. That is not going to happen.

As far as statements made in a moment of pique? I'd rather look at overall relations.

Jordan is a valued partner in peace. I am working to improve the relationship. Most of the time we understand each other. When we don't, friends have a way of getting through that.

Index